FRIEDRICH HÖLDERLIN

SELECTED POETRY

FRIEDRICH HÖLDERLIN, 1823

Pencil drawing by Johann Georg Schreiner and Rudolf Lohbauer
27 July 1823 (Deutsches Literaturarchiv, Marbach)

FRIEDRICH HÖLDERLIN

SELECTED POETRY

TRANSLATED BY
DAVID CONSTANTINE

BLOODAXE BOOKS

ISBN: 978 1 78037 401 7

First published 2018 by
Bloodaxe Books Ltd,
Eastburn,
South Park,
Hexham,
Northumberland NE46 1BS.

www.bloodaxebooks.com
For further information about Bloodaxe titles
please visit our website and join our mailing list
or write to the above address for a catalogue.

Supported using public funding by
**ARTS COUNCIL
ENGLAND**

Cover design: Neil Astley & Pamela Robertson-Pearce.

Printed in Great Britain by Bell & Bain Limited, Glasgow, Scotland, on
acid-free paper sourced from mills with FSC chain of custody certification.

CONTENTS

INTRODUCTION

Hölderlin was born in 1770, as were also Wordsworth, Hegel and Beethoven. That generation grew up believing the world – 'the very world, which is the world/ Of all of us' – could be changed for the better, and that love, reason and justice would prevail in it, here and now. They were disappointed. But disappointment does not annul hope. What we can still get from Hölderlin, as from Wordsworth, is a passionate and generous hope. That hope survives, in the teeth of every disappointment. Hölderlin, writing his best poems after things had gone badly wrong in France and after the possibility of improvement in Germany had been erased, constantly offers images and visions of fulfilled humanity. True, the poems demonstrate the absence of fulfilment; but their project is utopian and it is their drive towards fulfilment which lingers in the blood after reading them. That feeling is an equivalent of what it was like to be alive then, when 'the whole earth / The beauty wore of promise'. The excitement and the faith revive.

Hölderlin was born into the so-called *Ehrbarkeit*, the Respectability, who administered Church and State. He was brought up by an anxious mother; his father, and then his stepfather, had died before he was nine. He was brought up in and never quite escaped from a condition of dependence. First on his mother: though in fact comfortably off and with a large inheritance to pass on to her eldest son, she kept him throughout his life in want of funds and he never broke free. Secondly on the State: he was put through a church education free, on condition that he serve the State (through its Church), once educated. He spent his life resisting that obligation. He was schooled in theology, but also in philosophy and the classics. He took all three very seriously, and the tensions that engendered were hard to manage. He entered the seminary in Tübingen in 1788 and suffered there, with his eyes on France, as though it was the oppressive and anachronistic State in miniature. He had Schelling and Hegel with him as allies in republicanism.

Hölderlin was born in Lauffen, north of Stuttgart, but grew up in Nürtingen, also on the Neckar but south of the city. All his education was in Swabia – in Denkendorf, Maulbronn and Tübingen – and it was to Tübingen, to the clinic, that he was forcibly returned, and all the latter half of his life he spent in a tower in the town walls with a view of the river and the meadows and hills beyond. Swabia was his homeland. He sought employment outside it (he had to, or the Church would have claimed him) but when those employments failed, he returned. He idealised the homeland as the paradise of childhood and as the location for the New Republic; but in fact, until his collapse, he was debarred from settling in it. That fact, like so much in Hölderlin's life, is intrinsically figurative.

Hölderlin imagined his ideal largely in Greek terms. Quite simply, the civilisation of Periclean Athens seemed to him the best the human race had ever achieved and he wanted an equivalent of it for his own day and age and even believed the French Revolution might bring it about. Once disappointed, he risked becoming merely nostalgic, for an ideal sited irretrievably in the past. He countered that by committing himself to the present, to present time and to present place, and by imagining an ideal future for them. He created, poem by poem, a world having two poles: Greece, and what he called Hesperia. And the heart of Hesperia was his own homeland Swabia. He celebrates the world north of the Alps, his own world, its towns and hills and above all its rivers, as a land fit for the ideal, once realised in Greece, to be welcomed into; and again and again he connects Greece, now lost, with Hesperia, still to come. That way of thinking – an ideal past, an unsatisfactory present, an ideal future – was characteristic of Hölderlin's age; but the expression he gave to it was peculiarly concrete and precise. He embodied his poetic thinking in landscapes: in those he knew well (having walked through them), and in others, the Greek, which he had only read about in publications by French and English travellers. A similar luminousness lies over both zones.

When Hölderlin finished his education in 1793 he took immediate steps to avoid being drafted into the Church. He went 'abroad', that is, outside Swabia, and became a house-tutor. In all he had four such jobs. It was the usual thing for a young man to do if he wished to earn a living whilst chiefly to be furthering his own intellectual and artistic life; but it was a compromise and not a happy one. His task was to educate the children of the well-to-do. In that paid capacity he was a domestic, and liable always to be treated accordingly. But by his talents and his sensibility he was, very often, the superior of his employers. The predicament of the house-tutor was in epitome the predicament of artists and intellectuals altogether in Germany at that time: marginalised and dependent. They added culture to a household, as ornament and extra. In that they were allied naturally with the women, whose role also was subordinate and ornamental. Hölderlin's first post, in Waltershausen, on the remote estate of Schiller's friend and confidante Charlotte von Kalb, ended badly. He fell in love with and had a child by a young woman called Wilhelmine Kirms who had left her elderly and abusive husband and become Frau von Kalb's lady-companion. The baby died of smallpox one year old. His second post was in Frankfurt, the bankers' city. There he saw the spirit denigrated and pushed to the periphery. He saw money triumphant. His employer was Jakob Gontard, whose motto, despite being married to an intelligent, cultivated and beautiful woman, was 'Business first'. Susette was the mother of four young children; Hölderlin looked after the eldest, the one boy, aged eight. She became the Diotima of his poems and proof to him that ideal life was possible on earth. Her existence in Frankfurt, in the very city of mercantile dreadful night, seemed miraculous. Loving and being loved by her he was, for a time, in a condition of fulfilled humanity. She was Greece recovered and restored to life, she was the woman fit for the New Age. When in France the attempt to change the institutions failed, bringing a new tyranny, many idealists put their hopes in a change of hearts and minds instead. Susette in herself seemed to Hölderlin a guarantor of what humanity had been like and might be like again. The ideal was realised – then lost. They were severed, she died, his mind collapsed.

Hölderlin found his own poetic voice when he met Susette. Prior to that he had been much under the influence of other writers, notably Schiller (whom he adulated). He was writing a novel, *Hyperion*, when he came to Frankfurt; he re-wrote it when he met her. Its heroine is called Diotima. Forgive me, he said, giving her the second volume, that Diotima dies. The book was dedicated to

Susette Gontard, in the words 'Wem sonst als Dir' [To whom else but you]. Forced out of her house in September 1798 Hölderlin moved to nearby Homburg and there, for a while, lived on his earnings and tried to make his own way. He reflected on his art and began to write the poems for which he is best known. And he worked at a tragedy, *The Death of Empedocles*, pushing it through three versions, to no completion. Away from Susette, in Nürtingen, Switzerland and Bordeaux, he wrote the elegies, 'Bread and Wine', 'Homecoming', 'Menon's lament for Diotima' and the great hymns in Pindar's style, 'The Rhine', 'The journey', 'Germania' and, later, 'Patmos'. A whole unique oeuvre was produced. There cannot have been many days during his brief maturity when he was not writing at poems among the very best in German literature. It is a tremendous work, like nobody else's, his in every line and in its large project.

In the winter of 1801-02 Hölderlin walked to Bordeaux, over the Auvergne. He took up a job as house-tutor there, his last; but left in May and went home, via Paris (where he saw the classical statues Napoleon had stolen from Italy). Susette died in June, of German measles caught whilst nursing her children. When Hölderlin showed himself in Stuttgart and Nürtingen his friends and family thought him out of his mind. But it is not known for certain whether or not he had already learned Susette was dead.

Thereafter, for four years until his incarceration in the clinic, he struggled against fatigue and distraction, and wrote marvellous poems – 'Patmos', for example, 'Mnemosyne' and 'Remembrance'. He held a sinecure in Homburg, as librarian to the Landgraf, and it was from there that he was transported in September 1806, having become, so it was said, too difficult to manage in that little town. He had eight months in the clinic, and was discharged then as incurable with 'at most three years' to live. He lived another thirty-six, half his life, in good hands, in the loving and sensible care of a carpenter's family, his own wanting little or nothing to do with him. He became a celebrity, sightseers visited him and asked him for verses, which he readily gave. They are rhyming verses, and he signed them with strange names. Yes, he was much visited, by the ghoulish and by the truly devoted. He died peacefully in 1843.

Hölderlin is the poet of absence. His gods have departed, presence has been lost. There is no poet more honest and uncompromising in the depiction of absence and loss. Reading Hölderlin we know what bereavement, in its widest sense, is like. But we know also, with an equal or greater force, what fulfilment would be like, what it would be like to live lives full of love and joy; and the injunction of his poetry, always there, is to believe in the possibility of that fulfilment and to seek to make it real.

This new volume of my translations of Hölderlin's works supersedes the previous two (1990, 1996). I have added more than sixty poems and completed the 'Pindar Fragments' (till now represented solely by 'Concerning the dolphin'). Also included here, in my English, are Hölderlin's translations of Sophocles' *Oedipus* and *Antigone* (first published by Bloodaxe in 2001) and a few more important passages of Sophocles and Euripides. Still this is nothing like a complete edition of Hölderlin's work. For something closer to that – most of the poems and the second and third versions of his verse tragedy *Empedocles*, in German and in English – I am glad to direct readers to Michael Hamburger's *Friedrich Hölderlin: Poems and Fragments* (Anvil Press Poetry, 2004).

Hamburger thought of himself as a 'mimetic' translator; that is, he reproduced very closely not only the sense but also the forms – the stanzas, the lines, the metrics – of the originals. I have kept close, but not so close. In translating the odes ('To the Fates', for example, or 'Plea for Forgiveness') I adopted their syllabic count but not their metres; for the elegies, such as 'Homecoming' and 'Bread and Wine', and for the long poem 'The Archipelago' I attempted quite near but not exact equivalents of hexameters and pentameters; for the hymns and the hymnic fragments I imitated Hölderlin's rhythms, which are free, and allowed myself only as many lines as he used; in the last poems I rhymed, not always as strictly as he did. Beyond that, to use (roughly) Ewald Osers' distinction, I went for equivalence of effect rather than exact reproduction of the means of the effects.

I translated the poems as they appear in Volumes 1i and 2i of the *Sämtliche Werke*, edited by Friedrich Beissner and Adolf Beck (Stuttgart 1943-85); but for this third and greatly enlarged edition

I have made more use than I did before of the rival Complete Works edited by D.E. Sattler and others, published in Frankfurt (1975-2008), and also of Dietrich Uffhausen's *Hölderlins hymnische Spätdichtung* (Stuttgart 1989). Beissner, a classical philologist and an extraordinarily fine and scrupulous reader of Hölderlin's manuscripts, worked always towards establishing a 'finished text' and this, along with any finished or at least distinct versions of a poem, he published in 1i and 2i. Everything else, all the undecided, inconclusive and abandoned possibilities, he conscientiously presented in the accompanying volumes (1ii and 2 ii), for readers to study alongside the texts in 1i and 2i, if they wished and were able to. Sattler and Uffhausen both thought this editorial philosophy and practice improper; and in their editions they supply facsimiles of the manuscripts themselves, followed by typographical equivalents of those facsimiles, and finally a readable text as it were physically coming out of the often very convoluted drafts and revisions. I feel more inclined this time, having done more poems, and particularly more of the late hymns and fragments, to admit that a 'truer' translation would be one which followed exactly the genesis, progress and, quite often, failure of a poem on its way (we assume) to a final form. The 'truest' translation then would be one of all the words on every manuscript page exactly in their places relative to one another, a method which would tend to undermine the whole concept of linear progression since Hölderlin frequently began his poems in *Keimworte* [seed-words] scattered across a sheet of paper and out of them he released, like a series of starbursts, the life and shape of the poem. Often also he left variants – different epithets, for example – standing till a very late stage of composition; and in poems he did not finish, there they remained, as possibilities. And if you believe, as I do, that any alteration even of a single word, or a choosing one from two or three, affects more or less palpably and significantly the workings and sense of the whole poem, you may see in a Hölderlin poem in progress an abyss of co-existent possibilities, quite dizzying. Making a translation of such a phenomenon with its different inks, different thicknesses of nib, different layers of work (intermingled sometimes with stray elements from other poems), the earliest still visible through the latest – the translator would have to follow the creating mind itself, and to do that exactly and truthfully would take far longer than I've got. So I have translated Beissner's finished-looking texts and don't with these few remarks mean to impugn them in any way. But studying the work of Sattler and Uffhausen I have come closer to a sense of the fearful undertow beneath Hölderlin's strictly beautiful classical forms, the maelstrom of chaos which may actually be the same thing as creation at its highest pitch. And aware of that, I love and admire him ever more for his heroic struggle against the threat of dissolution inherent in his undertaking, and for his many triumphs.

For the most part I have ordered the poems according to the chronology of the Stuttgart edition, the chief exception being that I brought the nine 'Night Songs' together as a group and in the order in which they were first published in 1805.

Finally (since it may seem rather an eccentric exercise), a word on my translations of some of Hölderlin's translations. His, chiefly those from Greek, are central to, and an integral part of, his whole poetic oeuvre. He came into his own poetic language by doing them – a language that is uniquely his, thoroughly German, uand beautifully haunted by Greek. Anyone wishing to read into the heart of Hölderlin's poetry will be helped by his translations. So I have 'Englished' some – not the great Pindar translations of 1800, but others (including *Oedipus* and *Antigone*) less extreme in their procedure which could, I thought, be usefully 'brought across'.

ACKNOWLEDGEMENTS

This edition has been expanded from *Selected Poems* (Bloodaxe Books, 1990) and its second, expanded edition (1996), with the addition of a substantial number of new translations as well as incorporating the whole of *Hölderlin's Sophocles: Oedipus & Antigone* (Bloodaxe Books, 2001).

A part of my translation of Hölderlin's *Oedipus* first appeared in *Comparative Criticism*, 20 (1998), and a few of the poems in *Modern Poetry in Translation*.

A large part of this new volume has been closely read for me by Helen Constantine, Sasha Dugdale and Charlie Louth. I am deeply grateful to them for many corrections and improvements and much helpful discussion.

FRIEDRICH HÖLDERLIN, 1786

Pencil drawing by unknown artist, probably a fellow-student.
(Württembergische Landesbibliothek, Cod.poet.et.phil.fol.63,V.b.3)

Greece

(for Stäudlin)

Had I found you under shady plane trees
Where through flowers the Cephissus' waters flowed
Where the young men dreamed the ways to glory
Where Socrates was heard and hearts were swayed
Where Aspasia strolled through groves of myrtle
Where my Plato set the vision free
Where from the noisy agora the people
Raised the glad shouts of fraternity

Where the spring was spiced with festive singing
Where the rivers of inspiration
Poured from Athene's sacred hilltop giving
Thanks and praise for her protection,
Where by a thousand hours of poetry
Dreaming like gods, they stayed the fleeting years
Oh had I found you there and loved you dearly
As I have loved you in this age of ours

How different then would have been our embraces –
You'd have sung me the dead at Marathon
In your eyes, smiling on me in those days,
Lovely wild enthusiasm would have shone,
Your heart made young again by victories
Your spirit too, among the laurel leaves,
There would have felt the joyous cooling breezes
Stinted in our close oppressive lives.

Has your star of love been clouded over?
And youth's rosy-fingered dawning too?
Oh in the dance of Hellas' golden hours
The fleeing of the years would not touch you.
There in every heart eternally
Love and courage burned like Hestia's flame
There like the garden of the Hesperides
Always youth's proud pleasures were in bloom.

Oh your heart would not have beaten vainly
For the people in those better days.
In your loving strong fraternity
Joy would have brought the tears to your eyes.
Wait a while – the hour will come for certain
And set free the gods from where they're pent.
Die! You seek in this earth's habitation
In vain your noble spirit's element.

Attica, the heroine, has fallen
Where the children of the gods are lain
In the city's marble halls in ruin
Stands the crane in mourning now alone.
Spring returns, the smiling spring, the gracious
But she'll find her brothers never more
In the holy valley of the Illisus –
Under thorns and rubble: seek them there!

Let me cross into the distant country
To Alcaeus and Anacreon
In the narrow house I'd sleep more gladly
Among the holy shades of Marathon.
Oh, for Greece, beloved land, let these be
The last of all the tears I ever shed
Sever now my thread of life, o Parcae
For my heart is given to the dead.

The oak trees

Out of the gardens I come to you, sons of the mountain!
Out of the gardens where Nature lives patient and homely
Caring and cared for together with hard-working women and men.
But you like a race of Titans stand in a world that is tamer
Splendid, belonging only to yourselves and the heavens
Who nourished and raised you and to the earth, your mother.
None of you ever was put through the schools of humans
Each among all, joyously, freely, from vigorous roots
Forces upwards and seizes, as eagles their prey
Space with your powerful arms and towards the clouds
Large and serene you lift up your sunlit crowns.
Each of you is a world, you live like the stars in the sky
Each one a god, in a free confederacy.
If I could bear my servitude never would I envy these trees
But to the social world I would fit myself gladly.
Were I no longer shackled to the social world by my heart
That cannot stop loving, how gladly I'd live among you!

To Diotima

Come and look at the happiness: trees in the cooling breezes
      Are tossing their branches
Like dancers' hair and with sunshine and rain the sky
      Is playing on the earth
As though joy had hands and were raising a music
      And light and shadows
Pass in succession and harmony over the hills
      Away like the myriad
Notes that swarm in a loving quarrel
      Over a lute.
Gently the sky has touched his brother the river
      With silvery drops
And now he is near and he empties wholly the fullness
      Held in his heart
Over the trees and the river and…

And verdant copses, the sky's own face on the river
      Fades and we lose them,
The head of the mountain, alone, the little houses, the rocks
      He hides in his lap
And the hills that assemble around him like lambs
      Clothed in blossom
As soft as wool and that suck on the clear cold
      Springs of the mountain,
The misting floor with its seed and flowers,
      The garden here,
Close things and distant leave us and wane in a happy confusion,
      The sun goes out.
But now with a rush the floods of heaven have passed
      And purer, younger,
The earth with her lucky children steps from the bath.
      In livelier joy
The green of the leaves shines forth and brighter the gold of the flowers,

White as the sheep that the shepherd has flung in the dip,

Diotima

Heavenly Muse of Delight, who once reconciled the elements
    Come now, quieten for me the chaos of the times,
Settle the furious fighting with peaceful music of heaven
    Till in the mortal heart what is dissevered unites,
Till humankind's first nature, generous and equable, rises
    Out of the times in ferment, powerful and serene.
Return, living beauty, into the scanted hearts of the people,
    Return to the welcoming table, return to the temples.
For Diotima lives like the delicate blossom in winter,
    Rich in spirit of her own, she too seeks after the sun.
But the sun of the spirit, the lovelier world, has gone under
    And in the chilling night there is only the hurricanes' strife.

The peoples were silent...

The peoples were silent, slumbering, then Fate saw to it
They would not sleep for good and there came Nature's
Implacable, terrible son, the old spirit of unrest.
He stirred like fire that heaves in the heart of the earth
Shakes the ancient cities like ripe fruit trees
Shreds mountains and swallows oaks and rocks.

And armies came in like the furious weltering sea.
Like gods of the sea many a man held sway
In the weltering fight, much hot blood drained
Into the killing fields and every desire and every
Human energy spent itself in rage in one
Vast abattoir from the blue Rhine to the Tiber
And for years there all around the ordered
Unstoppable butchery manoeuvred.
In that time Destiny, the potentate, played
A bold game with all those mortal lives.

And golden fruits will gleam for you again
Like serene and gracious stars through the cool night
Of the orange groves of Italy.

Empedocles

Life you were seeking, life, and it sprang and shone
    As divine fire from deep in the earth for you
        And you in cold terror and desire
            Flung yourself into the flames of Etna.

So in her arrogance the Queen melted pearls
    In wine. Why should she not? But better if you,
        Poet, hadn't cast in sacrifice
            Your riches to the fermenting crater.

Yet you are holy to me like the power
    Of the earth that took and killed you for boldness.
        And into the depths I should gladly
            Follow that hero, did not love hold me.

To the Fates

Give me one summer, you with the power to,
    Only one, and an autumn of song, so that
        My heart having fed to its content
            On music will be happier dying.

A soul withheld its heavenly right in life
    Will be restless in Orcus also; but let
        The making of the holiest thing
            My heart wants, the poem, be given me

Welcome then the silence of the world of shades!
    I am at peace, although my music may not
        Accompany me down. Once I'll have
            Lived like the gods and more I'm not asking.

To her good angel

Send her flowers and fruit from a never-exhausting abundance
  Send her, friendly spirit, heaven's eternal youth.
Cloak her in your delights and let her not see the times
  She, the Athenian, lives in, lonely, a stranger here
Till one day in the land of the blessed she embraces her sisters
  Who ruled and joyously loved there in Phidias' time.

Plea for Forgiveness

Often I've lost you the golden tranquillity
    Of heaven, yours by nature, and what you have had
        From me are many of life's
            More secret and deeper sorrows.

Forget them now and forgive me and like the cloud
    Over the peaceful moon there I shall pass and you
        Will be what you were and shine
            In your beauty, beloved light.

To the Sun God

Where are you? The soul is shadowy in me
    And drunk on your happiness. A moment since
        I saw a dazzling god, like a young
            Man tired at the finish of a journey,

Bathing the hair of his head in golden clouds
    And my eyes can't keep from looking where he went.
        He has left us now, he has gone to
            Lands where they love him still and revere him.

I love you, earth, for you are grieving with me
    And our grief like the troubles of children turns
        Into sleep and just as the breezes
            Flutter and whisper in the strings until

More adept fingers coax a better music
    Out of them so mists and dreams play over us
        Until the loved one comes and life and
            The spirit are kindled in us again.

Hyperion's Song of Fate

You inhabit the light, you walk
   On easy ground, the shining
      Breezes of heaven play
         Around you, the blessed,
           As lightly as the lyre-
               Playing fingers of a girl.

Gods have no fate, they have
   The sleeping infant's
      Quiet breath;
         Their spirits, kept
           From spoiling in the bud,
              Blossom for ever;
               They have a still
                  Eternal clarity
                  Of gaze.

We have no footing anywhere,
   No rest, we topple,
      Fall and suffer
         Blindly from hour
           To hour like water
              Pitched from fall
               To fall, year in,
                  Year out, headlong,
                 Ignorant.

When I was a boy…

When I was a boy
  A god often rescued me
    From the shouts and the rods of men
      And I played among trees and flowers
     Secure in their kindness
      And the breezes of heaven
       Were playing there too.

And as you delight
The hearts of plants
When they stretch towards you
With little strength

So you delighted the heart in me
Father Helios, and like Endymion
I was your favourite,
Moon. O all

You friendly
And faithful gods
I wish you could know
How my soul has loved you.

Even though when I called to you then
It was not yet with names, and you
Never named me as people do
As though they knew one another.

I knew you better
Than I have ever known them.
I understood the stillness above the sky
But never the words of men.

Trees were my teachers
Melodious trees
And I learned to love
Among flowers.

I grew up in the arms of the gods.

Achilles

Glorious son of a goddess, when they took your beloved from you
    Weeping you went to the seashore, and into the tide
Lamenting with all your heart and into the holy depths there
    Cried to sink down to the stillness where far away
From the din of ships, deep under the waves, in her peaceful grotto
    Blue Thetis lived, your protector, goddess of the sea.
Mother of the youth, a powerful goddess, she on his island's
    Rocky shore had lovingly suckled the infant boy
And with the muscular song of the surf and proofing him in
    The bath of the Styx had raised him to be a hero.
Now the mother hearing the young man's lamentations
    Rose like a mist from the bed of the sea in sorrow
Hushed with tender embraces her darling's trouble and he
    Listened while soothingly she gave him her word, to help.

Son of a goddess, were I like you I could face to face with
    One of the dwellers in heaven utter my secret sorrow
Which I am not to see but must bear the shame of as though I were
    No longer hers who with tears thinks of me nevertheless.
Kind gods, but you hear every human being's supplication
    And oh! I have loved with a pious passion, earth
Your holy light since the day I was born and your springs and forests
    And this heart with too pure a longing has felt you
Father of the aether – o kind ones, quieten my sorrowing
    Let not the soul in me be silenced too soon but let
Me live in the fleeing of the days with grateful song, o heavenly
    Powers, to give you thanks for the good you have done me
Already, the joys of my youth that is already over
    And out of my loneliness then take me kindly to you.

Once there were gods...

Once there were gods on earth, with people, the heavenly muses
    And Apollo, the youth, healing, inspiring like you.
And you are like them to me, as though one of the blessed
    Sent me out into life, where I go my comrade's
Image goes with me wherever I suffer and build, with love
    Unto death; for I learned this and have this from her.

Let us live, oh you who are with me in sorrow, with me in faith
    And heart and loyalty struggling for better times!
For such we are! And if ever in the coming years they knew
    Of us two when the spirit matters again
They would say: lovers in those days, alone, they created
    Their secret world that only the gods knew. For who
Cares only for things that will die the earth will have them, but
    Nearer the light, into the clarities come
Those keeping faith with the heart's love and holy spirit who were
    Hopeful, patient, still, and got the better of fate.

If I heeded them warning me now...

If I heeded them warning me now they would smile and think
   Seeking to avoid us he fell sooner to us, the fool.
And they would see no profit in that,

Sing me, terrible goddesses, whatever evils await me
   Sing again and again the song of my fate at my ear
In the end I'll be yours, I know it, but before then I will
   Belong to myself and seize life for myself and fame.

Parting

When I am dead, in shame, when I can't get my soul
   Vengeance on her insulters, when by the spirit's
      Enemies I'm brought down
         Beaten, into a coward's grave

Forget me then, even you, who are kind, and let
   My name go under into oblivion, blush
      For me then, even you, my
         Friend always, but not until then.

But I know it already. Soon, oh my loving
   Comrade, beyond your help all the familiars
      Of death will play my heart and
         Tear at it till they untune me.

Now of my youth, my brave time, may the locks of hair
   As well go white today as wait for tomorrow,

        here where the ways part
   Into loneliness, where grief,
      The killing grief, has flung me down.

The Zeitgeist

For too long you have governed above my head
    You in the cloud of darkness, god of the times.
        All round it is too wild, too fearful:
            Toppling and ruin wherever I look.

Oh like a boy often I cast my eyes down
    Seek underground a place to be safe from you
        And wish like a fool there were somewhere
            Shaker of everything, where you are not.

Finally, father, let me encounter you
    With open eyes, for did you not waken first
        By your lightning the spirit in me
            And bring me bravely to the touch of life?

True, from young vines a sacred strength comes to us
    In the mild air when they are quietly
        Walking among trees a god may meet
            And encourage mortal humans, but you

With greater force wake up the untouched souls
    Of the young and teach the old wise arts. Only
        The bad get worse so they sooner end
            When you, earthshaker, lay your hand on them.

Evening fantasy

The ploughman sits at his door in the quiet shade.
  Smoke rises from his hearth. He is contented.
    For the wayfarer hospitably
      Vesper-bells ring in the peaceful village.

Sailors also will be making for harbour
  In distant towns; the busy din of markets
    Fades cheerfully; in the still garden
      The meal shines for a gathering of friends.

And where shall I go? Mortals live from wages
  And work, they toil, they rest from their toiling.
    All have joy. Why then only in me,
      In my heart, does the unease never sleep?

On the western sky a springtime is flowering;
  Roses bloom without number, the golden world
    Has a quiet look. O crimson clouds
      Carry me high above and there in light

And air let my love and sorrow dissolve. But
  The magic, as if my fool plea frightened it
    Flees away, the dark comes and alone
      As ever under the heavens am I.

Come, gentle sleep, come to me now. The heart asks
  Too much. But youth in the end, restless, dreamy
    Of course will cool and fade and old age
      Will have some peace then and serenity.

Morning

The grass glistens with dew; quicker already
  Now the woken stream hastens; the birch inclines
    Her swaying head, in her foliage
      A rustling, a shimmering; and around

The grey clouds reddish flames are drifting, they rise
  In a silent annunciation, heave
    Higher and higher like incoming
      Breakers, never fixed, ever shape-changing.

Come now, oh come, golden day, and don't too soon
  Hurry away to the summit of heaven
    For my sight can fly after you, see
      Your joy closer, more openly, so long

As the look of your beauty is youthful still
  Not yet too lordly for me, too proud. But you
    Wish always to hurry, oh could I
      Go with you, wayfarer god, but you smile

That I in the hubris of joy should desire
  To be like you. Bless then rather my mortal
    Occupations and in your kindness
      Brighten again today my quiet path.

The Main

Many a land of the living earth I wish
    I could see and often over the mountains
        The heart absconds and its longings cross
            The seas to the shores which are of all

I know most praised but of those in the distance
    None there are dearer to me than where the sons
        And daughters of the gods are sleeping
            The land in mourning, the land of the Greeks.

Oh one day I'd like to land on Sounion's
    Coast and question your columns, Olympieum
        Before the north wind buries you too
            With the Athenians' rubbled temples

And images of divinity. For you
    Have stood alone a long time, pride of the world
        Now lost. And you, o you beautiful
            Islands of Ionia where the sea's

Cool breezes waft on the warm shore and under
    A strong sun the grapes are ripening, oh where
        A golden autumn converts to song
            The sighing of the poor people when now

From their griefs their pomegranate trees, full of
    Crimson fruit, their lemon groves, and the sweet wine
        The drum and the zither summon them
            To dance the labyrinthine dance – to you

O islands, a homeless singer will perhaps
    One day find his way for he must wander from
        Strangers to strangers and the free earth
            Alas must serve him for a motherland

So long as he lives and when he dies – but I
    How far and wherever I wander never
        Will I forget you, lovely Main, your
            Shores, their many and manifold blessings.

Proud river, I came as a stranger to you
    You welcomed me in, you gladdened my eyes, you
        Taught me songs that glided softly on
            And how to live a life that made no noise.

Peacefully with the stars, you happy river
    You go your way from your morning to evening
        Towards your brother, the Rhine, and then
            With him joyfully down to the ocean.

That which is mine

The autumn days repose in their fullness now,
    The grapes are lit all through and the orchards red
        With fruit though, as a libation, some
            Of the lovely blossom did fall to earth.

And in the fields around where I follow
    The quiet path out contented men and women
        See how their land has ripened and what
            Happy labour its richness will give them.

The mild light of the skies looks down on them,
    Comes through their trees upon them busy working
        And shares the joy, for the fruits are not
            Only a work of the hands of humans.

Oh golden light do you shine for me too, does
    The air breathe on me again as though blessing
        Some joy such as once there was and came
            Visiting my heart like a happy man's?

I was so but like roses, passing as they,
    That good life went and yet, too often, the stars,
        Still flowering, which are all I have,
            The stars are my sweet reminders of it.

Happy the quiet love of man and wife, a
    Hearth and home in a country to be proud of.
        Over solid ground the heavens shine
            More beautifully and a man is steady.

For like the plant if it cannot root in ground
    Of its own the soul burns out of any man
        Who goes his ways on the holy earth
            Only with the daylight, a poor mortal.

O heights of heaven, the pull of you is strong,
  Too strong, in wild weather, on quiet days, I feel
    The force of the restless gods, they come
      And they go and it wastes my heart away.

Today though let me walk my familiar
  Path in peace among the trees whose leaves are lit
    In the crown with gold, dying, and wreathe
      My head likewise with kind memories.

And so that for me too, as there is for others,
  To save my mortal heart there will be a place
    To abide and the soul not leave my life
      And go beyond me, longing and homeless,

Let the poem be my place of asylum
  And friendly garden, tended for its joys with
    Careful love, and among the always
      Renewing flowers let me walk and dwell

In a secure simplicity while outside
  Wave on wave the colossal unsteady times
    Are roaring at a distance and the
      Quieter sun furthers the work I do.

Over mortal men the powers of heaven
  In their kindness bless for everyone his own.
    Oh bless for me too that which is mine
      And may the Fates not end the dream too soon.

Another day...

Another day. I follow another path,
  Enter the leafing woodland, visit the spring
    Or the rocks where the roses bloom
      Or spy out from the hilltop, but nowhere

Love are you to be seen in the light of day
  And down the wind go the words of our once so
    Beneficent conversation

Your beloved face has gone beyond my sight,
  The music of your life is dying away
    Beyond my hearing and all the songs
      That worked a miracle of peace once on

My heart, where are they now? It was long ago,
  So long and the youth I was has aged nor is
    Even the earth that smiled at me then
      The same. Farewell. Live with that word always.

For the soul goes from me to return to you
  Day after day and my eyes shed tears that they
    Cannot look over to where you are
      And see you clearly ever again.

The sun goes down...

The sun goes down. Beautiful, they have paid you
   Scant attention; holy, they knew you not
      Who without toil and in quietness
         Have risen over them, the toilers.

Me you are a friend to going down and rising
   And my eyes know you, o my sovereign light,
      For I learned a quiet reverence
         When Diotima made my senses whole.

My go-between with heaven, how I listened
   For you, love, Diotima, and how these eyes
      From you to the golden light of day
         Lifted, shining and thankful. Then the streams

Rushed with a greater life and blossom of the earth,
   Of our black earth, breathed on me lovingly
      And smiling above silver clouds
         Inclined to me with blessings the pure blue.

Peace

As though the ancient waters, the
                      transformed into
  A different rage, more terrible,
    Came again, to cleanse, that being needed

So war in a style unheard of ran and grew
  And seethed without halt from year to year and swamped
    The scared land far and wide and people
      Paled in the darkness coming over them.

Heroic force flew up like foam and vanished
  Away. Revenge, you shortened often and soon
    The work of your servants and fetched them
      Home from the fighting and they were quiet.

O you, the implacable and never defeated
  Who strike the unbrave and the over-mighty
    So that from the stroke the whole poor tribe
      Will shake unto the last generation,

You, Nemesis, the covert keeper of goad
  And bridle, holder-back, bringer-on, are you
    Still punishing the dead? Or under
      The laurel gardens of Italy you'd

Have let the old invaders sleep. Nor have you spared
  Even the leisurely shepherds and herdsmen
    And haven't the peoples by now done
      Penance enough for their easeful slumbers?

Who started it? Who brought the curse? It is not
  Of today and not from yesterday and those
    Who first lost the measure, our fathers,
      They didn't know and their spirits drove them.

For too long, too long, mortal humans with glee
　　Have trodden on each other's faces and fought
　　　　To rule, fearing their neighbours, and none
　　　　　　Even on his own ground has a blessing.

And this generation in ferment as if
　　In Chaos, its unsteady desires flit and
　　　　Drift and their poor lives are wild and have
　　　　　　Lost heart and are cold with anxieties.

But you, Mother Earth, continue quietly
　　Your firm course in the light. You flower in spring,
　　　　Out of your rich life the seasons grow
　　　　　　Melodically changing, and leave you.

O you the best-beloved of all the holy
　　Muses and the constellations, longed-for
　　　　Renewer of life, oh come now, Peace
　　　　　　And give us heart and our lives an abode.

Innocent peace, our children are wiser than
　　Us their elders almost, the conflict does not
　　　　Turn their goodness or their minds, they have
　　　　　　Some joy and clarity in their looks still.

And as with other spectators the judge looks
　　With an earnest smile on the young contestants
　　　　There on the hot track forcing faster
　　　　　　The chariots, raising the dust in clouds

So Helios, the happy god, stands smiling
　　Over us and is never alone but has
　　　　The aether's blossoming stars always
　　　　　　With him, dwelling in their holy freedom.

Heidelberg

I've loved you a long time. What joy it would give me
  To call you my mother and sing of you simply
    Who are of my country's towns
      The rural-loveliest I've seen!

As the bird of the forest flies over the heights
  So over the river that passes you shining
    The bridge reaches, light and strong
      And sounding with wheels and footsteps.

Once as though sent by gods an enchantment fastened
  Me on that bridge as I crossed and into the hills
    And upon me the light of
      The beckoning distances shone

And the youth, the river, made for the level land
  Sadly glad. So the heart, becoming to itself
    Too beautiful, in time's flood
      Will dive, to be sunk still loving.

You had given him, the fugitive, streams and cool
  Shadows and the banks were all watching as he passed
    And their pretty mirrorings
      Quivered upwards from the ripples.

But into the valley, down to the bed of it,
  Hung the vast castle, cracked by the lightnings, heavy
    With the learning of fate, but
      Over the ageing colossus

The eternal sun poured its rejuvenating light
  Everywhere the living ivy flourished green
    And the friendly woodland made
      A rustling down over the fort.

Bushes blossomed down to where in the bright valley
   Cleaving to the slope or gracing the river banks
      In among scented gardens
         Your cheerful alleys quieten.

The Gods

In the aether: stillness. This has kept my soul
   From scathing in its pain and under the eyes
      Of Helios the indignant heart
         Often will lift itself to steadfastness.

Kind gods, we are poor without you, a man then
   In his savage self has strife and no respite
      And the world is black in him and no
         Joy thrives and no singing for him ever.

Only you who are always young, you nurture
   In hearts that love you a child's understanding
      And in anxieties and error
         Never let the spirit sadden to death.

The Neckar

In your valleys the heart within me awoke
   To life, your waters played around me and of
      All the gracious hills that know you,
         Traveller, none is a stranger to me.

Often on those high places the airs of heaven
   Released me from the pain of servitude and
      Up from the valley, as life out of
         Joy's cup, the silver-blue waters sparkled.

The freshets of the hills hurried down to you
   And with them my heart and you took us with you
      To the quietly majestic Rhine
         Down to its towns and jovial islands.

Still the world looks lovely to me, my vision,
   Longing for the beauties of the earth, absconds
      To golden Pactolus, Smyrna's shore
         And the woods of Ilium. I should like

To land often at Sounion and consult
   The mute path to your columns, Olympieum
      Before the years and the storm winds
         In the rubble of Athens, the temples,

The graven images of the gods, bury
   You too, already so long alone, the pride
      Of a lost world. And oh you lovely
         Islands of Ionia where the breeze

From the sea cools the hot shores and through the groves
   Of laurel rustles, where the sun warms the vines
      Oh, where a golden autumn changes
         The sighs of the poor people to singing

When their pomegranates ripen, when through green
    Night the oranges gleam, when the mastic drips
        And drum and cymbal sound and summon
            The dancers to the labyrinthine dance.

To you, oh you islands, one day perhaps my
    Guiding angel will bring me but even there
        I'll hold my Neckar with her willowed
            Banks and her sweet meadows close in my heart.

Home

The boatman comes home glad to the still river
   From distant islands when he has harvested;
      So I should come home too had I as
         Much good harvested as I have sorrow.

Dear riverbanks, once my fosterers, can you
   Still the sorrows of love, can you promise me,
      Woodlands that I was young in, when I
         Come back to you my peace of mind again?

The cool beck where I watched the ripples playing,
   River where I watched the boats gliding away
      There I'll soon be, the familiar hills
         Who were my guardians once, the homeland's

Revered and safe frontiers, my mother's house,
   Sister and brother, their loving embraces,
      I will enjoy and they'll enfold me
         And swaddle my heart in healing bands for

They have kept faith with me. But I know, I know
   The sorrow of love will not be healed so soon,
      No lullaby that a consoling
         Human sings will sing it away from me.

For those who lend us heaven's fire, the gods,
   They give us the gift of holy sorrow too.
      So be it. I'm a son of the earth
         Made, as it seems, to love and to suffer.

Love

Forget your friends, if you must, vilify all
   Your own, your poets, and may God forgive you such
      Thanks, but only if you will
         Honour the souls of lovers.

For tell me where else now human life is alive
   Since all are in the grip of servile care? The god
      Left long ago, carelessly
         He strolls his ways above our heads.

But just as the year is always cold and songless
   At the determined time but out of the white fields
      Green shoots come through and often
         A solitary bird does sing

When slowly the forest opens, the river stirs
   Already the milder air wafts in from the south
      At the chosen hour and is
         A sign of the fairer times that

We believe in, so, like none other sufficient
   Like none else noble and good, yet over the iron
      And savage ground God's only
         Begotten daughter, love, will grow.

Love, heaven's seed in us, I wish you a kind earth,
   Song at your nursing, the clearest, purest air
      For your nourishment and sun
         The quickener, so you ripen,

Grow and become a woodland, a livelier world
   Fully flowering. May the language of lovers
      Be the language of the land
         Their souls the voice of the people.

Course of life

You also wanted greater things but love forces
   All of us down and sorrow bows us still harder
      But not for nothing and though
         They bend us back where we began.

Up or down! Are there not in the hallowed night where
   Nature dumbly ponders the coming days and in
      Crookedest Orcus also
         Right things, things that are straight and true?

So I learned. For never as mortal teachers do
   Have you, my deities, upholders of all things
      Led me, so far as I know,
         With caution on level pathways.

The gods say to humans, Taste everything and learn
   By that strong nourishment to give thanks for all things
      And know what it is to be
         Free to quit and go where you like.

Parting

(second version)

So intending to part, thinking it good and wise
　　Why did the doing it shock us like murder then?
　　　　How little we know ourselves!
　　　　　　Working in us there is a god

Whom to betray, creator for us at the start
　　Of sense and life, inspiriter and guardian
　　　　Angel of our love, only
　　　　　　That I don't have the strength to do.

Worldly sense however has other rules of wrong
　　Practises other strict service, another code
　　　　And day by day convention
　　　　　　Filches the living soul from us.

Oh I knew this already! Since between the gods
　　And humans, fear, that deformity, rooted
　　　　Lovers must die and blood must
　　　　　　Flow from their hearts in atonement.

Let me be silent, let me never again view
　　This killing thing but in peace may I go away
　　　　From here into loneliness
　　　　　　So the parting still be ours.

Hand me the cup yourself so that of the saving
　　Sacred poison, the Lethe drink, I drink enough
　　　　With you and love and hatred
　　　　　　Will all of it be forgotten.

I shall leave. Perhaps a long while hence I'll see you
　　Diotima here. But desire by then will be
　　　　Bled white and peacefully like
　　　　　　The blessed as strangers we shall walk

Conversation leading us, pensive, hesitant
   To and fro until here the place of the parting
      Alerts our forgotten selves
         Warmth comes into our hearts again

I look at you amazed, I hear voices, sweet songs
   As from a former age, the playing of a lute
      And the lily lifts, fragrant
         Golden, over the stream to us.

Diotima

You are silent, you suffer it. They cannot grasp
   A life lived nobly. You cast down your eyes,
      Silent in lovely daylight. You look
         In vain for your kindred under the sun,

Those royal people who, like brothers and like
   The sociable tops of trees in a grove,
      Enjoyed home and their loves once and their
         Forever-embracing heaven and who

Sang in their hearts and never forgot their source –
   I mean the grateful, the only loyal ones,
      The bringers of joy into the depths
         Of Tartarus, men like gods, the free men,

Gentle and strong, who are souls below now
   Whom the heart has wept for since the mourning year
      Began and the stars that were here then
         Daily turn us to thinking of them still

And this lament for the dead can never rest.
   Time heals, though. Now the gods in heaven are strong
      And quick. And Nature is assuming
         Surely her old and joyful rights again.

See, love, it will happen before our hill is
   Levelled and before my words are dead the day
      Will have come when you will be named with
         Gods and heroes, a day that is like you.

Return to the homeland

Mild breezes, messengers from Italy
  My beloved river with its poplar trees
    The undulating hills, the sunny
      Uplands, here still, all as you always were?

Quiet place, you came to me in dreams, far off
  After hopeless days, to me in my longing
    You, my house, and you, the hilltop trees
      My companions, my close familiars.

How long, so long ago, the child's peace of mind
  Has gone and gone are youth and love and delight
    But you, my motherland, holy in
      Your long-suffering, see, you have remained.

And because they suffer with you and with you
  Rejoice, dear land, they are yours, you watch their ways,
    And in dreams admonish them when they
      Wander far off and go wrong, unfaithful.

And when in the youth his self's own passion
  And headstrong desiring have calmed and quietened
    Faced by his fate then, clearer, truer
      He gives himself to you more willingly.

Farewell then, days of my youth, love's rosy paths
  And all you paths of the traveller, farewell
    And take up and give, o you homeland
      Heavens, once again my life your blessing.

Encouragement

(second version)

Free spirit, echo of heaven, our holy
   Heartener, why among the living are you
      Mute now? Or have the godless sent you
         Down into the night to sleep for ever?

Does not the light of the aether wake and Earth,
   Old mother, still blossom as they always did?
      And here and there do not the spirit
         And, smilingly, love still assert their law?

And you will not? But in the heavens there are
   Reminders and Nature, the quiet maker
      Who cheers all life and fills the soul's
         Lungs, breathes on you as on a bare field.

Hope comes that soon not only the groves of trees
   Will sing life's praises for now it is the time
      When from the mouths of men and women
         Newly a lovelier soul will speak

And the element allied with humankind
   Will be kinder then, only then will Earth come
      Into her riches in her children's
         Thanks, her infinite goodness will unfold,

Our days will again be like flowers and Sun
   In the heavens will see himself imparted
      In the still passing of time, his light
         Joyfully mirroring in the joyful

And he who rules without speaking and prepares
   Unbeknownst the future, the god, the spirit
      Will utter himself as once he did
         In the lovely daylight in human words.

Sung under the Alps

Holy innocence, the best beloved, the
Closest to the heart of gods and men, indoors
Or under the sky where you sit at the feet
                Of them, the elders,

Wise and wanting nothing; for although we know
All manner of good we stare like beasts still
Often at heaven, but how pure to you, pure
                Yourself, are all things.

Look at the brute beast of the fields: it serves
You willingly and trusts you, the dumb woods speak,
As they did formerly, their words to you and
                The mountains teach you

Holy laws, and whatever to us, who are
Experienced, the almighty now, the Father,
Lets be made clear, only you may utter it
                Shining innocence.

To be thus alone with the gods, light passing
By and the rivers and the wind and time that
Hurries to its end, and yet to be steady-
                Eyed before them

Is blessed, I know nothing more, nor want, so long
As the flood that uproots the willow does not
Take me too and I must go with the waters
                Cradled and sleeping.

Who truly houses God in his heart of hearts
Is content at home; in freedom then, so long
As I may let me sing and elucidate
                The tongues of heaven.

The calling of poetry

The banks of the Ganges heard the joyful god's
    Triumph when from the Indus conquering all
        The young Bacchus came with holy wine
            Waking the peoples out of their slumbers.

And you, the day's angel, will you not awake
    Those who are still sleeping? Give us the laws, give
        Us life, Master, prevail, you only
            Have the right of conquering, like Bacchus.

What otherwise in the home or out beneath
    The open sky is a human's fate and care
        When, nobler than the animals, we
            Feed and fend for ourselves, not such things are

Entrusted to the poet's care and service:
    The holiest is what we are suited for
        That closer, forever newly sung
            The befriended heart will hear and feel it.

And yet, o you heavenly pantheon, all
    You springs and shores and hills and groves of trees
        Where wonderfully first you seized us
            By the hair and unforgettably

The spirit of god the maker came over us
    So out of the blue, so beyond hoping, our
        Minds were dumb as if touched by lightning
            And every bone in the body shook –

You restless doings in the wide world, fateful
    Furious days when the god, musing for himself
        Steers wherever the gigantic
            Anger-maddened horses bring him, shall we

Say nothing of you and if in us still plays
   The melody of the ever tranquil year
      Will it not be as though in idle
         Daring a child of the Master fingered

For a joke the pure and dedicated strings?
   And, poet, was it for this you heard the East's
      Prophets and the singing of Greece and
         Lately the thunder only to enlist

The spirit to service and rush the presence
   Of that good and mock and heartlessly deny
      That innocence and for a game, for
         Money, drive it like a captured creature

Till goaded into fury it remembers
   Its origins and calls so the Master comes
      Himself and in volleys of fire
         And death evicts the soul from your body?

Too long already all holy things are made
   To serve and for pleasure, ungratefully, a
      Sly generation squanders, exhausts
         The kind forces of heaven and presumes

When the god himself ploughs their fields to know him
   The Light of Day, the Thunderer, and it spies
      With telescopes and numbers and names
         Every one of the stars of heaven.

But the Father so that we may still abide
   Here a while, closes our eyes with holy night.
      He dislikes unrule. Nor will a wide
         Violence ever force heaven open.

Nor is it good to be too wise. We know him
   By thanking. But not easily holding it
      Alone, gladly, a poet, to learn
         To help, will seek company with others.

But fearlessly, if he must, the man will stand
 Alone before God, safe in simplicity
  And he needs no weapons and no guile
   Not till God's desertion stacks against him.

Voice of the People

(second version)

You are the voice of God so I once believed
  In youth, that holy time, and I say so still.
    The rivers also never heeding
      Our wisdom rise and roar but nonetheless

All love them and they always trouble my heart
  When I hear them far off vanishing full of
    Presentiment not my way but more
      Surely hurrying off into the sea.

For self-forgetting, all too keen to do the
  Gods' desire, the living, who will die, going
    A while their own ways open-eyed will
      Seize too eagerly the way that takes them

Quickest back into the universe, the way
  The river, flung headlong, seeking rest, is tugged
    And dragged willy nilly down from one
      Falls to the next without his steering by

The wondrous longing towards the abyss,
  The itching to come undone, and this delight
    In dying seizes peoples too and
      Bold cities, when they have tried their best and

Driven on the work year after year, they meet
  A holy end, the earth greens again and there
    In silence flat on the sand as if
      At prayer before the stars of its own

Free will defeated the long art lies before
  The inimitable stars, himself to honour
    The highest with his own hand he broke
      His work in pieces, man, the maker, did.

But those are not less dear to human beings
    Who give in love as good as they are given
        And often slow, to lengthen our time
            Enjoying the light, our trajectory.

And not only the eagle, so they will not
    Stay home too long, evicts its young from the nest
        Us likewise the lord and master with
            A goad for the purpose he drives us out.

Happy are those already gone to their rest
    Falling before the time, they also, being
        Like the first fruits of harvest also
            A sacrifice, had their allocation.

In Greek times on the Xanthus the city stood
    But went like the greater cities now at rest
        In that land through an event of fate
            Out of sight of the holy light of day.

They did not die in the open battle but
    By their own hands. What happened there, the horror
        Of it carries all the way to us
            Out of the east in a wondrous story.

The kindness of Brutus riled them. For after
    Fire had broken out he offered himself to
        Help though he stood before the city's
            Gates as a commander, besieging it.

But they flung down from the walls the servants he
    Had sent. Whereupon the fire grew livelier
        And they rejoiced and Brutus reached out
            Towards them with his hands and they were all

Ecstatic, they raised a great noise of crying
    And jubilation. Husbands and wives then flung
        Themselves into the flames and boys some
            Leapt from the roofs some at their fathers' swords.

It is not advisable to test the nerve
    Of heroes. This was long prepared. Their fathers
        Also once being attacked and the
            Persian enemies pressing them hard

Seizing the reeds of the river, to break out
    Free, they set fire to the city. And the flames
        Took up houses and temples flying
            Into the holy aether and people.

So the children had heard and no doubt it is
    Good to have stories for they keep us in mind
        Of the highest but also needed
            Are ways of explaining the holy text.

The blind singer

ἔλυσεν αἰνὸν ἄχος ἀπ ᾽ ὀμμάτων Ἄρης.

SOPHOCLES

Light, youthful light, where are you who always at
 The hour of the morning have woken me?
  The heart is waking but still in a
   Holy spell the night compels and keeps me.

I used to love listening at the daybreak
 For you, at your hill, waiting, never in vain
  Never, sweet light, did your harbingers
   The breezes, deceive me, you always came

Inspiriting all things, came the usual path
 Hither in your beauty, oh where are you, light?
  Again the heart is waking but still
   The unending night compels and cribs me.

For me back then the leaves put forth, the flowers
 Shone for me like my own eyes, not far away
  Were the faces of the ones I loved
   They shone for me and above and around

The woods I saw the wings of the open skies
 Pass on their wanderings in my youthful time.
  Now from one hour to the next I sit
   Still and alone, and my thoughts make figures

From the love and sorrow of the brighter days
 For my own delight and I hearken into
  The distances whether some friendly
   Liberator might perhaps come to me.

Then often I hear the voice in the thunder
At midday when in bronze he approaches when
His house shakes and under him the ground
Reverberates and the mountains echo.

Then in the night I hear the rescuer, the
Liberator, hear him killing, life giving
In thunder hurrying from sunset
To sunrise and after him my music

Sounds, my singing comes to life with him and as
The stream follows the river's thinking likewise
I must leave and follow him who is
Sure of himself on the erratic ways.

Where to? Where to? I hear you close and further
And all around the earth sounds with your glory.
Where will you end? And what, what is it
Above the clouds and what working in me?

Day! Day! You above collapsing clouds, you are
Welcome to me, my eyes open like flowers
To you, o youthful light, oh the old
Happiness again, more spirited, as

Golden waters from a holy cup pour down
And you, green earth, my peaceful cradle, and you
House of my fathers, you, my loved ones
With me back then, come closer now, oh come

All of you, that this joy shall be shared with you
And the man who sees now give you his blessing.
Oh take for me, so I may bear it,
Life, the life of the gods, from off my heart.

Poetic courage

(first version)

Are you not kith and kin with every living thing?
    Does not Fate herself nurture you into service?
        Go forward then through life un-
            Armed and without anxiety.

Whatever happens, make it all a blessing, turn
    It to joy, for what thing is there that could befall
        Your heart insultingly if
            You are going the way you must?

For as by a quiet shore, in close, or among
    Silver resounding waves or over a silence
        Of depths of water the light
            Swimmer passes so too are we,

The poets of the people, eager to be where
    Living things move and breathe around us, glad, disposed
        To all and trusting, how else
            Should we sing to all their own god?

And even should one of the brave where truly he
    Trusted be tempted by the waters down and his
        Singing voice fall silent in
            Rooms of deeper and deeper blue

He died glad and those left lonely, his groves of trees
    They bewail the fall of their favourite and she
        His friend, often will hear his
            Singing still in the leafing boughs.

In the evening then if one of our kind comes by
    Where the comrade sank, he will think hard, many things,
        At the warning place and say
            Nothing and go more provided.

Poetic courage

(second version)

Are you not kith and kin with every living thing?
   And does not Fate herself nurture you in service?
      Go forward then through life un-
         Armed and be fearful of nothing.

Whatever happens, make it a blessing, turn
   It to joy, for what thing is there that could befall
      Your heart insultingly if
         You are going the way you must?

For ever since poetry on a breath of peace
   First left the lips of humans and our words, helping
      In good and bad times, touched their
         Hearts with pleasure, so we who are

The people's singers have liked to be where many
   Kinds of the living mingle, glad, disposed to all
      Open to all; for this is our
         Ancestor's way, the sun god's, who

To rich and poor allows the cheerful daylight and
   In the hastening times holds us, who cannot last,
      Upright on golden leading-
         Strings much as we do the children.

Him awaits, him also takes, when the hour arrives
   His crimson tide; see there now where the noble light,
      Adept at changing, travels
         Equably down the path it must.

So then let pass when it is time and the spirit
   Nowhere still lacks its due, let die then also in
      The seriousness of life
         Our joy but – die beautifully.

The fettered river

Sleeping and dreaming, youth, wrapped up in yourself
    Idle between the cold banks in sufferance
        Have you forgotten your origins
            Son of Ocean, friend of the Titans?

The loving messengers the Father sends you
    Do you not know them, the breezes breathing life?
        And does the word from the waking god
            Out of the brightness above not reach you?

Already it sounds, sounds in his heart, as when
    Still in the lap of the rocks he used to play
        It bubbles up in him now, and now
            He remembers his strength, his force, now he

Who was hesitant hurries, laughs at and takes
    The fetters now and breaks and flings them in bits
        Angry, so easy, this way and that
            On the resounding banks, and at the voice

Of this son of a god the mountains awake
    All round, the woods stir, the chasm from far away
        Hears the herald and in the bosom
            Of the earth joy shudders to life again.

Spring comes; new greenery is dawning; he though
    Has gone his ways to the immortals having
        Nowhere he is allowed to bide till
            The Father takes him up into his arms.

Chiron

Light, thoughtful light, where are you, who always must
   Go aside at times, where are you? My heart has
      Awoken but the astounding night
         Thwarts me in anger still. I used to go

For herbs into the woods, I was soft and shy,
   I listened by the hill and never in vain,
      Never once did your birds deceive me
         And almost all too eagerly you came

Wanting the refreshment of my garden or
   A foal or my counsel for your heart, oh light
      Where are you? My heart wakes again
         But still the heartless night pulls at me hard.

I remember what I was. The earth gave me
   Its first bouquet of saffron, corn and thyme.
      I learned under the cool stars, at least
         Such things as we can put a name to. Then

He came, the upright man, the demi-god, the hind
   Of Zeus, and took the magic from the wild fields
      And saddened them. Now I sit alone
         From one still hour to the next and my thoughts

Make figures from clouds of love and the wet earth
   For poison is between us, and hark into
      The distances whether some friendly
         Liberator might perhaps come to me.

Then I hear the chariot of the Thunderer
   Often at noon, approaching, I know him best,
      His house reverberates and the ground
         Is cleansed and my pain echoes after him.

I hear my rescuer in the night, I hear
    Him killing, my liberator, and I peer
        As though in visions down at the earth
            Luxuriant with growth like a fierce fire;

The days come and go, and when one watches them,
    The good and the bad, and suffers, when one is
        Two in shape and there is nobody
            At all who knows what would be for the best

That is the thorn of the god working, for how
    Could one love otherwise divine injustice?
        Then the god comes home and settles in
            And we are face to face and the earth is changed.

Day! Day! Now the willows can breathe again
    Along my streams, and drink, now the eyes have light
        And there are proper footings, and as
            A regent, spurred, local and home, you shine

Out in your self, my errant star of the day,
    And the earth also, a peaceful cradle, shines
        And the house of my fathers who were
            Not citizens and went in clouds of beasts.

Now take a horse and clothe yourself in armour
    And take up the light spear, child. The prophecy
        Will hold and with it will appear my
            Returning Heracles, so waited for.

Tears

Heaven's love, should I ever forget that love
 And the kindness of heaven, should I... And you
  They visited with fire and are full
   Of ash already and desolate and

Lonely, beloved islands that were the eyes
 Of the fabled places, you solely now
  Concern me, shores where idolatrous
   Love paid the price, but only to heaven.

For all too gratefully they served, those blessed
 With life there in the days of beauty and
  The heroes in a rage of life, and trees
   In plenty and the cities stood, were there

To be seen like a man in the senses; now
 The heroes are dead and the islands of love
  Almost disfigured. So love must be
   Everywhere, foolish and at a loss.

Oh may the light of my eyes not be put out
 Wholly with tears and death not shame me and let
  A memory live after though I
   ` Am weak now, robbed and deluded by tears.

To Hope

Hope, who are kind to us and busy yourself
    Even in the houses of mourners and go
        To and fro between us who die and
            The forces of heaven gladly, helper

Where are you? Over what little life I had
    The cold evening blows already and I
        Am quiet as the shades here, songless,
            Fearful already, cold and dead at heart.

In a valley, in a verdant place of pure
    Spring waters daily rushing forth, where the autumn
        Is lovely with open crocuses
            There in the silence I will look for you

And kindness from you then or when at midnight
    The invisible life among the trees moves
        And over me those flowers that never
            Sadden, the bright stars, are in bloom, oh then

Dear heaven's daughter from your father's gardens
    Come down and if not as a ghost of the earth if
        That can't be then come and with something
            Other startle, startle my heart somehow.

Vulcan

Come now, friendly spirit of fire, enfold
   In clouds, in golden dreams, the woman's gentle
      Temperament and protect the flower
         Of quiet in her and the lasting love.

And the man, let him like his thoughts and his work
   And his candle light and the coming day and
      Let not his portion of discontent
         And ugly anxiety be too great

When now the ever-angry Boreas, my
   Sworn enemy, overnight falls on the land
      With frost and late at the hour for sleep
         Sings his cruel mockery of humankind

And wrecks the walls of our towns and the hedges
   We so carefully set and the groves of trees
      This spoiler of all things and even
         In the making of verse troubles my soul

And with no respite havocking over the
   Placid river empties his black clouds so that
      Far and wide the valley seethes and like
         Falling leaves rocks fall from the bursting hills.

Pious more than other creatures the humans
   May be but when there's anger outside they too
      Look to themselves, in their meagre homes
         Bide safe and reflect on their freeborn state.

And always one of the friendly spirits with
   Her blessings lives with them, no matter how all
      The unteachable energies rage
         In anger, she, Love, despite and still, loves.

Timidity

Are you not acquainted with many living things?
    And where you walk is it not carpeted with truth?
        Go then, my soul, into life
            Naked, without anxiety.

Whatever happens, welcome the use of it, rhyme
    It to joy, for what thing is there that could befall
        Your heart insultingly if
            You are going the way you must?

Since humankind like the gods who are as alone
    In their way as the wild beasts, since poetry
        And the foremost choirs have led
            Gods and humans home so we the

Tongues of the people have liked to be where many
    Kinds of the living mingle, glad, the same to all,
        Open to all; for this is
            The sky god's way, our father's who

To rich and poor allows the thinking daylight and
    At the turning of the times holds us, the asleep,
        Upright on golden leading-
            Strings much as we do the children.

Good for something, useful to someone, we also
    Are who come with art and of the gods of heaven
        Bring one in. But ourselves we
            Bring our ready and able hands.

Ganymede

Son of the mountains, sleeping, lying at odds
   Freezing between the bare banks, sulking, patient
      Have you forgotten the grace you had
         At heaven's tables, when they were thirsty?

Down here don't you know the Father's messengers
   Nor the airs playing more sharply among the rocks?
      And the word a travelled man sends you,
         The old breathing word, does it not reach you?

Oh, now it sounds in his heart! Deep bubbling up
   In him, as once before high among the rocks
      While he was sleeping, and now, enraged
         He cleanses himself of the shackles now

Now races, who seemed slow, and laughs at the slag,
   Takes it, smashes it, casts it in bits aside
      Drunk with rage, easy, this way and that
         On the staring banks, and at this stranger's

Own voice the flocks leap to their feet, the woods
   Stir and deep in the land, distant, the river's
      Being is heard and the spirit again
         Shudders to life in the navel of the earth.

Spring comes. And everything after its fashion
   Flowers. But he is distant now, no longer there,
      He wandered, for the spirits are all
         Too kind, again he speaks heavenly language.

Half of life

The land with yellow pears
And full of wild roses
Hangs into the lake
O gracious swans
And drunk with kisses
You plunge your heads
Into the holy, the sober water.

Alas, for where in winter
Shall I come by flowers and where
The sunlight and
The shade of the earth?
The walls stand
Speechless and cold, the wind
Clatters the weathervane.

Ages of life

Euphrates' cities and
Palmyra's streets and you
Forests of columns in the level desert
What are you now?
Your crowns, because
You crossed the boundary
Of breath,
Were taken off
In heaven's smoke and flame;
But I sit under clouds (each one
Of which has peace) among
The ordered oaks, upon
The deer's heath, and strange
And dead the ghosts of the blessed ones
Appear to me.

Hahrdt Nook

The wood sinks down
And, like buds, the leaves
Hang inwards, under them
A ground blooms up
With things to say.
For there Ulrich
Walked. Often over the footprint
A large destiny broods
Ready at the remaining place.

Menon's lament for Diotima

1

Day after day I go out in search of what is not there,
    Long since I have questioned all of the country's paths;
Visited those cooling heights and all of those places of shade
    Also the springs; the spirit treks up and down, astray
Pleading for rest; so the deer when they hit him flees to the forest
    Where at midday he once rested safe in the dark.
Now that bed in the greenery salves his heart not at all,
    Pain drives him sleepless and whimpering to and fro,
Neither the warmth of daylight nor the cool of the night helps.
    Useless to dip his wounds in the swirls of the river.
And just as Earth offers him in vain her cheerful
    Healing plants and no breeze quietens his fevering blood
Like that, my dear ones, it feels in me and can no one
    Lift from my mind this dream of unhappiness?

2

Nor does it help at all when once death's divinities
    Seize and tight in their grasp hold the defeated man,
Once the demons have hauled him down into dreadful night
    Then to seek ways and means, plead or quarrel with them
Or even patiently to bide in the fearful banishment
    Hearing the truth of their cold refrain with a smile.
If it must be, forget your salvation and sleep without music!
    Yet, like a spring, a chord rises, hoping, in you
Still, o my soul, even now you cannot accustom yourself;
    Deep in the iron sleep, here in the depths you still dream.
I have no festive time but should like to be garlanded;
    Am I not all alone? Yet some friendly thing must
From far off be near me so that I smile in amazement
    Here in the midst of sorrow how joyful I am.

3

Light of love, so even on the dead you shine golden!
  Sights of a brighter time radiate into my night?
Sweet gardens, oh welcome here, and mountains reddened by evening
  And you, paths of the woodland, now silent, who witnessed
Happiness fit for heaven, and stars, you high observers
  Back then so often with a blessing glancing down on me.
And you my Mayday's loving and beautiful children
  Quiet roses, and you, the lilies, often I speak of you still.
True, the springtimes pass over, one year displaces another
  Changing and quarrelling there, time with a roar engulfs
The heads of those who will die but not the eyes of the blessed,
  And to lovers is given the gift of a different life.
For the days and the years of the stars, they were all
  Diotima, united around us, always, and close.

4

But we contented together like loving swans who are
  Quiet on the lake or ride rocked on its waves and gaze
Down at the mirrored silvery clouds in the water, the blue of the
  Highest and purest sky flowing under them passing
So on the earth we went our ways and even when Boreas,
  The enemy of lovers, the maker of mourning, threatened
 Stripping the branches of leaves and hurling the rain down the wind
  We were quiet, we smiled, feeling a god of our own in
Our conversation, our unison souls, and each with the other
  Wholly at peace, like children, joyously alone.
But now the house is desolate to me, they have taken
  My eyes, I have lost all myself with the loss of her, I am
All astray now and must so it seems like a shade live on
  Long after nothing left makes any sense to me.

5

Still I should like to celebrate – what? – and to sing with others
  But alone as I am all sense of the gods has gone.

This it is that afflicts me, I know it, a curse that lames my
   Sinews and flings me down at every beginning
So that I sit all day without feeling and dumb as a child and
   Tears are the only and frequent signs of life in my eyes
And the flowers of the fields and the singing of birds are a sadness
   Being themselves in their joy messengers of the gods
But in me in my freezing heart the inspiriting sunshine
   Flickers cold and fruitless like beams of the night
Oh and a nothingness, empty, like walls of a prison, the heavens
   Lour over my head, burdensome, weighing me down.

6

Once, oh my youth, so different you were and will prayers
   Not bring you again nor any path lead me back?
Must it be for me too as it is for those who, now godless,
   Formerly, light in their eyes, ate and drank with the blessed
Till soon these over-rapturous guests, being sated
   Lost their speech and now under the singing breezes
Under the flowery earth are asleep till one day some violent
   Miracle forces them, sunk deep below, to return
And over the greening earth, newly, to follow their lives.
   Holy breath of the heavens streams through the luminous forms
When the feast is ensouled and tides of love are stirring
   Supping from the heavens then the waters of life will roar
When it resounds down below and the night disburses her treasures
   And there in the rising streams glitters the buried gold.

7

Oh but you who already back then at the parting ways
   Showed me, dejected there, beauty, consoling me
And who once by silence and stillness taught and inspired me
   Till I saw greatness and sang the gods with more joy
Child of the gods you appear and greet me now as you once did
   Speaking to me, as then, of better than this?
See, I must weep before you and lament even though all the while
   Thinking of nobler times, my soul is ashamed.

For so long now, so long, on the weary paths of the earth
    Used to you, I have sought you, lost myself and astray
Joyful guardian spirit, in vain and the years running out
    Since we, opening, saw around us the evenings shine.

8

Lady, your light upholds only yourself in the light, your
    Suffering and lovingkindness uphold only you.
Nor are you even alone, companions enough are
    There when you with the year's roses blossom and rest
And the Father himself sends the gentle breezes, the soothing
    Lullabies of the Muses breathing around you.
Yes, still as she was, wholly, from head to toe, softly
    Here to me as she once did the Athenian woman appears.
Friendly spirit, your eyes, unclouded by troubled thinking,
    Cast the blessing of the light surely on mortal lives.
So you prove it to me, tell it to me, so that I'll tell it
    To others onwards for others also do not believe
That a more lasting life than trouble and anger is joy
    And daily at the ending still there is a golden day.

9

So then, heavenly powers, I too will give thanks and at last
    Prayers of a poet again breathe from a lightened breast.
And as when I with her stood on the sunny uplands
    Giving me life now a god speaks from within the shrine.
So then I too will live, already there's leafing and from
    Apollo's silver mountains his lyre seems to call me on.
Come, it was like a dream, the wings that were bleeding are healed and
    All my hopes, young again, now lift up with new life.
Much that is great, oh much, remains to be found and whoever
    Loved, he will go, he must, his path to the gods.
And you, the first solemn and youthful vows of our love, be
    Our companions still and you, the first dawnings on us,
Pleas we made for our love, incomings of the spirit, all you
    Good angels who like being with people in love

Stay with us until on a ground that is ours together
    There where the blessed will all gladly return and bide
There where the eagles are and the stars that speak for the Father
    There where the Muses are, where heroes and lovers belong
Stay till we there or here on dewy isles are united
    Where our kind were first blossoming in gardens joined
Where poems are true and springs are lovely for longer
    And from the start a new year of our souls begins.

A walk into the country

(for Landauer)

Come, friend, into the open! True, very little shines
    Down today and the heavens shut us tightly in.
Neither the mountains have nor have the tops of the forest
    Lifted as we should like, the air is empty of song.
Dull day, the footways and alleys are sleeping. We might
    Almost, the way it feels, be living in the Age of Lead.
Wishes prevail nonetheless, the faithful won't turn on a moment
    To doubters, so let the day's purpose be pleasure still.
For what we win from the heavens delights us greatly when we
    First are refused it, then, like children, given it at last.
Only let what we win be worth our speeches, our striding,
    Our faith and pains and wholly true be the joy in it.
Therefore I'll even hope that if we begin the thing we
    Wish for and loosen our tongues and once we have found
Words and our hearts are lifted and better imaginings
    Leap from the sparkling mind, then with our flowering
Likewise the flowering of the heavens will start and shining
    Down they will open on us already opened to see.

For the thing we intend, though nothing magnificent
    Does belong to life and feels both joyous and fit.
Also those bringers of blessings, the swallows, a few of them
    Always sooner than summer home to these parts.
So then up there with speeches to bless the ground where our host
    Knowing his trade, is building his guests a house
So they will taste and view the loveliest, the land's abundance
    So, as the heart desires, open, answering the spirit
With feasting, dance and song, that Stuttgart's joy be completed
    For this, desiring it, we climb the hill today.
Let the light of a May day, friendly to humans, speak of it
    Better, explaining itself to guests who are open to learn
Or, as once, if pleasing to others, the custom is ancient
    And so often the gods look upon us with smiles

Let the master builder speak his words from the rooftop
    We, as well as we could, have done what is ours to do.

Oh but the place is beautiful on holidays in the springtime
    When the valley lifts up, when with the Neckar come down
Pasture and forest, greening, and all of the greening trees
    Numberless, blossoming white, move in the cradling air
Or down the hill slopes vines, shrouded in wisps of cloud
    Dawn and thrive and warm in the scented sun.

Stuttgart

(for Siegfried Schmidt)

1

Here is a further good fortune. The dangerous drought is healing
  The scything edge of the light no longer sears the crop.
Rooms stand open again and health is restored to the gardens
  And refreshed by rain the valley rustles and shines
High with growth, the streams enlarge and the wings that were bound
  Dare to lift up again into the regions of song.
The air is full of the joyous and the town and the trees are
  Everywhere filled with the happy children of heaven.
Gladly they meet and mingle, flitting hither and thither
  Careless and, so it seems, nothing's too little, too much.
For the heart orders it thus, and so they will breathe in a fitting
  Grace, a good spirit grants it them as a gift.
But the travellers too are well conducted and have
  Garlands enough and songs and the sacred staff adorned
Fully with the grapes and the leaves of the vine and the fir-tree's
  Shadows, village exulting to village day after day
While like chariots drawn by wild free creatures the mountains
  Lead the way and the path dawdles and hurries along.

2

But d'you suppose that for nothing the gods have opened
  Wide the gates and made the way joyful for us?
Or in their kindness donate to the banquet's abundance
  Berries, honey and fruit along with the wine, in vain?
Donate for our festive singing the crimson light and, cool and
  Quiet, the night for closer talk between friends?
If something more serious holds you, save it for winter and if you've
  Courting in mind, be patient, May's the good month for that.
Now something else is needed, come now and celebrate the ancient
  Custom of autumn that still flourishes nobly with us.

All our concern on this day is the motherland, everyone
    Throwing to the festive flame what is their own. For this
Our communal god has adorned our hair with rustling garlands
    And in the wine dissolves, like pearls, the self's demands.
That is the sense of our gathering like bees and at time-honoured tables
    Encircling the oak tree, to sing; and that is the sense
Of the musical clinking of glasses, for this the choir forces
    Together the wild souls of the quarrelling men.

3

But so we don't, like the all-too knowing, allow this
    Lapsing time to escape us I hurry to meet you there
On the borders of the land where the river's blue waters
    Part round the island and past the dear place of my birth.
The ground is holy to me, both riverbanks, also the rock
    That with house and garden rises green from the waves.
There we meet. Oh light, friendly light where in the beginning,
    Touching me closer, one of your rays hit home.
There life, so lovely, so dear, began and begins now again.
    But, seeing my father's grave, shall I greet you with tears?
Tears, though I have and am holding my friend and hearing the words
    That once with heavenly art healed love's sorrow in me.
Other things wake! I must name him the country's heroes
    Barbarossa, and kindly Christoph, you too, and you
Conradin, as you fell, the strong fall, the ivy is green
    On the rock and bacchantic leaves cover the castle
But past things like things of the future are holy to poets
    And in the autumn days we placate our shades.

4

So with the mighty in mind and their fates that lift up the heart
    Deedless ourselves and slight and yet by the blue of heaven
Looked upon, even us, and pious, like the ancient poets raised
    For joy by the gods, in joy we stride through the land.
Large all around is the coming into being. There in the farthest hills
    Much youthful life begins and descends the slopes.

Springs rush down from there and a hundred industrious streams
    Descend by day and by night and labour the land.
But the Master himself ploughs the middle of the country, the river
    The Neckar, draws the furrows, draws down the blessings.
And the airs of Italy come with him, the sea sends her clouds
    She sends magnificent suns to accompany him. So it is
That the vast abundance grows almost over our heads for hither
    To the level ground the goodness was brought more richly
To my dear ones, my homeland's people, but none on the hills there
    Envies them the gardens, the vineyards, the luxuriant
Grass and the fields of corn and the shining trees that
    Lining the ways arch over the travellers.

5

But while we look about us and pass through the abundant joy
    The path and the day, as though we were drunk on them, flee.
For already the town, far-famed, and luminous now
    Wreathed in the holy green lifts up her priestly head.
Stands there in splendour and holds up the fir and the vinestock
    High into the crimson and blissful clouds. Be gracious
Sovereign of the homeland, to us, the guest and the son!
    Stuttgart, into your happiness, welcome the stranger, my friend!
Always, so I believe, you have encouraged the music
    Of flutes and strings, the innocent chatter of songs
Sweet forgetting of toil in minds still awake and attentive
    And willingly therefore you'll gladden the hearts of poets.
But you, the greater powers, you also, who live and move
    Forever in joy, whom we know of or when, more strongly,
In holy night, omnipotent, ruling alone, you work and create
    And raise up a people beginning to sense a future
Till the young remember the elders above and before you
    Come of age, stands a thinking humanity, shining –

6

Angels of the homeland, oh you before whom even the strongest
    Sight fails and who so unsteady the solitary man

He must hold on to friends, dear friends, and beseech them
    To bear with him all the burden of happiness
Oh you in your kindness I thank you for him and the others
    Who all are my life among mortals and all I possess.
But the night is coming. Let us hurry to celebrate the autumn
    This day, our hearts are full but our lives are short
And what the heavenly day has enjoined upon us to speak of
    For that naming, dear friend, the two of us will not suffice.
I will bring you excellent people, the fire of joy will leap high
    And the more daring words will be uttered more holily.
See: their pure selves! And the friendly gifts of the god that we share
    Only among the loving do they become what they are.
Otherwise not – oh come, oh make it true, for I am
    Alone and will no one take the dream from my mind?
Come, my dear ones, offer your hands and let that be enough
    But the larger delights we save for the children's children.

Bread and Wine

(for Heinse)

1

Town rests now, all around, the lit streets quietening;
    Carriages leave in a flare of lamps with a rush.
Full of a whole day's happiness people go home to their rest;
    Shrewd men weigh profit and losses
Pleased at home; empty the bustling market stands
    Of grapes and flowers and rests from works of the hand.
Distantly though there is music from gardens, perhaps
    Someone in love is playing or a lonely man
Thinking of distant friends or his young days; the unfailing
    Fountains come with a rush through greenery, sweet.
Sofly the rung bells ring on the dusky air and the watchman,
    Mindful of time, calls out the counted hours.
Now comes a stir through the air and troubles the treetops
    And see, our earth's shadower, the moon
Comes too now, stealing in, the night comes, passionate night
    Full of stars and not much concerned about us,
The astonishing night, the foreigner among humans, lifts
    Over mountains, sadly, in glory, shining.

2

Wonderful her goodness to us, from so high, and no one
    Knows what she causes in him nor when, thus
Moving the earth and the hopeful soul in people.
    Even the wise cannot fathom her, God
Wills it, the Highest, who loves you, and so, even more than
    She is, daytime is dear to you, sunlit. Still
Even a clear eye loves the shadows sometimes and may try
    Sleep sooner than need be, for pleasure.
And a tried and trusted man may be glad to look into the night.
    Truly it is right to offer her wreaths and songs
Sacred as she is to the strays and the dead, herself,
    Freest in the spirit, abiding eternally.

But she must grant us also lest in the hesitant time
    Here in the dark we have nothing to grasp
The gift of forgetting and merriment, drunk and holy,
    Grant us the babbling word, like lovers,
Sleepless, refilling the cup, and bolder lives,
    Holy memory too, to wake and watch at night.

3

Also, why smother the heart in us, why, for what reason
    Hold back our mettle, masters and boys, for who
Should prevent it, who would prohibit us joy?
    God's fire itself is driving us day and night
To leave. So come, let us face into openness,
    Seek out a thing that is ours, far as it may be.
This much is certain: be it at midday or should it
    Reach into midnight a measure remains
Common to all, but to each is due also his own
    To go for and come to wherever he can.
Jubilant madness rides over ridicule when it
    Seizes the singers, the makers, in holy night.
So! To the Isthmus, come! There where the open sea sings
    Around Parnassus and rocky Delphi is snow-lit,
Into the land of Olympus, on to the heights of Cithaeron,
    In among the pines, in among the grapes from where
The rivers Ismenus and Thebe rush through the country of Cadmus
    From where and pointing back there the coming god comes.

4

Greece, blessed land, the house of all the immortals!
    See, what we heard in our young days is true.
Hall for a feast, whose floor is the ocean and tables the mountains
    Truly for unique use built aeons ago!
But where are the thrones and the temples, where are the vessels
    Brimming with nectar, the songs delighting the gods?
Where are the words now that lighten, travel and strike?
    Delphi sleeps, where is there a coming, the roar

Of joy breaking – where? – over us, quickly, through all things
    Thundering over the vision from sunny air?
Father! they cried. Lord of light! And flung it from tongue to tongue
    Thousandfold, no one bore life alone,
Such good delights best dealt out and swapped with strangers
    Becoming a din of joy, sleeping the word's power grows,
Father! Light! It sounds to the limits of reaching, the ancient
    Sign, from parent to child, comes down and strikes and quickens.
For so they come in, the gods, shaking the heart arrives
    Thus from the shadows down among humans their day.

5

Their coming at first is not felt, the children
    Strive at them, joy comes too brightly, it blinds,
Humans are shy of them, even a demigod hardly
    Knows who they are by name approaching with gifts.
But the mettle from them is great, their joys fill his heart
    Full but what to do with such good he hardly knows,
Makes with it, wastes, the unholy became almost holy
    Touched by his hands, like a fool, to bless, to give.
A while, as long as they may, the immortals allow this, then
    Come in truth themselves and humans grow used to joy
And the day and to seeing their open faces whose name,
    Ancient and still, is One and All and who
Fathom the core of the heart with a liberal contentment
    Answering, first and alone, happily every want.
So humans are: when the good is there and with gifts a god
    Tends them himself, they neither know nor see it.
First they must bear it, now what they love they name,
    Now for it words must come into being like flowers.

6

Now in earnest they think to honour the blessed gods,
    Really, truly, all things must speak their praise.
Nothing must see the light ugly for gods to look at,
    Halfhearted things are not fit to be under the sky.

So to stand well in the presence of the heavenly gods
    In splendid orders the people of a place arise
With others and build the lovely temples and cities
    Steady and noble, they lift up over the shores –
But where are they now? The flower, the crowns of the feast?
    Thebes has faded and Athens, and is there no longer the rush
Of weapons and the race in Olympia of golden chariots?
    And are the ships of Corinth no longer garlanded?
And why are they silent too, the ancient, sacred theatres?
    And no more dance, the joyous dance for the gods?
Why will a god no longer mark, as they once did, a man
    And astound him, pressing the stamp on his brow?
Or he came even himself and took on the shape of a man
    As a comforter ending and shutting the revels of heaven.

7

But friend, we have come too late. It is true the gods live
    But over our heads, above in another world.
Work without end there and seem to care very little
    Whether we live, so much and so well do they spare us.
The vessel is weak and cannot always contain them,
    Only at times can humanity bear the gods' fullness.
Life is a dream of them, after. But wanderings
    Help, like sleep, and need and the night give strength
Till in the brazen cradle heroes enough have grown,
    Hearts of a strength, as they were, to be like the gods.
They come in the thunder then. Meanwhile it seems to me often
    Better to sleep than be so without comrades
Waiting thus and what to do in the meanwhile and say
    I don't know nor why be a poet in dead time?
But they are, so you say, like the wine god's holy priests
    Who wandered from land to land in holy night.

8

See, when a while ago, to us it seems long, they
    All ascended who were the joy of our lives

97

When the Father averted his face from the human race
    And grieving, rightly, set in on the earth
When at the last had appeared a comforter, quietly,
    A god, announcing the end of the day, and vanished,
Then for a sign that once they were there and would come again
    Some day the choir of immortals left gifts
Which in our human way we can, as before, enjoy.
    Here among humans, the greater thing, joy with the spirit,
Would be too much, for such joy, the highest, we lack the
    Strength still, but thanks lives, a little, quietly.
Bread is the fruit of the earth but is blessed by the light
    And from the thundering god comes the joy of wine.
Thus, having them, we think of the gods who were once
    Here and will be again when the time is right.
Singers sing for that reason in earnest the god of wine,
    The ancient god, they devise him ringing praises.

9

Yes, they are right to say he reconciles day and night,
    Leads the sky's stars for ever in setting and rising
Always merry like the green of the evergreen pine
    Which he loves and the garland he chooses of ivy
Because it lasts and even into the darkness fetches
    Down to the godless a trace of the vanished gods.
What the ancient songs foretold of the children of God
    Is us, we are it: the fruit of Hesperia,
Exactly fulfilled, a wonder, on humankind, as it seems.
    Prove and believe! But so many things happen,
Nothing can work, for we are the shades, heartless, till our
    Father of Light is known and belongs to all.
But in the meanwhile the son of the Highest, the Syrian
    Comes as the torchbearer down among the shades.
The wise are aware, the blessed; the imprisoned soul
    Shines, smiles; thaw of the eyes, to the light.
Titan dreams and sleeps more gently in the arms of the earth,
    Cerberus even, spiteful Cerberus, drinks and sleeps.

Homecoming

(for my family)

1

In the Alps it is still bright night and in there cloud,
    Dreaming up joyful things, covers the valley mouth.
All ways is flung and falls the jesting air of the mountain,
    Down through firs the abrupt light flashes and fades.
Slow haste, cold shivers of joy: Chaos is working,
    Young in shape but strong, revels in loving strife
Under the scarp, it ferments, it reels in the eternal confines,
    Morning is coming up, God's dancers are rising.
For the funds of the year are deepest in there and the holy
    Hours, the days, ordered and mixed more boldly.
But the storm bird watches time, between mountains
    High in the air he holds steady and calls out the day.
Now too, deep in the depths, the village has woken and looks
    Fearlessly, trusting the heights, up from under the peaks,
Scenting growth, for already, like lightnings, the ancient water
    Sources are tumbling, the ground, under their beating, steams.
Echo resounds: by day and by night a measureless
    Work of donation comes forth from the hands of that place.

2

Light meanwhile rests on the silvery heights over all,
    Up there the shining snow is already strewn with roses.
Higher still, over the light, the god, in his clarity,
    Lives and his lucid joy lifts on the play of its rays.
His life is alone and still, his face shines brightly, he seems
    Leaning to lend us life out of his heights of sky,
Creative of joy, with us, as often when, knowing the measure,
    Sparing us, holding off, knowing our limit of breath,
He sends the cities and houses a wellshaped fortune,
    Mild rains to open the land, teeming clouds and these
Familiar breezes and such sweet springtimes as this,
    Slowly his hands lifting up mourners towards joy again,

When he, the maker, renews the times and re-enters
    Freshly hearts in the stillness of ageing and works
Down and down and opens and brightens, which is
    What he loves and a life starts again here and now,
Grace, as it once did, blossoms and into our present comes
    Spirit, and courage and joy rise on wings again.

3

I said many things to him, for whatever poets
    Think and sing is mostly the angels' and his;
And I asked many things for my country to keep the
    Spirit from befalling us suddenly and unasked;
Also for you, many things, who in my country are anxious,
    Who welcome the exiles home smiling with their debt of thanks,
People of my land, for you. I was lulled by the lake, the boatman
    Sat in the stern at his ease, lauding our progress.
Over the levels of the lake one joyous movement extended
    Under the sails and now there in the daybreak the town
Blossoms and brightens forth and from under the shadowy Alps,
    Being led in, the boat enters and rests in the port.
The shores here are warm and the open and welcoming valleys,
    Beautifully lit by paths, face me in shimmering green.
Gardens are grouped together, bright buds are starting,
    Birdsong excites in a man love of the open road.
Everything looks wellknown, the hurried greeting in passing
    Seems a friend's and the faces all seem familiar.

4

This is the ground I was born in, the ground of my home,
    What you are looking for hurries to meet you here.
And a travelled man stands like a son in a din
    Of waves at the gate, staring and seeking names
Fair enough for you, in songs, and calling you blessed
    Lindau, one of the land's welcoming doors that lead us
Out where the distances promise so much, where the
    Wonders are, where God's wild animal, the Rhine,

Breakneck out of the heights comes down to the levels
    And the valley with a shout shows from among the rocks –
To enter there and to stride the bright mountains towards Como
    Or follow the daylight down the length of the open lake.
But through that door which is sacred to me I am beckoned
    Home on familiar roads under blossoming trees
To visit the land and the lovely vales of the Neckar,
    The woods, the green sanctum, oaks and the tranquil
Birches and beeches together in a company where
    Among hills a place lovingly captures me.

5

There I'm received. My mother, the town, when they speak
    Touch and awaken things learned by the heart long ago.
Still the same things! Oh my loved ones, the sunlight and joy
    Flower for you still and your eyes almost never were brighter.
All as it was, thriving and ripening, but nothing
    That lives there and loves loses its loyalty.
Meanwhile the best, to be found, is lying beneath
    God's bow of peace, put by for young and old.
I speak like a fool. Joy makes me. Tomorrow and when we
    Visit the living fields, outside, in future,
Under the trees in blossom in the holidays of the springtime
    More will come to me then, many things, many hopes,
Dearest, the things I have heard of the Father whom I
    Fell silent about, who freshens the wandering times
High in the heights, the Almighty who rules above mountains,
    Soon he will give us heavenly gifts and call forth
Brighter song and the many spirits we need. Oh come soon:
    Hold us, lift us, come now, angels of the year, and you,

6

Angels of the house, and into the veins, into all of life's veins
    Enter and heaven break over all and make nobler,
Younger and nothing that is human and good and not any
    Hour of the day be without cheerful angels and also

Joy such as this when loved ones are found again,
  Such as is fitting for them, hallowed as it ought to be.
Blessing our bread, whom shall I name and when we
  Rest from the life of the day, how shall I offer thanks?
By naming the Highest? A god will not like our mistakes.
  To grasp him our joy is almost too small.
Often we are bound to be silent, we lack holy names,
  Hearts beat yet speech lags behind.
But music may lend any hour its tones and pleases
  Gods perhaps, should they be drawing near.
Let us have music then, and with that the worry
  Is almost soothed that had entered among our joys.
Worries of this kind, willingly or not, in their souls
  Poets must bear, and often, but others they need not.

The Archipelago

Are the cranes coming home to you? Are the ships
Resuming their course to your shores? Do breaths of the breezes
We longed for move on your quietened waves? Does the dolphin,
Lured from the depths, sun his back in the daylight again?
Is Ionia in flower? Is it time? In spring
When the living take heart and their first love
Revives and the memory of golden times then always
You draw me. I come. I salute you: age-old and silent.

You live as you were, unlessened, the mountains lend you
Shade to lie in, you embrace with the arms of a youth still
A beautiful land, and of all your daughters, Father,
Of all the flowering islands, not one has been lost.
Crete stands and grassy Salamis and Delos lifts from among
Dark laurels spiked with light at every dawn
Her ecstatic head and Tenos has and Chios
Purple fruits in abundance, on drunken hills
The Cyprian drink wells up and from off Calauria silver
Streams fall, as they always did, into the sea, their father.
All live still, all the mothers of heroes, the islands,
Flowering from year to year, and though the abyss let loose
Sometimes a flame in the dark, a nether tempest, and seized
One hold and she died and sank in your cherishing lap,
You lasted, for much has gone down and
Risen in your depths and your darkness, sea-god.

Also the gods who inhabit the heights and the stillness
Far off, and who bring with the largesse of power
Sleep and the cheerful daylight and dreaming thoughts
Over the heads of sentient men, they are what they were:
Your companions, and often when evening falls
And over the mountains of Asia the holy moonlight
Lifts and the stars encounter themselves in your waves
You shine as if it were heaven lighting you

Under the travelling stars and your waters switch and your brothers'
Lullaby above echoes from your loving heart.
Then when the light comes, star of the east, the wonderworker,
When the daystar comes and illuminates all things
And the living begin their lives in the golden dream
That the sun, like a poet, presents them with daily
For you in your grief his magic is kinder still,
Kinder than his light, even more beautiful
Is the wreath that he still, as he always did, for a token,
Remembering you, winds in your wintry hair.
Heaven, clear blue, bends over you still and returns
Out of the heights your couriers, the clouds, with the gods' gift,
Lightning, and over the land you despatch them, the woods
On shore, where it burns, reel in the rain and with you
Billow and roar and soon, like a son gone astray
When his father calls, the Maeander, streaming in thousands,
Tears from its twists and turns and Cayster runs to you
Over the flats with laughter and the elder, the firstborn,
Too long hidden, your Nile, in majesty now
Strides from the mountainous distance, tall, like a triumph
Clanging with weapons, homesick and reaching for you.

   Still you think yourself lonely. Rocks in the dumb night
Hear you grieving and often the winged waves fly,
Angered, away from humans at heaven.
You miss them, the loved ones, the noble company
Who honoured you once and wreathed your seaboards
With cities and beautiful temples. The holy elements
Always must seek and pine for, like heroes for laurels,
Hearts to be crowned in, the hearts of a feeling humanity.

   Say, where is Athens now? Oh, grieving god, has your city,
The one you loved best, that reached from your sacred shores,
Collapsed under ash entirely and buried even her graves?
Or are there remains, might a sailor,
Passing, remember her name and call her to mind?
Were there not columns once, risen up, and did not

The figured gods shine down from the citadel roof?
And the turbulent voice of the people murmured
Louder out of the Agora, the streets hurried down
Through the boisterous gates to your port full of blessings.
Look where the trader, thinking into the distance,
Loosed his ship with a will, the flighted breezes
Blew for him too and the gods loved him like the poets
For balancing the earth's good gifts and joining near and far.
Distant Cyprus drew him and Tyre and he reached
As high as Colchis and down the sea to old Egypt
Winning crimson and fleeces and corn and wine
For home, for his city, and often by the wings of his ship,
By his hopes, he was carried through the pillars of reckless
Hercules, out to new blessed isles – but meanwhile
Differently moved, a youth sat alone on the shore of the town,
Listened to the waves, alone in a grave enquiry,
Listened and sat at the feet of Poseidon,
The master, the breaker, and learned from the god what was needed.

For Persia, hating the spirit and lord over millions,
Year after year has stockpiled weapons and slaves,
Laughing at the land of Greece and the few little islands,
Thinking them child's play. He understands slaves but not
People with lives, whose spirit the gods have armoured.
Gives the word carelessly: like fluid from Etna
Tipped when it seethes and spreading in fearful streams
And burning in crimson the cities and the flower gardens
And entering the shock of the sacred sea as a river of fire –
So with the King in a glorious riot the hordes run down,
Scorching and murderous to cities, from Ecbatana.
Athens, the beautiful, falls. Old men
Look back among listening beasts from the hills
In flight to the homes and beg for the burning temples,
Nor can the sons arouse the holy ashes with prayer
Ever again. Death on the plain. Towards heaven
Fireclouds vanish. To reap more of the country
Hot in the face the laden Persians pass.

Off Salamis then, oh that day off Salamis!
Waiting for the end the women of Athens, the girls,
Stand, and the mothers with children, saved, in their arms,
Listening: the voice of the god in the sea, deep down,
Rises with hope and promise, the gods in the sky
Look down, weighing the verdict. For there, off the shaken land
Since dawn, like a slowly manoeuvring storm,
The battle has swung, on frothy seas, and noon strikes
Into the anger unnoticed, exactly above the fighters.
And now the men of the city, children of children of heroes,
Face more brightly, they are the gods' favourites, the issue
Is theirs, they think, and the children of Athens won't haul
Their spirit, that spits at death, in yet.
For sand may be quenching the prey's lost blood but
Still, a last time, it rises, flushed with a nobler strength,
And sets back the hunter – like that, in the row of arms,
Ordered by masters, gathered in a fury, the wild
Enemy even as they fall recover some soul.
Fighting flares up again, like wrestling men
The ships seize hold, the rudder swings with the swell,
Planking breaks as they struggle and sailors and ships sink.

Sung silly by the day, dreaming a vanishing dream,
The King rolls his eyes, grinning all askew at the outcome,
Threatens, begs and rejoices, sends men out like lightning.
He sends them in vain. No one comes back, but
Thunderous, vengeful waves pitch without number
Bloody messengers, ships that have burst and the army's corpses
At his feet where he sits enthroned, by the shaken shore, the pauper,
Eyes on the rout, and the rabble in flight drag him with them,
He bolts, the god drives him, over the waters the god
Drives his lost squadrons and jeers and has smashed his show
To bits and found out the weakling under the armour.

Lovingly back to the waiting abandoned river
Come the people of Athens and down from the homeland's mountains
The shining crowds, meeting like waters, replenish

The emptied plain with joy. But like a mother grown old
After years when the child she thought lost comes
Home to her bosom alive, a young man, but meanwhile
Her soul has faded in grief and the joy comes too late,
Hoping has travailed her, what he recounts,
Her loving and thankful son, she can hardly seize –
Home appears thus to the people of Athens returning.
They look for the dear gods' groves, they look without finding.
Coming as victors, where is the gate to receive them
That welcomed the wanderer with open arms when he came
Home from the islands and looked up with longing and saw
Mother Athene's citadel shining ahead?
But they know their streets when they see them: desolate,
Gardens in mourning. In the Agora then –
The Stoa's columns are prone and the gods'
Statues face down – they take hands and obeying their hearts,
Trusting to love, renew their citizenship.
And a man goes looking for house and home and finds them
Under the rubble; his wife, thinking of the heart of the house
Where they slept, weeps in his arms; the children
Ask is the table there where they sat in the family
Order, watched by the elders, the smiling gods of the household.
Now, though, the people make themselves tents; neighbourhoods
Form as they were and after the heart's own custom the airy
Houses consort on the slopes of the round of hills.
So in the meanwhile they live, like the ancients, the freemen who,
Sure of their strength and trusting the coming day,
Like migrant birds travelled from peak to peak
Singing, the forest's lords, the lords of the trekking river.
Mother Earth enfolds, as she always did, steady in her love,
Her people again and under the holy sky
They have quiet nights and mildly the breezes of childhood
Waft over the sleepers, the murmur of Ilissus
Comes through the planes to them and at night the waves of the sea-god,
Promising new days, whispering of new deeds, comes
Out of the distance with cheerful dreams for his favourites.
Flowers have sprung up again, little by little, and bloom

Golden on the trampled fields and believing hands
Have greened the olive again, and the horses of Athens
Pasture as before in peace on Colonus meadows.

   Honouring Mother Earth and the god of the waves
Now the city flowers, becoming a wonder, starlike,
Founded firmly, the work of the spirit that puts on gladly
Fetters of love and in shapes of its own large making
Remains itself and is the perpetual mover.
And the trees serve the man as he works, Pentelicus
And every neighbourly mountain offers him marble and ore.
Living, as he is, the work leaves his hands
Like spring, full of joy, and splendid and light as sunshine.
Drinking-fountains arise and over the hills in pure
Channels springwater hurries to the shining basin;
Dwellings shine in a row all around like banqueting heroes
Passing the common cup and the high Prytaneum
Rises, gymnasia open to the air and the gods'
Temples come into being, like a bold and holy
Thought from the blessed grove into the aether the Olympieum
Climbs towards the deathless gods, and other heavenly halls,
Mother Athena, yours too, your glorious hill out of grief
Grew with a greater pride and flowered for years and,
God of the waves, your favourites sang in a happy
Gathering frequent thanks to you on the headland again.

   Where are the children of happiness now, the believers?
Home with the distant fathers, their great days forgotten,
Strolling by Lethe, and longing won't bring them
Back into sight, you will never appear
On any of the thousand paths of the flowering earth
Like gods, wherever the search goes, and I, whom your language
Reached and the legend of you, must I grieve and grieve
And my soul go down to your shades before its time?
Let me nearer at least, where your groves are still growing
And the gods' own mountain hides its sorrow in cloud,
Let me come to Parnassus, let my wanderings end

With a sight of Castalia sparkling through the darkness of oaks
And there from a scented and blossoming bowl I will pour
Water, with my tears, on the growth of new green and to you,
Asleep, shall be given the dues of the dead.
There in the silenced vale, in Tempe, under the cliffs
I will live with you and call up your glorious names
Here to me in the night and when you appear in anger,
Ploughs having raped your graves, with the voice of the heart,
Singing its love, I will soothe your shadowy lives
And my soul will accustom itself to living with you.
Like a priest I will question the holy dead but
Question the living too, the high powers of heaven
That pass with their years and years above our ruins,
Secure in their course, for often under the stars
Like freezing winds distraction assaults my heart
And where shall I look for counsel? The comforting
Voice in Dodona's oak was stopped long ago,
At Delphi the god is dumb and the paths are empty
And wild where once, being led by his hopes,
A questioning man climbed up to the prescient town.
But above us the light, the light still speaks to mankind,
Full of beautiful pointers, the thundering god
Cries do we think of him and the grieving waves of Poseidon
Echo it back: do we think of him ever as we did?
For gods are glad to repose on a feeling heart;
The inspiring powers, gladly as they always did,
Go with our aspirations and over the mountains of home
Rests and rules and lives the unending sky
And a people might be as they were, gathered in the Father's arms,
Loving, humanly joyful and sharing one spirit.
But alas this race of ours inhabits the night, it lives
In an Orcus, godless, every man nailed
Alone to his own affairs, in the din of work
Hearing only himself, in a crazy labour
With violent hands, unresting, pitiable, and all
Their trying, like that of the Furies, brings nothing forth.
Thus till the dream of anxiety ends and our souls

Lift up, youthful and gay, and the blessing breath of love,
As often it did when the children of Hellas flowered,
Blows through the new times and over our lightened brows
Nature's spirit again, the wanderer, the god,
Appears in golden clouds, serenely biding.
But daylight is holding off. Those born with the gods still
Inhabit, so it seems, the depths of the earth,
Lonely below, asleep, whilst an undying spring,
Unseen, is brightening over their heads.
Surely no longer! I hear in the distance that festival
Day's chorale on the green hill, the echoing groves,
Youth breathing again and the soul of the people
Collected and still in a freer song and the god
Honoured who belongs in the heights but the valleys are his too.
For where the river in its growing youth hurries out
Happily into the flowering land and the tall
Corn ripens on the sunny plain and fruit, there too
The people are wreathed with love, on the city's hill
The heavenly hall of gladness shines like a human home.
Life, all of life, has filled with the sense of God
And everywhere nature returns to her children, the old
Fulfilment returns and as if from a hill of springs
Blessings water the seedling soul of the people.
O festive Athens, o Sparta remembered for bravery,
Sweet springtime of Greece, when our
Autumn comes, when the spirits of the old world return
Ripened and the year moves to fulfilment
Then on a day that will hold the past in its arms
Weeping in thanks let the people look towards Hellas
And soften the pride of their triumph with memories.

Blossom meanwhile until our fruition begins,
Ionian gardens, blossom, and over the rubble of Athens
May greenery hide that grief from the light of day,
Laurel woods wreath with their lasting leaves the hills
Housing your dead, at Marathon, there where the boys
Won and died and there on the fields of Chaeronea

Where the last men of Athens ran with their weapons and bled
Fleeing from a shameful day, and the travelled streams
Sing down from the hills into the battle valley
Sing down from the peaks of Oeta the facts of fate.
But you, undying, though the Greeks have ceased
Singing your praise, o Poseidon, from out of your waves
Sound in my soul still, often, and on the water
My spirit will move like a swimmer, bravely, and practise
New happiness such as the gods have, and know what the gods mean
And how things change and grow, and when these tearing times
Assail my head too roughly and the need among mortal men
And bewilderment shake my mortal life
Let me think of the stillness then that you have in your depths.

Those sleeping now

One unenduring day I lived and grew with my dearest.
    One after another they slept, one by one they have fled.
Still you, sleeping, wake near my heart, the images of you
    Fleeing, rest in my kindred soul and you live there
Livelier now where joy, the gods' own spirit, where youthful
    Joy reappears in all of my ageing and all of my dead.

As when on a holiday…

   As when on a holiday a countryman
Walks out to see the fields, early
When all the while from a night of heat the cooling
Lightnings fell and in the distance there's still thunder
The river returns between its banks
The ground is green and fresh
And from the heavens' delighting rain
The vinestock drips and shining
In the quiet sunlight stands the grove of trees:

   So for them too it is a promising time
Whom no master alone but by her beauty she
The goddess Nature in her strength and everywhere
Wonderfully with light embraces teaches.
So when at times of the year she seems asleep
In the heavens or among the plants or among the peoples
The faces of the poets sorrow also
They seem to be alone but feel an expectation.
For she, lying quiet, does too.

   But now day dawns! Waiting, I saw it come
And what I saw, the word for it is holy.
For she herself who is older than the seasons
And above the gods of the West and of the Orient
Now with a din of arms Nature has woken
And from the aether down into the abyss
By a settled law, as formerly, born out of holy Chaos
The spirit breathes, is felt again
In her, creator of all things.

   And as fire shines in the eyes of one whose thought
Is bravely taking shape, so now
Again by the signs and the doings of the world
Fires have been lighted in the souls of the poets

And what occurred before, then hardly felt,
Is only now apparent
And they who smilingly have ploughed our fields in
Servant-shapes, the liveliest
Energies of the gods, we recognise them now.

　　Their whereabouts? Their spirit blows through the songs
That spring from the day's sunlight and the warm earth
And from weathers moving in the air and those that
Longer preparing in depths of time, more
Signifying and more audible to us
Travel between heaven and earth and among the peoples.
So the thoughts of the communal spirit come
To rest in the soul of the poet

　　Who then, struck swiftly and long cognisant
Of everlasting things, shakes with memory
And by the holy lightning quickened to flame
The poem, conceived in love, the work – that it may speak to both –
Of earth and heaven, with luck and grace succeeds.
Thus, so poets tell, when she desired to see
Divinity visible his lightning fell on Semele's house
And she, struck by the god, gave birth to
The child of the thunderstorm, holy Dionysus.

　　And so it is that the children of the earth
Now drink the fire of heaven without danger.
But, poets, by our calling we are asked to stand
Bare-headed under God's thunderstorms and to grasp
The Father's very lightning with our hands
And clothing it in song to pass
The gift of heaven to the people. For if
We are only pure of heart
Like children and our hands are guiltless, the Father's

　　Naked lightning will not sear us and deeply
Shaken, suffering in ourselves the suffering

Of the stronger, when the god, highriding, approaches
In storms upon us, the heart will stand its ground.
But ill betide me if from *a self-inflicted wound*
My heart bleeds and my peace is lost
Deep down and my chosen modest contentment
And restlessness and want drive me
To the abundant tables of the gods while around me

Ill betide me

  And if at once I say

I have come to look upon the gods they would
Themselves fling me, the false priest, back among the living
Down, deep down, into the dark to sing
Those quick to learn, a warning song.
There

To Mother Earth

Song of the brothers Ottmar, Hom and Tello

Ottmar

There being no congregation, I sing alone.
So one string touched as though
For a trial by pleasing hands
Plays at the start. But soon with delight and a greater seriousness
The master bows his head
Over the harp and the notes
Shape up for him, they fledge
Many as they are and under the waker's strokes
Together, fully, as though out of oceans
Into the moving air without end the cloud of melody lifts.

But still another thing
Than the music of the harp will be
The singing
The choir of the people.
For although the Father has signs enough
And floods and lightning in his power
Like thoughts
he would surely be inexpressible
And nowhere truly find himself again among the living
Did not the congregation have the heart for singing.

As yet, however

But when the rocks first became
And in a shadowy workshop were forged
the iron strongholds of the earth
Before streams hurried down from the hills
And groves and cities blossomed along the rivers
Already he in the thunder
Had created a pure rule
And established pure harmonies.

Hom

Meanwhile, God of Might, spare him
Who sings alone and give us songs enough
Until it has been spoken as we mean it
The soul's secret.
For often I heard
The hymns of the old priest

        and so
Prepare in me also the soul for thanksgiving.

But in the armoury the men
In idle times wander with tied hands
And view the weapons
In great seriousness they stand and one relates
How formerly the fathers drew the bow
Sure of the mark at a great distance
And all believe him
And none is permitted to try.
Like a god   the people
Let fall their hands
Nor is it right to dress festively for the everyday.

The temple columns stand
Abandoned in the days of need
True, the north wind howls an echo
          deep inside the halls
The rain washes them clean
And moss grows and the swallows return
In the days of spring but the god
Within is nameless and the bowl of thanks
And the vessels of sacrifice and all the sacred things
Are buried from the enemy in the unspeaking earth.

Tello

And who wants to give thanks before he has received
Or answer before he has heard?
Not   while one higher is speaking
To interrupt the music of that speech.
He has much to say and a different right
And there is one, hours will not suffice him
And the times of the creator
Are like ranges of mountains
That billowing upwards from sea to sea
Progress over the earth

Many travellers speak of this
And the wild beasts wander lost in the gorges
And the herds roam over the heights
But in holy shadows
On the green slope dwells
The shepherd and views the peaks
So

At the source of the Danube

[I greet you, Mother Asia
I say your name, not out of my own strength
for, so that thanks shall reach you soon, by the spirit of them, as
     from a holy mountain
I was called to sing

and far away in the shade of the ancient woodlands
you rest and remember your deeds
and energies when you, filled with heavenly fire
drunk on it, lifted up an endless rejoicing and still that voice
out of your thousand years sounds in our ears

But now you rest and listen whether perhaps from lively hearts
an echo of love might not come to you

with the Danube when down from the head of the Black Forest
     she goes towards the East and seeks
        the world and gladly
bears the ships, on her strong waves
I come to you and further, further, before
   it all happens I announce it to you and say
that now at last at last with the waves of the Danube
       the answer comes, Mother Asia]

   For as when from the organ tuned in splendour from on high
In the sacred space
The morning waking prelude's clear springs start
And through the pipes from the well that will never be exhausted
And all around from room to room
The refreshing river of melody flows
And the house, into its cold shadows
Fills with the spirit
And wakes and now in song
The congregation lifts and answers it

This sun of their celebration, so
The word came out of the East to us
And on Parnassus' cliffs and on Cithaeron, o Asia
I hear the echo of you and it breaks
On the Capitol and sheer down from the Alps

    The foreigner comes
To us, the wakener comes
The voice that shapes our humanity.
Then astonishment seized the soul
Of each and everyone of those she touched and night
Fell over the eyes of the best of them.
For humans can do much
And with cleverness and craft bring flood
And rock and the violence of fire under their control
And with careless courage will face the sword
But confronted by the divine
Our strength is cast down

    Rather as the deer
Sweetly driven by youth
To range restlessly over the mountains
Feels its energy
In the midday heat but when
Drawn down through playful breezes
The holy light and with the cooler radiance
The spirit of joy comes
To the blessed earth then unused to this uttermost beauty
The creature succumbs and slumbers in a waking sleep
Even before the stars approach. And we likewise. For in many
The light of the eyes went out before the friendly

    Gifts of the gods came to us from Ionia
And from Asia too and the souls of those
Who were sleeping had no joy
Of the precious teachings and the sweet songs.
But some were awake. And they moved

Contentedly among you dwellers in beautiful cities
At the contests where, otherwise unseen, the hero
Sat secretly among the poets and watched the wrestlers and with a smile
Acclaimed, who was himself acclaimed, the leisurely-earnest children.
It was and is an unceasing love.
And for that, well parted from you, we think of you nonetheless
All of you in the joy of life on the Isthmus
And by the Cephissus and under Taygetus
And you also, valleys of the Caucasus
Ancient as you are and you, paradisal places there,
We think of you and of your patriarchs and your prophets

  O Asia, Mother, your strong ones
Who fearlessly before the signs of the world
And heaven on their shoulders and every fate
Rooted for days on the mountains
First learned
To speak alone
With God. They are at rest now. But if you
And that is to say all
You ancients have not said what
We shall call you, in holy compulsion we call you
Nature and from you, as from the bath
Steps all life born of the gods.

  True, we go almost like orphans
And doubtless do not have the care we used to have
But the young, remembering their childhood
Even they are not strangers in the house.
They live threefold just like
The first sons and daughters of heaven.
And faith was not given us
Into our souls for nothing.
It upholds not ourselves but what is yours also
And in the sacred things, the weapons of the word
That you, the offspring of destiny, departing
Left for us who are less adept

Good spirits, there you are
Often when the holy cloud wafts around one of us
We are astounded and cannot interpret it.
But you spice our breath with nectar
And often then we rejoice or a deep musing
Befalls us but if ever you love any too much
He cannot rest until he is one of you.
Therefore be kind, surround me lightly
So that I abide, for much still wants singing.
But now, blissful and weeping
Like a legend of love
My poem ends and so it has gone
With blushes and pallor
From the start. But so everything goes.

Celebration of peace

(first version)

Reconciler, never believed in
Who are here now   assuming
For me the shape of a friend, an immortal but
I can recognise   kneeling
I look up to and almost
Like a blind man am compelled
To ask you where you have come from
And why to me, heavenly peace, blessed peace.
This I do know, you are not a mortal, for a wise man
Or one of the friends who look honestly at the world
May cast light on many things but when
A god appears then over heaven and earth and the seas
Comes an all-renewing clarity.

We also once were glad
In the early morning when the works were still
On a holiday and the flowers also in that stillness
For certain bloomed more beautifully and the living waters sprang
    forth brightly.
The singing in the church, I shivered, hearing it at a distance
When the more secret utterances like a hallowed wine
Aged but more potent then, growing
In summer from God's thunderstorms
Did still the anxieties
And the doubts in me but I never knew what was happening
For scarcely born, why did you so soon
Spread a night over my eyes
So that I could not see the earth and had
To breathe you effortfully, heavenly breezes?

It was predetermined. And God smiles
When unstoppably but hemmed in by his mountains
Angry with him between the iron banks the rivers roar

Deep down, buried, where no daylight mentions them.
And oh, preserver of all things, may you always
Hold me too and spare my soul, who is so light she will escape me.
Hence my festival today and in the stillness in an evening fashion
The spirit flowers around and even if my hair were silver grey
Nevertheless, friends, I would urge that we prepare
For the supper and the singing and enough wreaths and melodies
For this time as though we were young for ever.

   Be present, youth, now at last, who before you had finished speaking
Were summoned below and rapidly that joyous thing you offered
Was shut from sight and a destiny
A vast and terrible shadow spread over you
So rapidly the things of heaven pass, but are not in vain.
Always deft with the measure a god touches
The dwellings of human beings
With a sparing hand, only for a moment
And they do not know it but for a long time
Think of it and ask who it was.
But when some time has passed, they know.

   And on a human good deed, thanks follow
But on a divine gift
First years of error and tribulation
So that on the following times
The light from above
Through a holy wilderness will shine more mildly.
Therefore as a god be present
And lovelier than before, o you
Reconciler be reconciled now so that we in the evening
May name you with the friends and sing
Of the high ones, and that others may be there with you.

   For the sacred fire was almost exhausted
All breathed out in flames of sacrifice
When, swiftly kindling, the Father sent down
Of all he had, the most loving

And burning with this
Consuming, if from generation to generation
Humankind became too full of the blessing and they
Should think themselves sufficient and in their arrogance forget heaven
Then   he said   there shall be a new beginning
And see, what you said nothing of
The completion of the times has brought it.
Which you surely knew but you were sent to die, not live
And always greater than his sphere, like the god of gods himself
One of the others must also be.

  But when the hour strikes
He steps like the master from his place of work
And robes himself no other than festively
As a sign that in the work
He had left things to do.
Less he appears and greater.
And likewise you
And you grant us, the children of the loving earth
That we, however many
The festivals have become
May celebrate them all
And not count the gods, one is always for all.
Like the sunlight to me, I salute
Divinity in you at the evening of your days.
And now may we remain.

Celebration of Peace

(final version)

I ask that this poem be read with goodwill. It will surely then not be unintelligible, much less will it give offence. If some should even so find the language here not conventional enough, I have to tell them: I can do no other. On a fine day, as we know, almost every kind of singing may be heard; and Nature, from whence it comes, will in turn receive it.

The author proposes to present a whole collection of such poems to the public, and this may be taken as a foretaste.

Aired through and filled with the heavens'
Still echoing, still peaceably proceeding
Harmonies stands the ancient
Sweetly familiar hall, joy drifts in fragrances
Over the cloths of green and laden
With ripest fruits and gold-wreathed chalices
Over the levelled ground, this side and that in a long
Well-ordered splendid shining
The tables rise. For here
At this hour of evening
From distant places a loving company
Is called to meet.

And with dawning eyes I think I see him already
Smiling after the serious labours of his day
Himself, the Prince of the Festival.
And though you like to disavow your foreign land
And as if weary from the long campaign
Lower your eyes so your look is absent, lightly shaded
And assume the shape of a friend, you who are known to all, yet
Eminence brings me almost to my knees. Before you
I know nothing, only this: you are not a mortal.
A wise man may cast light for me on many things; but when
Also a god appears
There is a different clarity.

But he is not new to us nor unannounced
And one who never shied from fire or flood
Marvels that now there is stillness with good reason
And dominance nowhere to be seen among the spirits and the people.
For they hear the work
So long preparing from east to west, only now
As the Thunderer's reverberations, the millennial storm
Colossally resounding fainter and fainter into the depths
To sleep, are eclipsed by the ringing of peace.
But you, grown precious to us, you days of innocence
Beloved days, you bring us this festival and in this stillness
In an evening fashion the spirit flowers around
And even if my hair were silver grey, nonetheless, my friends
I would urge we prepare for the supper and wreath our hair
Now, as though we were young for ever.

And there are many I should like to invite but you
With a friendly seriousness disposed to people
There under Syrian palm trees
In the place you loved at the well close by the town
Amid the rustling cornfields, in the cooling soft breathing
Of the sacred mountain's shadow
And your dear friends, the faithful cloud, likewise shaded you
So that your radiance, your youthful forthright holiness
Came to people through a thicket, mildly.
Oh, but a killing fate, decisive, terrible
Shaded you more darkly then in the midst of your words. So soon
The things of heaven pass, but not in vain.

For always deft with the measure a god touches
The dwellings of human beings sparingly
Only for a moment, unlooked-for, and no one knows when.
And thereupon insolence passes over it
And licence from all quarters comes to the holy places
Lays hands on them and practises its delusions
And doing so, works as a destiny, but thanks
Never follows at once on the god-given gift

Which will be grasped through ordeals.
Also if the giver were not sparing
Long ago by the blessing of the hearth
From floor to rafters the house would have been in flames.

Yet of the gods
Much has been given us. Fire
Was put into our hands and the sea's tides and the shore.
Far more than in their human ways
We are familiar with those alien energies.
And the stars instruct you
That are in front of your eyes, but you can never be like them.
But from the spring of all living things, from whom
There is much joy, much singing
There comes one, a son, a calm power,
And now we know him
Now that we know the Father
And to hold days of celebration
The high spirit of this world
Has disposed himself to human beings.

For he has long been more than Lord of the Times.
His zone ran far and wide but when did it ever exhaust him?
But even a god on occasion may choose a daily labour
Like mortals and share all that comes at them.
Then fate decrees that all shall know the lives of others
So when the quiet returns there will be a language too.
But wherever the spirit works there we are also and quarrel
What might be best. And now seems best to me
Now that the Master has finished and his picture is accomplished
And himself transfigured by it he steps from his place of work
As the quiet God of the Times and henceforth only the law of love,
Sweet reconciler, counts from here onwards to heaven.

Much since morning time
When we became a conversation and began to hear from one another
Has humankind experienced; but soon we shall be song
And the image of the times the great spirit has unfolded

As a sign it lies before us that between him and others
There is a covenant between him and other powers.
Not he alone, the unbegotten, the eternal
Those powers too are knowable by it, as by the plants
Mother Earth and light and air are made known to themselves.
And lastly now, you holy energies, for you
This love-sign, this testimony
That you still live, this festival

Gathering all in, where the gods of heaven
Are not revealed in miracles nor work unseen in the weather
But in the singing hospitably with one another
Are present in choirs, a holy number
The blessed in all their guises
Are together, nor is their dearest absent
To whom they are devoted, and for that
I summoned you, unforgettable youth
Here to this banquet prepared at the evening of time
To be the Prince of our festival, and our generation
Will not lie down to sleep
Till all of you who have ever been promised us
All you immortals
Are there in our house
To speak to us of your heaven.

Lightly breathing airs
Announce you already
The smoking valley announces you
As does the ground still sounding from the thunder
But hope brings roses to the cheeks
And in the door of the house
Sit mother and child
And gaze at peace
And few seem to die
Presentiments keep the soul, a promise
Dispensed by the golden light
Keeps the oldest here.

The essences of life
Are indeed prepared from above and from there also
The toils are carried through.
And now all is pleasing
But a simple thing
Most, for it is the long sought after
Golden fruit
Fallen in battering storms
From an ancient tree
And then, as the dearest good,
Guarded by holy fate itself with gentle weapons,
It is the shape and form of the powers of heaven.

Like a lioness you lamented
When you lost your children
Mother Nature. For your enemy
Stole them from you when, too lovingly
You had received him almost like a son of your own
And put gods into the company of satyrs.
So you built much
And you buried much
For what you in your omnipotence
Dragged forth into the light before its time
Hates you.
And now you know this and you desist.
For those things in their fearful workings
Like better to be left without feeling
Till they ripen, below.

The journey

Suevia, my mother, happy land!
You also are, like your more shining sister
Lombardy over there,
Flowed through by a hundred streams
And trees in plenty, white with blossom or reddish
And the darker, deep, full green, the wild trees
And the Alps of Switzerland overshadow you too,
Neighbourly; for near the hearth of the house
Is where you live and you can hear
Inside from silvery vessels
The spring rushing that issues
From pure hands when touched

By warm rays
Crystal ice and tipped over
By the lightly quickening light
The snowy summit drenches the earth
With purest water. For that reason
You are born loyal. Hard
Living near the source to quit the place.
And your children, the towns
On the long lake in the haze
On the willowy Neckar and on the Rhine
All think
Nowhere would be better to live.

But I am set on the Caucasus.
For I heard it said
On the winds even today
That poets are as free as swallows.
Besides, in younger days
This was imparted to me:
That ages ago
Our ancestors, the German people,
Tugged gently hence by the flow of the Danube

On a summer day encountered
Children of the sun
On the Black Sea
When these were seeking shade
And its name is for good reason
'Kind to strangers'.

For having regarded one another
They approached first, then ours too
Sat down in curiosity under the olive tree.
But when their clothes touched
And no one could understand
The other's own speech a discord
Might well have arisen had not from among the branches
Come down the cooling
That often over the faces of quarrelling men
Will usher a smile, and a moment
They looked up in silence then one with another
Lovingly took hands. And soon

They were swapping weapons and all
The lovely goods of the house
And speech too, swapped, and at joyful weddings
Fathers in friendship
Wished the children nothing that did not come true.
For from them wedded
Out of their sacrament issued forth
More beautiful than anything before or since
Belonging to humankind, a people. Where
But where are you now, dear ones, my kith and kin
That we might enter again into the bond
And lovingly remember the ancestors?

There on the shores, under Ionia's
Trees, on the levels of Cayster
Where cranes delighting in the clear blue
Have in an arc around them hazy distances of mountains

You were there too, surpassing them all in beauty; or tended
The islands wreathed in vines
And sounding out with song, and others lived
Under Taygetus, under famous Hymettus
They flowered last, but from
The springs of Parnassus to Tmolus'
Streams glinting with gold one
Everlasting song was lifted up; for over the trees
In those days strummed
The mild breezes of heaven
And over the lyrestrings.

   O land of Homer
By the purple cherry or when
Arrived here from you in the vineyards my
Young peaches leaf
And the swallow comes a great distance with much to tell
And builds her house on my walls in
May time, and also under the stars
Ionia, I think of you, but people
Want presence. So
I have come to the islands and the rivermouths,
The halls of Thetis
Woods and the clouds over Ida.

   But do not think to stay.
Unfriendly and hard to win
Is the mother I come from, and shut.
One of her sons, the Rhine,
Would have taken her heart by storm but vanished
When she rebuffed him who knows where into the distance.
I should not like to have gone like that
From her and only to invite you
Graces of Hellas, I have gone to you
Sweet daughters of heaven
That if the journey is not too great
You might come to us.

When the air breathes more gently
And morning sends down loving arrows
On us who are all too patient
And light clouds flower
Over our diffident eyes
Then we shall say what brings you,
The Charites, here to barbarians?
But the handmaidens of heaven
Are a wonder
Like everything born of the gods.
It turns to a dream should anyone
Come at it by stealth and punishes
Anyone violently setting himself up as equal;
Often the one it surprises
Has scarcely been thinking it.

The Rhine

(for Isaak von Sinclair)

I sat in the dark ivy, at the forest's
Gate, just as the golden noon,
To visit the spring,
Came down the stairs of the Alps
Which are to me the stronghold
The gods built for themselves
After an old opinion, but from where
In secret many a resolution
Reaches men; from there
I learned without expecting it
Of a destiny when my soul
Conversing on this and that
In the warm shade
Had wandered towards Italy
And far away to the coasts of the Morea.

But now in the mountains
Under the silver summits at a depth
Under cheerful greenery
Where the woods with a shudder
And the peering heads of the peaks
Look down at him, all day, it was there
In the coldest pit
I heard him yammering to be released,
The youth, he was heard as he raged
And railed against Earth his mother
And against the Thunderer who fathered him
By mother and father with pity but
Humanity fled from the place
For it was terrible how he
Lightless in chains
Writhed and raved, that hero.

It was the voice of the noblest of rivers
The freeborn Rhine
And high at the outset he had other hopes
When he parted from his brothers Ticino and Rhône
And wanted to wander and his royal soul
Drove him impatiently to head for Asia.
But it makes no sense
To wish one's own wishes in the face of fate
But the blindest in this
Are the sons of gods. For men know
Their homes and to beasts it is given
To know where to build, but they
Start out
With souls that want direction.

Pure origins are a riddle. Even
The poem may hardly disclose them. For what
You began as you will remain
However necessity
And discipline work, and most
Is done by birth
And the ray of light
That greets us newborn.
But where else is there one
More made by a happy nativity
For lifelong freedom and only
To gratify the heart
Than the Rhine
Who was born of the blessed heights
And the holy womb of our earth?

His voice therefore is exultant.
He never loved mewling
Like other infants in swaddling bands.
When the crooked banks
First crept alongside
And thirstily twining around him

To lead him their way before he knew it
And guard him perhaps
In their own jaws, he laughed
And ripped these snakes asunder
And ran with the spoils and if swiftly
He were not mastered
And made to grow, he must like lightning
Have split the earth, and the woods flee after him
As though enchanted and the hills subsiding.

But a god likes to save his sons
Their fugitive lives, and smiles
When headlong but baulked
By the holy Alps his rivers bridle
As this one does in the depth.
For purity comes
Out of such a smithy
And it is beautiful then
Leaving the mountains
How he contents himself
Dawdling through Germany and quietening his longing
With works and he ploughs the land
Our father Rhine and nourishes children
In towns he founded.

But he never forgets.
For house and home
And law will perish and the days
Of man become monstrous before
One like the Rhine forgets his beginnings
And the pure voice of his youth.
Who were the first
To spoil the ties of love
And make them fetters?
So overweening that they mocked
Their own justice and surely
The fire of heaven too and then

Despising human paths
Elected overboldness
And strove to equal the gods.

But the gods have enough
In their own immortality and need
If anything
Heroes and men
And other mortal creatures. For since
The supremely blessed feel nothing themselves
Doubtless another must
If it is permissible to say such a thing
Feel in their name, in sympathy and that
Someone they need; but their judgement is
That he shall topple his house
And mix his dearest and his enemies in one scolding
And bury the old and the new generations
Under the rubble
Whoever seeks to be like them
And will not suffer the difference, the fool.

Better for a man to have found
A measured fate
On a safe shore where the memory
Of wanderings still
And suffering sweetly surfaces
To look here and there without rancour
And see the limits
Set him at birth
By God to live within.
He has peace, he is blessed, he is undemanding
For everything he desired,
Heaven's good, of itself
Comes over him smiling, unforced,
Now that he rests from his boldness.

I am thinking of demigods.
And should I not know them for whom

My heart has often quickened with love and longing?
But one whose soul like yours, Rousseau,
Endured and became invincible
To whom sure sense was given
The gift of hearing and speech
To speak like the god of wine
From such abundance
Holy, foolish and according to no law
Which is the language of the purest in heart
And the good understand it but it smites
The heedless, the sacrilegious hirelings
Rightly with blindness, what
Shall I call such a stranger?

The sons of the earth are, like the mother,
All-loving, for which they receive
Everything effortlessly and are blessed.
It startles a man
With fear
When he thinks of the heaven
His loving arms have piled
On his shoulders
And the burden of joy.
Then often what seems to him best
Is Biel, the lake, the breezy greenery,
In woodland shade
Where the light does not burn
And poor in tunes and cares
To learn like a beginner from the nightingales.

And to rise from the sacrament of sleep
How good that is, waking
From the cool of the woods, at evening then
To approach the milder light
When he who built the mountains
And drew the rivers their paths
Has filled the sails of our busy lives
So poor in breath

And steered us, smiling, with his breezes
When he too rests and towards
His pupil now the maker
Finding more good than bad
Towards this present earth
The day inclines. –

    Then men and gods will have their bridal feast
Everything that lives will celebrate
And fate for a while
Is entirely even-handed.
And the fugitives look for shelter
And the brave a sweet sleep
But the lovers are
What they were, they are
At home where flowers delight in
Harmless fire and the foreboding trees
Are breathed about by the spirit, but people at odds
Have turned in their tracks and are hurrying
To take hands now before
The friendly light
Goes down and the night comes.

    And some this hurries by
But others
Retain it longer.
The eternal gods
Are full of life for ever; but unto death
A man also
Can retain the best in mind
And crown his life with it.
To everyone his measure.
Unhappiness is hard
To bear, but happiness harder.
One wise man managed
From midday to midnight
And until the morning brightened
To keep his wits at the symposium.

Sinclair, on a burning path among pines
Or in the darkness of an oakwood if clad
In steel God appears to you or if in clouds
You will know him since you know in your own youthful self
His strength and his goodness and he never smiles
The smile of power but you discover it
In daylight when
Feverish and chained it seems
The quick of life or else
At night when everything mixes
Without order and the ancient
Chaos returns.

Germania

Not those, the blessed, the living images of the gods
Who appeared once in the ancient land
Of course I may not summon them any more, yet when
You waters of home, with you
The heart's love grieves, what else does it desire
What else is it in holy mourning for? The land lies
Full of expectation and as in days of heat
Louring, full of portent, the sky today
Lays a shadow over the yearning
And is full of promises and seems
Threatening also, but I will stay under it
My soul shall not desert me and fly back
To you who are past and whom I love too well.
For to look upon your lovely faces
As though it were then, I fear is fatal
And scarcely is it allowed to wake the dead.

Past gods, and you, still present but back then
More real, you had your time!
Nothing will I deny here, nothing plead for.
For when it is over and the day extinguished
The priest will feel it first but lovingly
Temple and image and his rule and custom follow him
Into the dark land and no light still shows.
Only as if from funeral flames a golden smoke
Legend, then wafts over it and faintly now
Flickers around our doubting heads
And none knows what is happening. We feel
The shades of those who once have been,
The ancients visiting the earth again.
For those who are to come, they press upon us
And not much longer will the blessed host
Of human gods linger in the blue heavens.

Already the field, in the prelude of a harsher time
Prepared for them, is greening now, the offerings are ready
And the valleys and their rivers are
Wide open around prophetic mountains
So that a man may see into the East
And many changes coming from there will move him.
Out of the aether
The true image falls, oracles without number
Rain down from there and the innermost grove resounds
And coming from the Indus
And overflying
The snowy peaks of Parnassus and Italy's
Celebrant hills, seeking some welcome prey
But not as he once did, for the Father, the eagle
Older and more practised now in flight at last and rejoicing
Lifts over the Alps and views the many different lands.

He seeks the priestess, God's quietest daughter
Who in a deep simplicity, too readily holds her peace
Seeks her who in all the noise of late
In the storms then threatening death above her head
Stood open-eyed as though not knowing it
Childlike, sensing better things
Until there was amazement throughout the heavens
That there should be one great in faith as is
The high power itself that gives us blessings.
Therefore they sent the messenger who quickly knowing her
Smiled and thought: Whom nothing breaks
A different word must test you. And, youthful again
Looking towards Germania, he cried:
'You chosen for your boundless love
To bear a heavy happiness
Are now grown strong enough

Since the time when, hidden in the forest and the flowering poppies
Dazed in a sweet slumber, you paid me no heed
And long before others, lesser, also sensed your maiden pride

And marvelled and asked whose child you were and whence you came
And you yourself not knowing. I did not mistake you
And secretly while you lay dreaming I left
At midday a farewell sign of friendship
The flower of speech and you spoke in solitude.
But in the joy of it you sent also an abundance
Of golden words out into the rivers and they issue forth
Into all the localities. For like the holy
Mother of all things
Whom people once called "the hidden"
Like hers almost your heart is full of love and sorrow
And of presentiments
And peace.

   Oh drink the morning airs
Till you are open
And name what is before your eyes
The unspoken can no longer
Remain a secret
Having been so long enshrouded
For shyness is fitting in humans
And most of the time
It is wise to speak of the gods so.
But where more plentifully than clear stream waters
The gold overflows and the anger in the heavens is in earnest
Then between day and night
For once a true thing must appear.
Circumscribe it thrice
But unspoken too, as it is here
So, innocent girl, it must stay.

   O daughter of the holy earth, say now
The name of the mother. Roaring of waters below the rocks
And stormwind in the forest and at her name
Out of the ancient time the lost gods sound again.
How different it is! And on the right, from the distances
Future things also shine and speak, and gladden us.

But in the middle time
The aether lives quietly
With the hallowed virginal earth
And willingly, in remembrance
They, wanting nothing, are present
Hospitably at your festivals
Germania where you
As priestess, wanting nothing
And unarmed, give counsel all around
To the kings and to the peoples.'

The only one

(first version)

What is it that
To the ancient blessed coasts
So binds me that I love them
More than my motherland?
For as if sold into
Heavenly captivity
There I am where Apollo walked
In the form of a king
And where Zeus from the heights
Abased himself to innocent youths
And in holy fashion
Got sons and daughters among humans.

High thoughts in plenty
Have sprung from the Father's head
And great souls
Come down
From him to humans.
I have heard
Of Elis and Olympia, have stood
On the summit of Parnassus
And over the mountains of the Isthmus
And beyond also
By Smyrna and down
By Ephesus I have walked

Seen many beautiful things
And sung
God's image abundantly
That lives among humans, yet
You ancient gods and all
You brave sons of the gods
I seek one more I love

Among you and whom you conceal
The last of your race
The jewel of your house
From me, the foreign visitor.

My master and lord!
O you, my teacher!
Why have you kept
Your distance? And when
Among the ancients
I asked the heroes and
The gods for you, why were
You missing? And now my soul
Is full of sorrow as though
The immortals jealously competed
So that if I serve one
I will lack another.

And yet I know
The fault is mine. For I cling
Christ, too much to you
Although the brother of Heracles
And boldly I profess
That you are brother also of Evius
Who to his chariot
Hitched the tigers and down
As far as the Indus
Commanding cheerful worship
Established the vine and
Tamed the fury of the peoples.

But I am shy
Of comparing the worldly men
With you. And indeed I know
That he who begot you, your father
The same who

For he never rules alone.

But love attaches
To one. For this time
The poem has come
Too much from my own heart.
I will make good the error
When I sing other songs.
I never hit, as I should wish
The measure. But a god knows
When that comes that I wish, the best.
For as the Master
Walked on earth
A captive eagle

And many who
Saw him were afraid
While the Father did
His utmost and the Son
Truly worked his best and very
Troubled was he also
All the while till he
Passed on the breezes towards heaven.
Such is the captivity of the souls of the heroes.
The poets, even
The spiritual, must be worldly.

The only one

(ll. 50-97 of the second version)

And yet I know
The fault is mine. For I cling
Christ, too much to you
Although the brother of Heracles
And boldly I profess
That you are brother also of Evius who
Holds up the peoples' death-wish and tears the snare
So that humans see clearly not to go
The way of death and keep a measure so that all
Are something for themselves and feeling
The great time's destiny and
Its fires, they strike the moment and where
The way goes otherwise there they too see
Where it might be a destiny but make it safe
Aligning it with humans or with laws.

   But his anger flames up, that
The sign is touching the earth, gradually
Going out of sight as though down a ladder.
This time. Wilful, excessive
Unbounded, that humans
Lay their hands on what lives and more than is proper
Even for a demigod, the project
Exceeding what is set and sacred. For since an evil mind
Took possession of the happy Ancient World, unendingly
For ages now a thing has governed that is the enemy of song,
     tuneless, that
Transgresses in portions, violence of the mind. But God
Hates dissolution. But interceding

   The daylight of these times, a quiet maker
Going its way, the bloom of the years, restrains him.
And the din of war and the history of the heroes, obstinate destinies

The sun of Christ, garden of the penitents and
The wanderings of pilgrims and peoples, the watchman's
Song and the writings of the Bard or the African. Also the fates
Of those without fame hold him, those who into the daylight
Are only now coming fully, the fatherly princes. For that estate
Is far more godly than it was. For the light belongs now
To grown men. Not to youths.
The motherland also. Fresh

   Not yet exhausted, and with abundant locks of hair.
For the Father of the Earth takes delight in this also
That there are children, so there remains a certainty
Of goodness. So also it delights him
That things remain.
And there are people saved as on
Beautiful islands. They are learned.
And temptations without number
Have visited them.
Countless fell. So it went
When Earth's Father was preparing what would endure
In the tempests of the times. But that is finished now.

The only one

(third version)

What is it that
To the ancient blessed coasts
So binds me that I love them
More than my motherland?
For as if bent into
Heavenly captivity, my speech following the daylight
There I am where, as stones say, Apollo walked
In the form of a king
And where Zeus from the heights
Abased himself to innocent youths
And in holy fashion
Got sons and daughters dwelling mute among humans.

   High thoughts in plenty
Have come out of the Father's head
And great souls
Come down
From him to humans.
I have heard
Of Elis and Olympia, have stood
Forever at springwaters on Parnassus
And over the mountains of the Isthmus
And beyond also
By Smyrna and down
By Ephesus I have walked

   Seen many beautiful things
And sung
God's image abundantly
That lives among humans. For, like space
Divinity is very richly calculable
In youth   and yet
You ancient gods and all

You brave sons of the gods
I seek one more I love
Among you and whom you safeguard
The last of your race
The jewel of your house
For me, the foreign visitor.

My master and lord!
O you, my teacher!
Why have you kept
Your distance? And when
Among the ancients, in the midst of the spirits
I saw the heroes and
The gods why were
You missing? And now my soul
Is full of sorrow as though
The immortals jealously competed
So that if I serve one
I will lack another.

And yet I know
The fault is mine. For I cling
Christ, too much to you
Although the brother of Heracles
And boldly I profess
That you are brother also of Evius who shrewdly long ago
Straightened the headstrong errancy
Of the earth for God and accorded
A soul to the beast that living
On its own hunger wandered and followed the earth
But he decreed right ways at once and places
And everyone's belongings
These too he ordered

But I am shy
Of comparing the worldly men
With you. And indeed I know
That he who begot you, your father is

The same. For Christ too of course
Stood alone under the visible heavens and the stars, those visibly
Governing freely over the established order with God's permission
And the sins of the world, the unintelligibility
Of knowledge for example when human busyness
Overgrows the things that last and the stars' courage was his charge also.
    For the world is
Forever ecstatically lifting away from the earth and would
Denude it where there is no hold in humane things. But there remains
    a trace
Of a word nonetheless which a man may seize. But the place was

  The wilderness. So they are one. Full of joys, abundantly. A trefoil
Greens in splendour. This would be unshapely, for the sake of the
    spirit, if of such
One versed in the knowledge, as a bad prayer, were not permitted to say
They are like commanders to me, like heroes. Mortals are allowed this
    because
Without some hold God has no understanding. But as upon carriages
Humble   with the daylight's
Violence or
With voices God appears as
Nature from without. Mediated
In holy writ. Gods are
And humans on earth together the whole time. A great man and likewise
    a great soul
Even if in heaven

  Desires to be with one on earth. Always
This remains always interlocking every day is
The world. But all the days they stand as over an abyss
One by another. Those three, however, are such
That they stand under the sun
Like a huntsman or
A ploughman who, drawing breath,
Bares his head, or a beggar. To make comparisons
Is sweet and right. The earth
Does one good. It cools. But always

Patmos

(for the Landgraf *of Homburg)*

    The god is near and
Hard to grasp but
Where there is danger some
Salvation grows there too.
Eagles live
In the dark and the sons of the Alps
Cross over the abyss without fear
On lightly built bridges.
Then since the summits of time
Are piled around us
And our loved ones close and fainting
On peaks far apart
Oh give us innocent water
Give us wings that we
Loyally go over and return.

    Those were my words, and quicker
Than I had supposed and far
To where I had never thought I should come
A spirit took me away
From my own house. The shadowy wood
And the longing streams
Of home were darkening
In twilight when I left
And I never knew the lands
But soon in a light
That was fresh, and mysteriously
In a golden smoke
Growing rapidly
With the strides of the sun
And the scent of a thousand summits

    Asia flowered, and blinded I looked
For something I knew

Unused as I was to the broad streets where
Down from Tmolus
Pactolus comes in gold
And Taurus stands and Messogis
And the garden full of flowers,
A quiet fire; but high in the light
The silver snow blossoms
And showing the life eternal
On unclimbable walls
The ancient ivy grows and the majestic
God-built palaces are borne
By living columns
Of cedar and laurel.

   But around the doors of Asia
Here and there
Over the uncertain levels of the sea
Shadowless roads in any number go,
But the boatman knows the islands.
And when I heard
That one lying near
Was Patmos
It made me long
To put in and approach
The dark cave there.
For Patmos is splendid
Not as Cyprus is
That abounds in streams
Nor like any other but

   In a poorer house
Is nevertheless
Hospitable and when
Shipwrecked or
Crying for home or
The departed friend
Some stranger
Nears her she welcomes the sound and her children

The hot grove's voices
And where the sand falls and the surface of the field
Cracks, those noises too
Hear him and give a loving echo
Of the man's laments. So once
She cared for God's
Beloved seer who was blessed in his youth

   With the company of
The son of the Highest, they went
Inseparably for the Thunderbearer loved
The disciple's simplicity and he was attentive
And saw the countenance of God exactly
When at the mystery of the vine
They sat together at supper and the Lord
Foreknowing and at peace from his large soul
Spoke out his death and the last love
For at that time
There was no end of his words of lovingkindness
And good cheer when he saw the world
Angry. For everything is good. Thereupon he died. Much might
Be said about this. And one last time his friends
Saw him in the look of victory, at his most joyful

   But they grieved since now
It was evening, and they were astounded
And a decision was weighing in their hearts
But they loved life in the sun
And were loath to leave the countenance of the Lord
And home. But it
Was driven into them like fire in iron
And the shadow of their beloved kept them company.
Therefore he sent them
The spirit and the house
Shook and God's turbulence rolled
Thundering into the distance over
Their guessing heads when,

Thinking heavily, they were assembled
Like sentenced heroes

    And he appeared
Once more to them and departed.
For the sun put out his light now,
The royal day, and snapped
The straight beams of his sceptre himself
With a god's pain
And intended returning
When the time is right. It would have been wrong
Later, abrupt and untrue,
The work of mankind, and it was a joy
From now on
To live in the loving night and preserve
In simple eyes, unflinching,
Abysses of wisdom. And lively images
Are verdant under the mountains too.

    But the way God scatters life
This way and that to the uttermost
Is terrible. Not only to lose
Sight of the dear friends' faces
And far over the mountains go
Alone when between two
The heavenly spirit was recognised
In unison and not as a thing to come but
Present and tugging at the hair
When suddenly
Hurrying away the god looked back at them
And swearing an oath
To hold him as though bound
Henceforth by golden cords
They said the worst and took one another's hands –

    But when thereupon he dies
On whom more than on anyone

Beauty hung so that his shape
Worked a miracle and the gods
Pointed him out and when they are left
For ever a riddle to one another
And cannot comprehend and yet they lived
Together in the memory and when it takes away
Not only the sand or the willow trees
And seizes the temples but down the wind
Goes the honour of the demigod and his kin
And the Highest himself
Thereupon averts his countenance
And nowhere in the sky is anything
Immortal to be seen nor on
The verdant earth – tell me, what is this?

It is the throw of the winnower when he catches
Corn in the fan
And flings it towards daylight over the floor.
The chaff falls at his feet but
The wheat gets through
Nor is that bad if some
Is lost and the living sound
Of speech disperses for
God's work resembles ours and he does not wish
Everything at once.
True, there is iron in the shaft
And glowing resin in Etna
So I would have the riches
To shape a shape and see
Him how he was, the Christ,

And what if one spurred himself and waylaid me
Conversing sadly when I was defenceless
So that I marvelled and of the god
I wished, a serf, to copy the image –
In his anger once I saw the Lord
Of heaven visible. Not to be anything myself. Only

To learn. They are kind, but what they loathe above all,
So long as they rule, is falseness and nothing
Human counts then among mankind
Who do not govern, the immortals do, their work
Proceeding of itself
Is hurrying to its destined end.
For when the triumph of heaven rises higher
The strong will name him like the daystar
They will name God's joyful son

    As a watchword, and here is the staff
Of song beckoning him down.
Now nothing is ordinary. The dead
Not coarsened yet
Will be woken. But many eyes
That are shy of looking are waiting to see
The light. They will not flower
When the beams are sharp
Although a golden bridle holds in their eagerness.
But when as though
Through shielding brows
Away from the world
A gently luminous power falls from the scriptures
Glad of the grace they may try themselves
On those quiet glances.

    If now the gods, as I
Believe, love me
How much more you
For I know this:
The will
Of the eternal Father weighs
With you. His sign is quiet
In the thundering sky. And one stands beneath it
His whole life long. For Christ still lives.
And all the heroes who are the Father's sons
Have come and holy scriptures

From him and the deeds of the earth
Explain his lightning still,
A race that cannot be halted. But he is there. For known
Unto God are all his works from the beginning.

   The honour of the gods has been
Too long, too long invisible.
For they must almost
Guide our fingers and do
A shameful violence to wrest the hearts from us.
For the gods want, all of them, oblations.
And neglect has done us
Nothing but harm.
We have served Mother Earth
And lately the light of the sun
In ignorance, but the Father
Governing all
Loves best that we tend
The solid letter and make good sense
Of what we have. And German poets try to.

Patmos

(fragments of the later version)

Full of kindness is; but none
Grasps God alone.
But where there is danger some
Salvation grows there too.
Eagles live
In the dark and the sons of the Alps
Cross over the abyss without fear
On lightly built bridges.
Since, then, around clarity, the summits of time
Are piled around us
And our loved ones close and fainting
On peaks apart
Oh give us innocent water
Give us wings that we
Loyally go over and return.

Those were my words, and with more art
Than I had supposed and far
To where I had never thought I should come
A spirit took me away
From my own house. The shadowy wood
And the longing streams
Of home were clothing themselves
In twilight, like people, when I left
And I never knew the lands.
Yet much have we suffered together, many times. So
In a light that was fresh, and mysteriously
In a golden smoke
Growing rapidly
With the strides of the sun
And the scent of a thousand tables now

Asia flowered, and quite blinded I looked
For something I knew

Unused as I was to the broad streets where
Down from Tmolus
Pactolus comes in gold
And Taurus stands and Messogis
And the garden almost sleepy with flowers,

O island of light!
For when fame is extinguished, the eyes' delight, and, no longer kept
    by people,
The paths, without shade, become unsure of themselves and the trees
And realms, lands where the eyes were young, have passed away
More athletic,
In the ruin,   and innocence, native innocence,
Is ripped to shreds. For from God unalloyed
Conscience and revelation come, the hand of the Lord
Signals richly from the directing heavens, then and for a while
Law and office are indivisible, and to lift
The hands, that too, and to order
The falling loose of evil thoughts. For cruelly
God hates know-all minds. But John
Stood pure and firm on the undoing ground. If any
Declare the prophetic word to be earthly

From Jordan and from Nazareth
And far from the lake by Capernaum
The airs of Galilee and from Cana.
I shall stay a while, he said. And so with drops
He stilled the sighing of the light that was like
A thirsty beast in those days when around Syria

The homely grace of the butchered infants wailed
In dying and the head
Of the Baptist, plucked, lay like never-withering scripture
Visible on the abiding platter. God's voices
Are like fire. But it is hard
To retain in great things that which is great.
It is not a pasture. That one
Remains in the beginning. But now
This passes as formerly.

    John. Christ. Him I should like
To sing as I would Heracles or
The island, nearby, with its cool sea-waters
That out of the waste of the wide tide
Held fast to Peleus and rescued and refreshed him. But
That cannot be. Fate decrees otherwise. More full of wonders.
To sing more richly. Since him
The story looks neverending. And now
I should like to sing the journey of the nobles
To Jerusalem and the suffering, all astray, in Canossa
And Heinrich. But let not my very
Courage for it expose me. First
We must grasp this. That since Christ
The names are like the morning air. Turn to dreams. Fall
Like error and lethally on the heart unless

    One weighs and grasps what they are.
But he was attentive
And saw the countenance of God
When at the mystery of the vine
They sat together at supper and the Lord
From his large soul choosing carefully
Spoke out his death and the last love. For at that time
There was no end of his words of lovingkindness
And to strengthen what strengthens us. But his light
Was death. For the world's quarrels are wearing.
But he knew that. Everything is good. Thereupon he died.

But at the last the friends
That notwithstanding saw before God the bowed
Figure of Denial as if, thoughtfully,
A century inclined itself in the joy of the truth,

But they grieved since now
It was evening. For to be pure
Is a destiny, a life that has a heart
Before such a countenance and lasts more than half.
But much is to be avoided. But too much
Of love where there is adoration
Is perilous, strikes most. They were loath
To leave the countenance of the Lord
And home. Born
Like fire in iron it was in them
And the shadow of their beloved kept them company, like a plague.
Therefore he sent them
The spirit and the house
Shook and God's turbulence rolled
Thundering into the distance, creating men, as when dragons' teeth,
    of a splendid fate,

Patmos

(ll. 136-195 of work on a final version)

From Jordan and from Nazareth
And far from the lake by Capernaum where they
Sought him, and the airs of Galilee and from Cana.
I shall stay a while, he said. And so as if with drops, with holy drops
He stilled the sighing of the light that was like a thirsty beast or
The shrieking of the hen that day when around Syria, sere
The homely grace of the butchered infants wailed
Eloquently as it disappeared and the golden head
Of the Baptist, fell and lay like inedible and never-withering scripture
Visible on the dry platter. God's voices
Are like fire in cities, deadly amorous. But for certain it burns
To retain equally in great things that which is great.
It is never a pasture. That one
Remains in the beginning. But now
This passes as formerly.

   John. Christ. Him I, as a bearer of burdens,
Should like to sing as I would Heracles or
The nearby island with its cold sea-waters
That out of the waste of the wide tide enchanted and adorned with
       meaningful flowers
Peleus, refreshing. But not
Enough. Fate decrees otherwise. More full of wonders.
To sing more richly. Since him
The story looks neverending. And also
I should like to sing the journey of the nobles
To Jerusalem and like swans the movement of the ships and the
       suffering, all astray, in Canossa, burning hot
And Heinrich. But let not right at the outset
My very courage for it expose me. First
We must look with conclusions
Of invention. For it is dear
The countenance of the dearest. For suffering
Colours its purity which is as pure

165

As a sword. But then
The attentive man
Saw the countenance of God
When at the mystery of the vine
They sat together at supper and the Lord
From his large soul choosing carefully
Spoke out his death and the last love. For at that time
There was no end of his words of lovingkindness
And to strengthen what is snow-white. But afterwards
His light was death. For the world's quarrels want names and concepts.
But he knew that. Everything is good. Thereupon he died.
But at the last the friends
That notwithstanding saw before God the bowed
Figure of Denial as if, thoughtfully,
A century inclined itself in the joy of the truth,

But nonetheless they were bound to grieve since now
It was evening. For mostly to be pure
Is a destiny, a life that has a heart
Before such a countenance and lasts more than half.
But much is to be avoided. But too much
Of love where there is adoration
Is perilous, strikes most. But they were loath
To leave the tears and the brows of the Lord
And home. Born glowing
Like fire red in iron it was in them. And harming the countenance
    of the god really
Like a plague the shadow of their beloved kept them company.
Therefore he sent them
The spirit and the house
Shook and God's turbulence rolled
Thundering into the distance, creating men, wrathful   as when
    dragons' teeth, of a splendid fate,

Remembrance

    The nor'easter is blowing
The dearest of the winds
To me since it fires the sailor's
Spirit and promises a prosperous voyage.
But go now and greet
The lovely Garonne
And the gardens of Bordeaux
At a place where the banks are abrupt
And the path goes along and down
Into the river the stream drops but
Over it looks out a noble pair
Of oaks and white poplars.

    I am mindful of it still and how
The elms in a copse incline
Their broad crowns over the mill
But a fig tree grows in the yard.
On holidays
There the brown women walk
On silken ground
At the March time when
Day and night are equalised
And over the leisurely paths
Heavy with golden dreams
Drowsing breezes pass.

    Now let me have
Full of the dark light
A scented glass
So that I rest; for sleep
Would be sweet among shades.
It is not good
To have our souls
Emptied by mortal thinking. But talk

Is good, with one another, and to speak
The heart's opinion and to hear
Abundantly of days of love
And deeds that have happened.

But where are the friends? Bellarmin
With his companion? Some
Are shy of going to the source
For riches begin
In the sea. And they
Like painters bring together
The beauties of the earth and take to
Winged war if they must and live
In loneliness, years at a time, beneath
The leafless mast, their nights
Not lit by the city's holidays
Nor music nor the dances of a native place.

But now the men
Have gone to the people of India
Past the airy point
And the vineyard hills
Where the Dordogne comes down
And together with the superb
Garonne as wide as the sea
The river leaves. But the sea
Takes memory and gives it
And love, too, busily engages our gaze
But the poets found what lasts.

The Ister

    Come now, fire,
For we are ravenous
To see the day
And when the proof
Has flung us to our knees
We may hear the forests in uproar.
We have sung our way from the Indus
A long way and
From the Alpheus, we have searched
Years for what would serve.
Lacking wings
No one can reach across
Straight to the next
And come to the other side.
But here we shall build.
For rivers dig up
The land. And when things grow
By them and beasts go down
To them in summer to drink
So people may.

    They call this river the Ister.
His course is beautiful. The columns' foliage
Burns and moves. They stand upright
In the wilds, together; and over them,
A second measure, the roof
Juts from the rocks. So I do not wonder
The Ister invited Heracles
Who shone on Olympus
Far off and came
From the hot Isthmus
Looking for shade. Down there
They were full of fire but for the spirits
Coolness is needed too, so he came here

To these sources of water
And tawny banks
And the high scents and the blackness
Of fir-forests where in the depths
A hunter strolls
At noon and growth is audible
In the Ister's resinous trees.

But he seems almost
Reversing and
Must come, I think,
From the East
And much
Might be said about that. And why
Does he cling to the hills so? The other,
The Rhine, went off
Sideways. Never for nothing
Do rivers run in the drylands. Then for what? To be a sign,
Nothing else, a forthright sign, and carry the sun
And moon inseparably in mind
And continue by day and by night and keep
The gods warm together.
That is why rivers
Delight the Almighty too. How else
Could he come down? And like the earth's green places
They are the children of heaven. But he,
The Ister, seems too patient,
Unfree, almost derisive. For when

The day should start
In his youth, when he begins
To grow, when the other there
Pushes his pride high and grinds the bit
Like a colt and the air
For miles hears his tumult
He contents himself.
But rock needs gashes

And the earth furrows
Or how should we plant and dwell?
But what this river is doing
Nobody knows.

Mnemosyne

(second version)

We are a sign with no interpretation
Painless we are and abroad
Have almost lost our language.
For when over mankind
There is quarrelling in heaven and the moons
Go violently, the sea
Speaks too and rivers
Must seek themselves a way. But One
There is without a doubt. He
Can change it any day. He hardly needs
Law. And the leaves resound, the oaks move in the wind
Then beside the snows. For the gods in the heavens
Cannot do everything. Mortals indeed
Reach sooner to the abyss. So the echo turns
With them. Time
Is long but what is true
Will happen.

But the things we love? We see
Sunshine on the ground and dry dust
And deep with shadows the woods and the smoke
Flowers from the roofs about the old crowns
Of towers, peaceably; and lost in the air
The larks trill and under the daylight
Shepherded forth the sheep of heaven graze.
And snow like lilies of the valley
Denoting nobleness
Wherever it be is shining with
The Alps' green meadows
Half and half where
Speaking of the cross set for the dead
Along the way a traveller went
The steep road and
The other with him, but what is this?

    At the fig tree my
Achilles died
And Ajax lies
By the caves near the sea
By streams that neighbour Scamander.
The spirit bold in him   in a roaring of the winds, after
His native Salamis' sweet
Custom, great
Ajax died abroad
Patroclus however in the king's armour. And others died,
Many besides. By their own hands
Sad, many, wild in the soul, but forced to
By gods in the end, but the others
Standing in their fate, in the field. For he riles the gods
Who will not compose himself
And spare his soul, although he must. And grief
Likewise goes wrong.

Mnemosyne

(third version)

Ripe and dipped in fire and cooked
Are the fruits and proved on earth and the law now is
That everything enters, snake-like,
Prophetically, dreaming on
The hills of heaven. And things
Want keeping like
A burden of logs on the shoulders
A lot of things. But the paths
Are wicked. The imprisoned
Elements and old
Laws of the earth go wrong
Like horses. And always
There is a longing to dissolve. But a lot
Wants keeping. Faith.
Let us look neither before nor behind, instead
Be cradled as though
On the lake in a rocking boat.

But the things we love? We see
Sunshine on the ground and dry dust
And the shadows of the woods are homely and the smoke
Flowers from the roofs about the old crowns
Of towers peacefully. The day's marks are good
When something of heaven
Has hurt our souls with contradictions.
For snow like lilies of the valley
Denoting nobleness
Wherever it be is shining on
The Alps' green meadows
Half and half where a traveller
Speaking of the cross set for the dead
High on the road
Rages forward full

Of the far future
And the other with him, but what is this?

   At the fig tree my
Achilles died
And Ajax lies
By the sea caves
By the streams that neighbour Scamander.
With a roaring in the temples once, after
The invariable custom of
Unmoved Salamis, great
Ajax died abroad,
Patroclus though in the king's armour. And others died,
Many besides. But on Cithaeron lay
Eleutherae, Mnemosyne's city. She too when God
Put off his coat at evening
She too undid her hair. For he riles the gods
Who will not compose himself
And spare his soul, even though he must. And grief
Likewise goes wrong.

As birds slowly pass over...

As birds slowly pass over
The prince of them looks ahead
And coolly around
His breast the happenings waft
And he is in silence high
In the air and below him lies
Richly shining the wealth of the lands and with him are
For the first time his young ones looking for conquest.
With strokes of his wings however
He calms.

As upon seacoasts...

As upon seacoasts when the gods
Begin to build and the work of the waves
Ships in unstoppably wave
After wave, in splendour, and the earth
Attires herself and then comes joy
A supreme, tuneful joy, setting the work to rights,
So upon the poem
When the wine-god points and promises
And with the darling of Greece,
Seaborn, veiling her looks,
The waves beach their abundance.

Home

And nobody knows

Let me walk meanwhile
And pick wild berries
To quench my love of the earth
On her paths

Here where – – –
                    and the thorns of roses
And lime trees scenting sweetly by
The beeches, at noon, when in the dun cornfield
Growth rushes through the straight stalks
And the corn bows sideways at the neck
Like autumn, but now beneath the high
Vault of the oaks, where I wonder
And ask upwards, the familiar bell
Strikes from a distance
Golden notes, at the hour
When the birds wake again. This is wellbeing.

For when the juice of the vine...

For when the juice of the vine
The mild growth looks for shade
And the grape grows under the cool
Vaulting of the leaves
A strength to the men
Sweet-smelling to the girls
And bees
Drunk on the scent of spring
When they are touched by the spirit of the sun
Hither and thither they chase after it
Driven but when
Beams burn they home
With a hum, full of presentiment
       above
   the oak rustles,

On pale leaves...

On pale leaves
The grape rests, the hope of wine, so on the cheek
The shadow rests of a golden earring
Worn by a girl.

And I'm to stay single
But the calf
Easily tangles in the rope
It broke.

Working hard

But the sower loves to see
One fallen asleep
In daylight
Over her darning.

A German mouth
Lacks euphony
But sweetly
On a prickly beard
A rush of kisses.

When over the vineyard...

When over the vineyard it flames
And black as coal
The vineyard looks around the time
Of autumn because
The pipes of life breathe more fierily
In the shadows of the vine. But
It is beautiful to unfold our souls
And our short lives

To the Madonna

Much have I suffered on account of you
And of your son
O Madonna
Since I heard of him
In my sweet youth.
For not only the seer
But those who serve, they also
Stand under a common fate. And because I

And many a song that I
Was minded to sing to the Highest,
The Father, melancholy
Ate to nothing in me.

Still, Lady of heaven, still I
Will celebrate you and no one
Must mind
The local beauty of
My speaking
While I walk alone
Into the fields where wild
And fearless the lily grows
To the ancient vault of the forest
Hard to reach,
        the West,

                and over humankind
In lieu of other divinity she,
All-forgetting love, has ruled.

    For in those days was to be the beginning
When

Born from your womb
The god-child and near him
The son of your friend, by his dumb father
Named John
To whom was given
The power of the tongue
To be a bold interpreter

And the fear of the peoples and
The thunder and
The tumbling waters of the Lord.

For laws are good but
Like dragon's teeth they cut
And kill life when an underling
Or a king sharpens them in anger.
But equanimity is given
To God's best-beloved. So they died.
Both,   and so you
In your strong soul grieving as immortals grieve
Saw them die. And for that reason dwell

                        and when in the holiness of night
We think of the future and are burdened with cares
For those who are sleeping and have no cares
The freshly blossoming children
You come smiling and ask what we, where you
Are queen, need fear.

For you never were able
To envy the budding days
And to you it is and always was a joy
If the sons are greater
Than their mothers. And it never pleases you
When looking back

The old deride the young.
Who does not with pleasure remember
The father he loved
And with pleasure speak of his deeds,

                    but when outrageous things occurred
And ungrateful men have
Given   offence
Too readily then
They look   to heaven
And wary of acting
Remorse without end and old age hates the children.

Therefore our Lady
In heaven protect
The young plants as they grow and when
The north wind comes or poison dew
Wafts in or the drought overstays and when
At their utmost flowering they fall
Under the scythe's
Severity give renewal of growing.
And may the fresh generation
Not split too many ways
Run weakly, essaying too much
And scatter its strength but be strong
To choose out of many the best.

Evil is nothing. Let one
Grasp that as the eagle
Grasps its prey.
The others too. So they will not
Confuse the nurse
Who brings the day to birth
And falsely clinging
To the homeland and heedless of the weight
Sit for ever
In the mother's lap. For he

Is great whose wealth they will inherit.
He

Above all spare
The wilderness made
By gods and decreed
Clean to their children to walk in
Among the rocks as they please
Heatherlands bloom
In purple for you
Lady and dark springs too
For you and your son but for
The others also
Or the gods will take back what is theirs
By force, as they would from serfs.

On the frontiers, however, where
The Knochenberg stands, as it is called
Today but in the old tongue
Ossa, Teutoburg
Is in that place and the land around
Abundant in spirited springs and there
The heavenly powers have all
Temples for themselves

    An artisan

But to us who
That

And not to fear fear too much!
For not you, gracious lady

                                        but there is
A grim race that will not willingly

Listen to a demigod nor when among humans or
In waves divinity appears, shapeless, nor honour the countenance
Of the pure, the near
The omnipresent god.

But even if the unholy
                a multitude
                    and insolent

But what are they to you
O song, pure song, true I
Shall die but you
Go your different way, in vain
Envy seeks to thwart you.

And when in times to come
You meet with a good man
Greet him and he will think
How indeed our days have been
Full of happiness and full of sorrow.
Going from one to another

But a further thing
Wants saying. For almost
Too suddenly
Happiness would have come to me
Lonely so that I at a loss
In the possession of it
Might have turned to the shadows
For since you gave
Mortals a trial
Of the shapes of gods
Why say a word? So I thought. For whoever husbands

The light of life, the nourishment of the heart,
Hates speech. In ages past
Poets were indeed heaven's interpreters
Having taken that power from the gods.

But we force unhappiness
To surrender its colours and hang them
High for the god of victory, the liberator, and on that account too
You sent riddles. They are holy
They shine, but when these powers of heaven
Become everyday and miracles
Begin to seem commonplace, yes when Titanic princes
Seize the Mother's gifts like so much booty
Then a higher help is given her.

The Titans

But it is not yet
Time. They are still
Not leashed. The spirit will not come to those taking no part.
Then let them reckon
With Delphi. May I in leisure hours meanwhile
So that I rest, remember
The dead. Many have died
Commanders in the ancient days
Lovely women and poets
And in the modern
Many men
But I am alone.

            and shipping into the ocean
Ask the scented islands
Where they have gone.

For things concerning them
Survive in faithful writings
And in the sagas of the times.
God reveals much.
For the clouds
Have long worked downwards
And the sacred wilderness, nursing many things, has rooted.
The riches are hot. For there's a lack
Of song to release the spirit.
It would devour
And be against itself
For never will heavenly fire
Suffer imprisonment.

But there is joy
In a feast or when at a festival

Eyes shine and with pearls
A young woman's neck.
And games of chivalry too

                        and down the garden
Allées the memory
Of battle crashes and the loud
Heroic weaponry of the ancestors
Lies hushed
On the slim bodies of children.
But I am hummed about
By bees and where the ploughman
Makes his furrows the birds
Sing on the light. Heaven
Has many helpers. The poet
Sees them. Good to hold on to others.
For no one can bear life alone.

But when the busy day
Is lit
And on the chain that leads
The lightning down
The heavenly dew
Of the hour of rising shines
Then feeling climbs
High in humans too.
So they build houses
Work starts up
And shipping on the rivers.
And men and women offer their hands
To one another, give and receive, sense
Is earthed and for good reason then
The eyes fix on the ground.

But you have also
A different way of feeling.
For in the measure

There must be coarseness too
So that purity may know itself.
But when

And into the depths
So they will come alive
He reaches who shakes all the earth
They suppose heaven's lord himself
Descends to the dead and violently
In the unleashed
All-witting abyss it dawns.
But I should not like to say
This ferment proves
The forces of heaven are weakening
But when
    and it goes

To the crown of the Father's head so that

    and the bird of heaven
Indicates it to him. Thereupon
He comes in wondrous fury.

Once I asked the Muse and she...

Once I asked the Muse and she
Answered me
At the end you will find it.
No mortal can grasp it.
I will not speak of the highest.
But forbidden fruit, like the laurel, is
More than any other thing, the motherland. But let everyone
Taste it last,

Beginning and end
Are largely deceptive.
But the last thing is
The sign from heaven that tears
        and   humans
Away. Surely Heracles
Feared that. But since we
Are born slothful it needs the falcon
Whose flight a rider
Follows when he hunts.

In the   when
And the prince

        and fire and a welter of smoke
Blossom on the parched grass
But unmixed there
From strong lungs, balm
In the battle, issues the voice of the prince.

An artist makes vessels
And they are bought

but when
It comes to the judgement
And chastely the lip
Of a demigod has touched it

And never now will he give his dearest things
To the unfruitful, henceforth
What is holy
Is there to be used.

But when the heavenly powers...

But when the heavenly powers
Have built, there is
Stillness on earth and the astounded mountains
Stand shapely. Their brows
Are marked. For they were smitten
By the Thunderer's shuddering lightnings
While his own forthright daughter
Ungently held him
And the turmoil then, quenched
From above, smells sweet.
Where now indwelling here and there
The fire   stands
Quietened. For the Thunderer
Pours out joy and would almost
Have forgotten heaven
In a passion then, had not
Wisdom warned him.
And now it blossoms
In poor places.
And wonderfully tall
It desires to stand.
Mountains hang   lake
Warm   depth   and the breezes cool
Islands and headlands
Caves, to pray,

A shining shield
And swiftly, like roses

                        or there is creation
Of other kinds too
Much sprouting

                        of envious luxuriant
Weeds, they dazzle, shoot up

Gawky, faster, for the Creator
Jests, which they
Do not understand. Too angrily
It reaches out and grows. And like the fire
That devours houses, it leaps up high
Without heeding, and leaves no room
And covers the paths
Fermenting far and wide, a boiling cloud
                              the hapless wilderness.
So it may seem the work of a god. But
Through the garden slinks your fearful
Guest without eyes
Madness. For the way out
Will hardly be discovered now by anyone
With clean hands. He goes, sent
And seeks, like the animals,
What is necessary. A man
It is true, with his arms
Filled with presentiment may
Hit on the goal. For where
The heavenly powers need a hedge or a sign
To point their way
Or a place to bathe
There in the hearts of men
It stirs like fire.

But the Father
Has others with him too.
For above the Alps,
Because the poets,
So they will explicate
More than their furious selves,
Must steer by the eagle,
Above that bird's flight around the throne
Of the god of joy
And covering the abyss for him
Dwell those, the prophets, who in the hurtling times

Around the brows of men are like a yellow fire
For which they are envied by
The fear-loving
Shades in Hell,

But these
The cleansing Heracles
Opening a clear destiny
Drove   from the holy
Tables of the earth
And himself still pure in heart
He abides with the Ruler even now, and bringing breath
The Dioscuri ascend and descend
Steps out of reach when from the heavenly citadel
The mountains go into the distance
At night and likewise
The times
Of Pythagoras

But Philoctetes lives in the memory,

They help the Father.
For they want rest. But when
The useless busyness
Of the earth provokes them and from
The heavenly powers is taken
                                the senses, burning
They come then,

The breathless ———

For the god
Deep in thought, detests
Untimely growth.

But formerly, Father Zeus...

But formerly, Father Zeus

Because

Now, however, you have found
Other counsels

Terrible therefore over the earth
Diana, huntress, walks and angrily
The Lord lifts over us
His countenance brimming with
No end of signs. The sea meanwhile
Sighs when he comes

Oh would it were possible
To spare my motherland

Not all-too-timidly, though,

It would   but rather
Let my life be not as it ought to be and pass away
With the Furies.
For above the earth
Violent powers are moving
And their destiny seizes
Whoever suffers it and watches
And seizes the hearts of the peoples.

For everything a demigod or a human
Must grasp in the measure of his suffering
Who hears, alone, or being
Himself transformed, distantly senses
The horses of the Lord,

The Eagle

My father travelled, he was on
The Gotthard where
The rivers go down and went
Aslant to Etruria and also
Straightways over the snow
To Olympus and Haemus
And where Athos casts
Its shadow at the caves of Lemnos.
But came in the first place
From the Indus with my mother
Among the spice forests.
But our first father
He was a sharp-eyed king
Who crossed the sea
Shaking his golden head
At the mystery of the waters
As the clouds steamed red
Above the ship and the beasts
Looked dumbly at one another
And wanted foddering, but
The hills indeed stand still:
Where shall we stay?

We have the rocks
For pasture, the drylands
To drink and for our meat
We have the wet.
Who wants a dwelling-place
Let it be by steps
And where a little house hangs down
Rest by the water
And what you have
Is to draw breath

And sleep restores
What you drew up
By day. For where
The eyes are covered and
The feet are bound
There you will find it.
Where will you see,

Nearest and best

(third version)

       the windows of heaven being opened
And the night spirit unleashed,
The stormer of heaven who has swayed our land
With tongues, many and ungovernable,
And shunted
Rubble till now.
But come the thing I want
If
So like the starlings
With a clamour of joy when in Gascony, places with many gardens,
When in the olive country and
Somewhere sweetly foreign
Fountains along grassy ways
The trees unknowing in the desert
The sun stabs
And the heart of the earth
Opens where round
The hill of oaks
Out of a burning land
The rivers and where
On Sundays amid dancing
The thresholds are hospitable
On roads slung with blossom, going quietly.
For they sense home
When straight   out of pale stone
The waters trickle silver
And green shows
Holy, on wet fields in Charente

Husbanding their clever senses.   but when
The air makes way
And the north-east wind blowing sharp
Quickens their eyes, they lift

And point to point
Spying things dearer to them
For they keep always exactly to what is nearest
They see the sacred woods and the blossoming scented flame
Of growth and the clouds of song in the distance and breathe the breath
Of songs. This is
Understood humanly. But the gods too
Have something of this in them and in the morning they watch
The hours and evening the birds. It is
The gods' way too. Well then. In the former time
Of secrecy I should as a natural thing have said
They are coming, in Germany. But now because the earth
Is like the sea and the lands like men
Who almost cannot pass by one another or be together
Without scolding words, I say: westerly well-wrought
From the Oberland the mountains bend where on high meadows the
    woods border
The Bavarian plain. And the mountains
Go far and stretch behind Amberg and
The Franconian hills. This is famous. Not for nothing
Was the range bent from the mountains of its youth
And directed
Home. For the Alps are a wilderness to it and
The mountains divide the valleys and along their length
Go over the earth. But there

That may suffice now. Almost impurely let itself and the bowels of the
    earth
Be seen.   But at Ilium
Also there was the light of eagles. But in the mid-time
The heaven of song. But close by
Angry old men on the shore, of the outcome, that is. All three
Are ours.

Tinian

Sweet to stray
In a sacred wilderness,
And to wander where you will, timeless

                                          for like
Chariot-racing or
Like wild-beast combat, as birthmark
Showing what manner of children
The Westerners are, the gods have decreed us
This bright-as-a-falcon ornament;

                                     There are flowers
Not spawned by the earth
They sprang of themselves from a loose ground
Answering a beam of the day, it is not
Fitting to pluck them
For they stand golden
Not prepared
Yes, even the leafless
Like thoughts,

And, o kindly spirit, at the she-wolf's dugs
Of the waters that through
This homeland of mine
Stray,
                             , more wildly once
And now accustomed, to drink, like foundlings
In spring when in the grove's
Warm ground foreign wings returning

                          resting in solitude,
And on Palm Sunday branches
Sweet smelling

With butterflies
The bees come together
And on your Alps

Divided by God

Zone of the world,

                       true they stand
Armed,

And to feel the lives…

And to feel the lives
Of the demigods or the patriarchs, sitting
In judgement. Not that everywhere
They go unheeded, but life, humming with heat, also echoes of shade
As though gathered
To a burning point. Golden desert. Or well-kept like the steel that
    lights
The life-warm hearth, the night strikes sparks then from the whetstone
Of the day and around dusk still
A lute is playing. The hunt's gunshots
Spit at the sea. But the gypsy woman sits, bare-breasted
Forever singing, the pains of hardship in her limbs
In the forest at the fire. Denoting a true knowledge
Of the planet's clouds and seas
In Scotland then as at the lake
In Lombardy a stream rushes by. So boys accustomed
To life as fresh as pearls will play around the figures
Of the masters or of the corpses, or thus around the crowns of the
    towers
The gentle swifts rush, screaming.

No, in truth, daylight
Is no maker
Of human forms. But first

An old thought, science
Elysium.

                              and lost love
Of the tournaments   horses, shy and damp

Where we began…

Where we began it was
The abyss, we went
Like the lion vexed and doubtful
For men have sharper senses in
The desert
Fire, they are
Drunk with light and the spirit of beasts
Is with them. But soon my voice
Will go about like a dog in the heat of the day
In the lanes behind gardens where people live
In France
The creator
But Frankfurt, to speak of it after man's
The print of nature's
Shape is this
Earth's navel, these times too
Are time and coloured German.
But above the slope of my gardens
There is a wild hill. Cherry trees. But a sharp breath wafts
Around the holes of the rocks. And here I am
And everything with me. But a tree bends
A miraculous slim nut-tree
Over the water-sources and   Berries like coral
Hang on the branches over wooden pipes
From which
Of corn once, but, to confess it now, the assured song of flowers when
New culture from the town where
To the point of pain in the nostrils
The smell of lemons rises and oil out of Provence and this
Gratitude the Gascon lands
Gave me. But, still to be seen, what tamed and nourished me was
The pleasure of rapiers and roast meat on the feast days
The table and swarthy grapes, swarthy
                          and glean me, o

You blossoms of Germany, my heart will be
Trustworthy crystal on which
Light tests itself when   Germany

...the Vatican...

                        the Vatican,
Here we are   in the solitude
And down below the brother goes, and a donkey too following the
    brown veil
But when the day   , because of the mockery, seeing good in
    all things
Makes destinies, since from the Goddess
Nature's rage, as a knight has said of Rome, in such
Palaces nowadays much error walks and knowing the keys of all secrets
Bad consciences ask questions
And meanwhile the spirit of Julius who changed
The calendar and over there in Westphalia
My honest master.
It is entrusted to us
To keep God pure and with discrimination
Lest, because much hangs
On this, to atone, over an error in
The sign
God's judgement come.
Oh do you no longer know him
The master of the forest and the youth in the wilderness who
Nourishes himself on honey and locusts? Stillness of spirit. Women
                        Up there perhaps
On Monte   , sideways too perhaps
I have strayed down
Through the Tyrol, Lombardy, Loretto, where the pilgrim's home
                on the Gotthard, hedged, casually in the midst of glaciers
He has his frugal dwelling where the bird
With the down of an eider, a pearl of the sea
And the eagle strikes its accent before God where the fire runs on
    account of human beings
But the watchman's horn sounds over the guards
Majestically, chastely
The crane holds upright over there
In Patmos, the Morea, in the pestilential air.

Turkish. And the owl well-known in scripture
Speaks like hoarse women in destroyed cities. But
These preserve the sense. Often like a conflagration
Comes confusion of tongues. But like a ship
Lying in the harbour, at evening, when the church tower's
Bell rings and it echoes below
In the bowels of the temple and the monk
And the shepherd say goodbye after their walk
And Apollo, likewise
From Roma, from such palaces, says
Farewell! And that, an unclean bitterness, is why!
Comes then the bridal song of heaven.
Peace accomplished. Golden red. And the ribs
Of the sandy ball of the earth resound in the explicit
Architecture of the work of God, in green night
And spirit, truly in the whole proportions
Of the columns' order, together with the centre
And with shining

Greece

(first version)

                    Ways of the traveller!
For   the trees' shadows
And hills, sunny, where
The way leads
To the church,
                laburnum, like a rain of arrows
And trees stand slumbering but
Step by step comes the sun
But just as it burns
Hotter over the mists of the towns
So it rises too
Over the walls hung with laburnum

For like ivy having no branches
The laburnum hangs. But more beautifully
The roads blossom for travellers
        in the open   changes like corn
Avignon, woody, over the Gotthard
The horse feels its way, laurels
Rustle around Virgilius and, so
The sun will not search
In an unmanly fashion, his grave. Moss roses
Grow
In the Alps. Flowers begin
Outside the gates of the town, on the levelled ways without favour
Like crystals growing in the waste of the sea.
Gardens grow around Windsor. In high style
The King's coach
Draws out of London.
Lovely gardens feel the season.
Along the Channel. But deep
Lies the level ocean, glowing.

Greece

(a part of the second version, lines 13-21)

      For Nature
Still lives. But when all too keenly
Unrestraint longs for death
Heaven falls asleep, and God's loyalty,
Good sense is wanting.
But as the dance
To a wedding
Also to humble things
A great beginning may come.

Greece

(third version)

O you, voices of destiny and you, the traveller's ways
For on the blue of the school
From far away, on the riot of the sky
Sounds like the blackbird's song
The cheerful mood and music of the clouds
Tuned by God, his being in the storm.
And shouts, like a looking out
To immortality, and heroes;
Many memories. When thereupon
Ringing like the calf's hide
Earth, coming from desolations, temptations of the saints
For in the beginning the work is shaped
And proceeds in accordance with great laws, science
And tenderness and far and wide the heavens' whole covering
        afterwards
Clouds of song appear, singing.
For the navel of the earth
Is fast. Bound within shores of grass are
The flames and the common
Elements. But above as of utter consciousness the aether lives. But
        on clear days
The light
Is silver. As a sign of love
Violet-blue the earth.
Also to humble things
A great beginning may come.
Everyday but wonderful, to please mankind
Are the garments God puts on.
And his countenance hides from understandings
And artfully covers the airs.
And air and time cover
The terror of him so that no one
With prayers, nor the soul herself

Will love him too much. For like leaves
Or lines and angles nature has long been open
To learn
And yellower the suns and the moons
At times however
When the earth's old culture
Looks to be ending, in stories, that is
That have come to pass, fighting bravely, as God
Leads earth to the heights. But he limits
Rash strides but then like blossom
Golden the soul closes over her powers and affinities
So that beauty is happier
To live on earth and one or another spirit
Comes more communally among people.

Sweet then to live under the high shadows of trees
And hills, sunnily, where the way
Is paved to the church. But for travellers whom
For the love of life, always measuring,
The feet obey, the ways
Blossom more beautifully where the country

Severed and at a distance now...

Severed and at a distance now and in
   The past if I were able still to show you
      Something good and you with a sorrow
         Equalling mine should you still know my face

Then say how might she expect to find you now,
   Your friend: in the gardens where we met again
      After the terror and the dark or
         Here by the rivers of the unspoilt world?

I will say this: there was some good in your eyes
   When in the distances you looked about you
      Cheerfully for once who were a man
         Always closed in his looks and with a dark

Aspect. The hours flowed away. How quiet
   I was at heart thinking of the truth which is
      How separate I would have been, but
         Yes I was yours then and I told you so

Without a doubt and now you will bring and write
   All the familiar things back into mind
      With letters and it happens to me
         The same and I will say all of the past.

Was it spring or summer? The nightingale's
   Sweet singing lived with the other birds that were
      Not far away among the bushes
         And trees were surrounding us with their scents.

On clear pathways, walking among low shrubs
   On sand, we thought more beautiful than anywhere
      And more delightful the hyacinths,
         The tulips, violets and carnations.

Ivy on the walls, and a lovely green
 Darkness under the high walks. In the mornings
  And the evenings we were there and
   Talked, and looked at one another, smiling.

In my arms the boy revived who had been still
 Deserted then and came out of the fields
  And showed me them, with sadness, but the
   Names of those rare places he never lost

And everything beautiful that flowers there
 On blessed seaboards in the homeland that I
  Love equally, or hidden away
   And only to be seen from high above

And where the sea itself can be looked upon
 But nobody will. Let be. And think of her
  Who has some happiness still because
   Once we were standing in the light of days

Beginning with loving declarations or
 Our taking hands, to hold us. Such pity now.
  That was our beautiful daytime but
   Sorrowful twilight followed after it.

You were so alone in the beautiful world,
 Beloved, how often you told me! But you
  Cannot know you were...

I have enjoyed …

I have enjoyed the pleasant things the world could show,
The hours of my youth went by so long, so long ago,
The months of April, May and June have gone,
I'm nothing now, I don't like living on.

When out of heaven...

When out of heaven brighter and brighter joy
   Pours down, happiness comes to human beings,
      Visible things are a wonder then
         And higher things and things that gladden us

And a holy singing with it, delightful,
   And the heart laughing and singing at the truth
      For the joy there is in a picture –
         Over the bridge the sheep are beginning

Their trail, almost into the dimming woods.
   The meadows however that now with pure green
      Are covered are like that common land
         Which in the ordinary way is near

Where the dark wood is. There in the meadows too
   These sheep are sojourning. The tops of the hills
      Around are naked heights except for
         Some cover of oaks and single pine trees.

Where the lively ripples of the river are
   So that a person coming along that path
      Looks at them gladly, the gentle shapes
         Of the hills ascend and the vineyards, high.

True, steps come down from high up under the vines,
   A blossoming fruit tree standing over them
      And scent still lingers on wild hedges
         Where the violets put forth in hiding;

Waters however trickle down and softly
   A rustling is audible all day long there
      But the dwelling places thereabouts
         Rest and are silent through the afternoon.

Spring

When new joy quickens in the fields and how
    Things look again becomes beautiful and on
        The mountains where the trees are greening
            Lighter breezes show themselves and clouds

What happiness people have then, the lonely
    Walk the riverbanks cheerfully, peace of mind,
        Zest and good health open like flowers,
            Friendly laughter is also not far off.

A happy life

Let me out into the meadow
Out into the fields as now
Here I'm tame again and pious
Seem unhurt by thorns and briars
And my cloak flaps in the breeze
And the merry spirit enquires
What an inner being is
Till the day it vanishes.

Seeing this picture, kind on the eye,
Seeing these trees stand leafy green
Like refreshment, like an inn sign
I can scarcely pass them by.
Peace, you see, a quiet day,
Seems an excellent thing to me.
Never ask me why I say so,
I'm not here to answer you.

However, to the pretty brook
I shall find a path I like
One that rambles under cover
Wildly down the bank deep down
Where the footbridge crosses over
Climbs then through the lovely trees
Where the footbridge feels the breeze
There the eyes look up and shine.

On the hill up there, up high
Many an afternoon I lie,
Hear the wind go through the branches
Hear the clock tower striking time.
Contemplation gives the heart
Peace, for so the picture is,
Soothes the ills that I have wrought
Cunningly until they rhyme.

Blessed landscape, where the road goes
Through the middle very level
There the moon, the white moon, shows
Through the evening comes a wind
Nature there is very simple
Nobly there the mountains stand
Home at last I go and try
The golden wine that I laid by.

The walk

Lovely the woods either side
Steeply depicted green
And I pass in between
With peace now sweetly paid
For every stab in the heart
And darkness in the head,
The harm that thinking did
And art from the very start.
Dear images in the valley
For example, garden and tree
And then the bridge, so narrow
And the river, hard to see,
How lovely from far away,
Where joy is, the image shows
Of the land it makes me happy
To visit on quiet days.
The friendly blue of heaven
Starts us on our way
Then clouds are added in
Like domes in shape and grey
And thunder comes and lightning
That sears and quickens the earth
With beauty welling forth
From where the images spring.

The churchyard

You quiet place, greening with the young grass
And crosses stand and men and women lie there
And friends go out and are conducted where
Windows are and shining with bright glass.

When on you shines the heavens' lifted lamp
At noon there when the spring will linger on
When there the spirit cloud, the grey, the damp
When softly day with beauty hurries and is gone.

How quiet it is at that grey wall
And over which a tree with fruits is hanging
With black and dewy fruits and foliage in mourning.
The clustering of the fruits is very beautiful.

The church has a dark quietness inside
And the altar too in this night hardly shows
And in there are some lovely things beside
But many crickets sing in the summer meadows.

And when one listens to the minister's address
And while the host of friends is standing near
With the dead man, what an own life is here
And what a spirit, what untroubled godliness.

Not all days...

Not all days he will call the best of days who
   Wishes he were back where happiness was where
      Friends loved him, where fellow humans
         Over the boy lingered a while, kindly.

Spring

How blessed to see the dawn of days again
When people in the fields look round contentedly
When people ask how you are getting on
When people shape themselves to living happily.

Just as the curved sky stretches far and wide
So joy too then on plains in the open air
When hearts hunger for life to be renewed
Comes singing then, comes the songbirds' screaming choir.

A man who often has asked himself questions
Then speaks of life from which our speech issues
Unless his soul is eaten at by sorrows
A man looks cheerfully on what he owns.

When a house is splendid, built high in the skies,
Fields for a man are roomier and ways
Far out, so one man turns to look
And well-built bridges go across the brook.

Autumn

The stories that are leaving earth that are
About the spirit that was here and will return
They turn our way again and we can learn
Much from time that wastes faster and faster.

The pictures of the past are not forgotten
By Nature when in high summer the days
Go white, autumn comes down to earth again,
Again the ghost of cold is in the skies.

In a brief while many things have ended,
The ploughman who was visible at the plough
He sees the year declining gladly now,
With pictures such as these our days are rounded.

The ball of the earth with rock for ornament
Is not like evening cloud that fades away,
It makes itself seen with a golden day
And in perfection there is no complaint.

Spring

The new day comes down from the far mountains,
The morning wakening is out of twilight,
Adorned and cheerful, and it smiles at humans,
It pierces humans, gently, with delight.

A new life for the future is unveiling,
With blossom, sign of happy days,
The wide valley, the earth seems to be filling,
And far away when springtime comes grief goes.

Obediently yours
Scardanelli

3 March 1648

View

To us with images the open day is bright
When from the level distance greenness shows,
Before the evening light inclines to twilight
And hazes gently damp the sounds of day.
Often the innerness of the world seems clouded, closed,
The minds of people full of doubts, morose,
Splendidly Nature brightens up their days
And doubt's black question stands some way away.

Obediently yours
Scardanelli

24 March 1671

In a lovely blue

In a lovely blue the church spire with its metal cladding flowers. Around it go the screams of the swifts, around it lies the most touching blue. High over it climbs the sun and colours the metal, but above, in the winds, the weather cock crows quietly. If anyone goes down then under the bells, down those steps, life has stillness then, because, when shapes are so separate, the plasticity of man emerges. The windows, through which the bells are sounding, are like gates in their beauty. For since gates are after nature still they have the appearance of trees of the forest. But purity is beauty too. Inside, from a variety, an earnest spirit arises. But so simple are the images, so very holy, that truly one is often fearful of describing them. But the heavenly gods, who are always kind, all together, they own like kingdoms these: virtue and joy. A man may imitate that. May a man, when life is all toil, look up and say: I too will be like that? He may. So long as friendliness, pure friendliness, still lasts in the heart a man may measure himself not unhappily with the Godhead. Is God unknown? Is he as apparent as the sky? The latter, I should say. It is man's measure. Full of merit, but poetically, man lives on this earth. But the shadow of the night with the stars, if I could say it thus, is not purer than man, who is called an image of God.

*

Is there a measure on earth? There is none. For the Creator's worlds never slow down the course of the thunder. Even a flower is beautiful, since it flowers under the sun. Often in life the eye finds living things that might be called much more beautiful than the flowers. Oh, I have known that very well. For to bleed at heart and in one's shape and wholly cease to be, is that pleasing to God? But the soul, as I believe, must remain pure, or the eagle with songs of praise and the voices of so many birds will reach to the sources of power, on wings. It is the being of things, it is their shape. Beautiful brook, how touching you seem, rolling so clearly, like the eye of God, through the Milky Way. I know you well enough, but tears start from the eye. I see a cheerful life flowering around me in the shapes of creation, because, with some justice, I compare it to the lonely pigeons in the churchyard. But people's laughter seems to grieve me, for I have a heart. Should I like to be a comet? Perhaps I would. For they have the speed of birds; their fire is such that they flower and for purity they are like children. Human nature could not presume to wish for anything greater. And the good humour of virtue deserves to be praised by the earnest spirit that blows between the three pillars in the garden. A beautiful girl must crown her head with flowers of myrtle because in her nature and in her feelings she has simplicity. But there are myrtles in Greece.

*

When a man looks in the mirror and sees his image there, as if in a portrait; it looks like the man. The image of the man has eyes; the moon, on the other hand, light. King Oedipus has an eye too many perhaps. These sufferings of this man, they seem indescribable, unsayable, inexpressible. If that is what the play depicts, that is the reason. But what do I feel if I think of you now? I am pulled as streams are by the ending of something – something that expands like Asia. Suffering of that sort Oedipus had, of course. Naturally that is the reason. Did Hercules suffer too? Indeed he did. And the Dioscuri in their friendship, did they not bear some suffering too? For to quarrel with God, as Hercules did, that is suffering. And in the envy of this life to share one's immortality, that is suffering too. But to be covered in freckles, to be covered all over with them, that is a sort of suffering too. The beautiful sun is to blame for that: it brings everything out. The sun encourages the young men along their way with its beams as with roses. The sufferings Oedipus bore are as if a poor man were crying that something was wrong. Son of Laius, poor stranger in Greece! Life is death, and death too is a life.

TRANSLATIONS FROM THE GREEK

Chorus from Sophocles' *Oedipus at Colonus*

Among the fine steadings
Of this land rich in horses
On Colonus' white ground
You have arrived
O stranger to these parts
Where the returning nightingale
Piercingly laments
Among the green bushes
And the vaults of dark ivy
And the god's impenetrable foliage
Fruitful, sunless
That no stormwind agitates.
But here the bacchantic
Dionysus who dwells among
The nurturing goddesses
Comes and goes and here
On the scents of heaven the narcissi
Lift their lovely clusters day by day
That are the ancient garlands
Of the great goddesses
With the crocus, shining gold.
Nor do the sleepless springs that part
Into the waters of Cephissus
Ever dwindle, but always and daily
Over the fields comes the quick begetter
With pure showers of rain
Over the bosom of the earth.
Nor do the choirs of the Muses nor
Does golden Aphrodite shun this place.

From Euripides' *Bacchae*

I come, the son of Jove, here into the Theban land
Dionysus, born in a former time of Cadmus' daughter
Semele, fathered on her by the thunder's fire
And taking a human shape instead of a god's
I am among Dirce's woods and Ismenus' waters.
I see the tomb of my mother on whom the lightning fell
There close by the houses, I see the ruined halls
The smoking, still living, flames of divine fire
Hera's everlasting violence against my mother.
But I praise the good man Cadmus who in the field here
Planted a fig tree for his daughter. I have encircled it
With the vine-stock's scent of grapes and greenery
And far from the gold-filled country of the Lydians
The Phrygians' and the Persians' land that the light strikes
Near Bactra's walls, through the stormy fields
Of the Medes, through Arabia called the fortunate
And traversing all of Asia that on the salty
Waters lies for them both, Greeks and barbarians
Mingled as they are and rich in cities with lovely towers
So I came here first into a Greek city
To bring my choral dance and to institute
My mystery, that I shall be visible, a spirit, to men.
First in Thebes here in the land of the Greeks
I have raised the shouts of joy, seizing the deerskins.

Chorus from Sophocles' *Antigone*

Much there is that is mighty. But nothing
Is mightier than man.
For he roves the grey seas
In stormy southerlies
In winged dwellings
In the roar and rush of the waves.
The holy earth of the gods
The pure, the effortless earth
He works it over year upon year
Driving the race of horses to and fro
And the lightly moving plough.

For the lightly living family of birds
He lays snares, he hunts them
And the wild race of the beasts
And the salt-sea tribe
With cunningly twisted cords
Man, with his lore.
Commands by his art the land's
Wild creatures that wander the mountains.
Around the neck and the mane of the steed
He flings a yoke and likewise the wild
The untamed bull.

From Sophocles' *Oedipus at Colonus*

ANTIGONE. My father, poor Oedipus, the towers here cast shadows
    Around the city, so that to the eyes it seems distant.
    The place, however, as may well be thought, is holy.
    It rustles with laurels and with the olive and the vine.
    In it, densely flocking, nightingales sound sweet.
    And it bends its limbs up the hard rock and around.

    —   —   —   —   —   —   —

OEDIPUS. What manner of place is this? Which god does it belong to?

TRAVELLER. Untouchable, uninhabitable. For the shy
    Goddesses have it, maidens of the earth and of the night.

OEDIPUS. Who are they? Their pure name I should like to hear.

TRAVELLER. They who see all things, the Eumenides. So say
    The people here. Other things are lovely elsewhere.

OEDIPUS. May they be gracious and take in this supplicant
    That never from this abode, this ground, I shall depart.

TRAVELLER. What is this?

OEDIPUS.   Very essence of my fate.

TRAVELLER.   But I to speak
    Before the town, doubly I do not have the boldness
    Till I have let be known what I am doing.

OEDIPUS. Here by the gods, o stranger, do not rate me lightly,
    Such a man astray, when I have the wish to speak.

TRAVELLER. Speak. You will have from me no disrespect.

OEDIPUS. What manner of place is this then where we are?

TRAVELLER. As much as I know myself you will hear all of it.
    The whole zone hereabouts is holy and the pure
    Poseidon has it. Within however
    Is the firebringer, the god, the Titan

Prometheus. But where you tread, the place is called
The bronze-footed path of this country,
The shield of Athens.

From Sophocles' *Ajax*

AJAX. Ah night, my light, o Erebus shining at me
    Take me, take
    Me home to you, take me. For
    Not to the race of gods nor among
    Everyday men am I
    Fit to look for a help. But I am thrashed
    To death by Zeus'
    Terrible goddess.
    Where must one flee to,
    That being so, where shall I go
    And stay?
    When it withers this side, dear ones,
    And I lie wholly othered
    And wildly out of my mind.
    But let all the army from both sides
    Kill me with their hands.

TECMESSA. Unhappy woman. That such a man of sense
    Lets go. He never dared before.

AJAX. O streams that enter the sea, o caves by the sea, and you
    My grove that hangs over the shore
    A long long time
    You held me up, at Troy,
    Now no more, no more
    Drawing breath. Let a man
    Come to his senses here and remember.
    Alas, by the Scamander, streams
    Kind to the Argives
    One of us you will never
    See again, I speak
    Big words: like him
    Troy saw no other in the host
    That came from Greece
    And my state now

Is all dishonourable.

[Lines 394-427]

CHORUS. Famous Salamis, somewhere
        You dwell among the sea-waves, fortunate,
        And anyone may find you.
        But I have suffered
        A long time now
        A same and countless time
        On Ida on the grassy pastures
        Time has been eating me and I entertain
        Bad hopes that soon
        I'll chase my elusive death
        To earth in Hell.
        I have a new enemy, his name:
        Ajax, who serves me roughly, oh me, oh me, his
        House is a godly madness.
        You sent him forth once
        Splendidly in a wild
        War mood. But now
        His brains are all alone and to his dear friends
        He is a large sorrow
        And the works once of our hands
        The high works of our virtue, these have fallen
        From favour now with the ill-favoured
        Useless sons of Atreus.

            True, the mother whom the ageing days
        Look after but
        Snow-white in years
        When she hears of his sickness
        Something of his madness
        She will lament, lament, and not
        With the dirge of the grieving nightingale
        She won't, but shrilly
        She'll wail and blows dealt by

237

Her hands will fall on her breasts
And locks from her grey hair.

    Better to sleep in Hell than be
Sick and good-for-nothing when one of our race
Of tribulated Greeks comes home
No longer master of
His native rage, but beside himself.
O Father suffering to an end
What unbearable harm awaits you when
You learn of your child!
For time has never reared the like
Among the Aeacides, this excepted.

[Lines 596-645]

CHORUS. I shake with love, good all around, I open.
    Oh Pan! Pan! Oh, joy!
    O Pan! o Pan! be seized by waves from upon
    Cyllene on the rockfirm hill
    In driving snow, appear, o you
    King of the given gods, you gatherer
    And fit together the Nysian steps you
    Taught yourself, and the Cnossian, for me, with me
    Now that I long to dance.
    And you who open over the Sea of Icarus
    King Apollo
    Famous on Delos
    Favour me evermore.
    For Ares has loosed the torment from his eyes.
    Joy, oh joy! And now
    Now Zeus appear in the white light
    Of lovely day driving
    The rapid ships, now that Ajax
    Forgetting his pains
    Ushers to the gods the lovely smoke of sacrifice
    Lawfully serving

And eminent again.
For mighty time drags everything away, to make
It pass. And there is nothing now I call unsingable
Since in his mind beyond our hope Ajax
Has ended his quarrel with the sons of Atreus.

[Lines 693-718]

Pindar Fragments

Wisdom's infidelities

> O child most likening your mind
> To the skin of that wild ocean creature
> Who loves the rocks, enter into all the cities
> And, looking kindly
> Praise what is there present
> And in other times think otherwise.

Fitness of solitary schooling for the world. The innocence of pure knowledge as the soul of shrewdness. For shrewdness is the art of remaining true in different circumstances, knowledge the art of being secure in one's understanding even among errors of fact. If understanding is practised intensively it retains its strength even amidst distraction, against its own honed edge recognising that which is foreign to it, and so will not easily go wrong in uncertain situations.

Thus Jason, a pupil of the Centaur, comes before Pelias:

> I believe I have
> The teaching of Chiron. For I come from the cave
> Of Chariclo and Philyra where I
> Was raised by the Centaur's
> Holy girls. Twenty years I have spent
> And neither an unclean work
> Nor word did I ever speak
> To them and have now come home
> To bring back my father's rule.

*

On Truth

> Beginner of great virtue, Queen Truth
> May you not cause my thinking
> To collide against rough lies.

Fear of truth, out of delight of it. For the first lively grasping of truth in a living sense is, like all pure feeling, exposed to confusions; so that one errs not by a fault of one's own, nor from any disturbance, but on account of the higher object, for which, relatively, the mind is too weak.

*

On Quietness

> If once a citizen in a calm time
> Has grasped the common weal
> Let him study the holy light
> Of quietness in some great person
> And thoroughly fend off the winds
> Of unrest from his heart; for they bring poverty
> And are hostile to the educators of children.

Before the laws, the holy light of quietness in a great person, are studied, someone, a law-giver or a prince, must when the fate of the country is more tumultuous or settled and according to the people's receptivity, grasp the character of that destiny, be it more monarchic or more wholly in the circumstances of the people, in times without disturbance, more usurpatory, as in the case of the Greek sons of nature, or more experienced, as in the case of people of education. Then laws are the means of holding that fate steady and undisturbed. What for the prince is originality is for those more truly citizens imitation.

*

Concerning the Dolphin

> Whom in the depths of the waveless sea the song
> Of lovely flutes has moved.

The song of Nature, in the weather of the Muses, when over blossom the clouds hang like flakes and over the lustre of golden flowers. Around this time every creature gives out its tone, its self-fidelity, the manner of its own fitting together. The only separation in Nature then is that of the differences among the species, so that everything is more song and pure voice than accent of need or, as it might be, language.

It is the waveless sea where the agile fish feels the pipes of the tritons, the echo of growth in the soft plants of the water.

*

The Highest

> The law
> Of all, mortals and immortals
> King; and for that reason
> In power it wields
> The justest justice with the highest hand of all.

The unmediated is, strictly speaking, impossible for mortals as for the immortals. The god must differentiate different worlds in accordance with his nature because divine goodness, for its own sake, must be holy, unmixed. Man, as that which sees and knows, must also differentiate different worlds, because seeing and knowing are possible only through contraries. Accordingly, the unmediated is, strictly speaking, for mortals and for immortals impossible.

The strictly mediated is, however, the law.

And accordingly it wields the justest justice with the highest hand of all.

Discipline, in so far as it is the form in which human beings and the god encounter one another, the laws of the church and the state, and inherited statutes (the holiness of the god and, for humans, the possibility of knowing and seeing, of an explanation) these wield the justest justice with the highest hand of all, more strictly than art they hold firm the living relations in which, with time, a people has encountered and continues to encounter itself. 'King' here is the superlative which is only the sign of the highest ground of seeing and understanding, not a sign of the highest power.

*

Old Age

> With those living lives
> In righteousness and holiness
> Sweetly nourishing their hearts
> Making a long life
> Hope walks who most
> For mortals directs
> Many-sided opinion.

One of the loveliest images of life, how innocent custom upholds the lively heart from which hope comes; which gives then a flowering to simplicity in its manifold experiments and directs the mind and so makes a long life in its hurrying and tarrying.

*

The Infinite

> Whether I climb the high wall
> Of justice or of twisted
> Deceit and thus
> Circumlocuting myself live

Myself out, I have
A mind viewing two ways
To speak of it exactly.

The wise man's jest, and the riddle is scarcely to be solved. The wavering and quarrelling between right and shrewdness can in fact only be resolved in their thorough interplay. 'I have a mind viewing two ways to speak of it exactly.' It is so I may discover the connection between right and shrewdness ascribable not to them but to a third thing through which they are infinitely (exactly) connected, that I have a mind viewing two ways.

*

The Sanctuaries

First the heavenly powers
On golden steeds
Conducted the wise counsellor
Themis by
The ocean's salt and tides
To the holy ladder of Olympus for
Her glorious return
As Zeus the Saviour's
Ancient daughter
While she of her goodness
Gave birth to the resting places
Set in gold
And shining with fruit.

How man, a son of Themis, settles himself when in the feeling for perfection his spirit has found no peace on earth or in heaven till, meeting in fate, by the traces of the ancient order the god and the man recognise one another and in the memory of original need he is glad to be there where he can have a hold.

Themis, lover of order, gave birth to the sanctuaries of humankind, the quiet resting places, which nothing alien can approach because in them the workings and the life of Nature were concentrated, and around them, like remembering, a sense of experiencing the same as formerly they experienced.

*

The Life-Giver

> The overcomer of men, after
> The Centaurs had learned
> The power
> Of the honey-sweet wine, suddenly they thrust
> With their own hands the white milk, the table, away
> And drinking from the silver horns
> Bemused themselves.

The concept of the Centaurs is doubtless that of the spirit of a river insomuch as it makes its way and its borders by force on the originally pathless and upwards-growing earth.

For that reason their image is to be found at places in Nature where the banks are rich in rocks and caves, especially in localities where in the beginning the river had to leave the chain of the mountains and break its way through their direction.

In the beginning for that reason Centaurs were also teachers of the science of Nature because from that point of view insight into Nature may best be got.

In such districts in the beginning the river was obliged merely to wander, before seizing itself a course. And thus, as they do near ponds, wet meadows formed and caverns in the earth for suckling beasts and the Centaur was meanwhile a wild shepherd like the Cyclops in the *Odyssey*; and longingly the waters sought their direction. But the more the drier parts of both its banks became firmer and gained direction by trees and bushes and the vine rooting fast, the more the river also, taking its movement from the shape of the banks, gained direction until, driven since its beginnings, it broke through at a place where the mountains confining it hung together at their lightest.

So the Centaurs learned the power of the honey-sweet wine, from the firmly fashioned tree-rich banks they took movement and direction and flung away the white milk and the table with their hands, and the waves taking shape ousted the stillness of the ponds, on the banks the way of life also changed, the invading woods with storms and the steady princes of the forest roused the idle life of the heathland, the stagnant water was for so long repulsed by the steepening banks it grew arms and thus with its own direction, itself drinking from silver horns, made its way, assumed a destiny.

Especially the songs of Ossian are true centaur-songs, sung with the river-spirit and as though by the Greek Chiron who also taught Achilles how to play the lyre.

HÖLDERLIN'S SOPHOCLES

INTRODUCTION

Hölderlin, a great translator, said very little about the theory and practice of translation; but in the spring of 1794, before he had attempted much himself, he did elaborate two principles or considerations in letters to a friend who was translating Virgil. The first is that translation is good for our native language; he calls it 'a salutary gymnastics'; our language, he says, will become skilful, strong and supple in the struggle with the beauty and greatness of the foreign original. The second is a view of translation as travel and residence abroad, like a journeyman's when he goes to learn his trade. The risk is, Hölderlin warns his friend, that in foreign service or servitude we may lose ourselves, our own identity, our own tongue, and have no serviceable speech at our disposal when we come home. Translation as combat, and as a necessary journeying abroad, for the sake of, but at the risk of losing, our own tongue.

'Abroad', for Hölderlin, meant time as a well as place; it meant a combat with and a dwelling in the language of the poetry of Ancient Greece. In 1800, in order to come into full possession of his own poetic language, he risked his identity and the identity of the German language altogether in a slavish translation of the great lyric poet Pindar, adhering to the syntax, the word-order, the literal senses of that original, producing for the most part a German unintelligible without the Greek, but now and then, by mechanically cleaving as close as possible, hitting on a language truly poetic, strange and beautiful, the true language of elsewhere, poetry at its best; and he wrote, as we might say, in that tongue thereafter.

Advertising the translations of *Oedipus* and *Antigone* in July 1804 the publisher, Friedrich Wilmans, said in their favour that Hölderlin had worked on them for ten years. This may not be much of an exaggeration. The earliest surviving evidence of Hölderlin's pre-occupation, as a translator, with Sophocles is a fragment of *Oedipus at Colonus* done in 1796; next is a version of an *Antigone* chorus from 1799 (see pages 231 and 2333). He had a version of this play and of *Oedipus* ready by the summer of 1802, when he began to look seriously for a publisher. Then in the winter of 1803-04, when he and Wilmans had come to an agreement, Hölderlin worked over the two plays, especially *Antigone*. It was probably his intention to translate all seven of Sophocles' extant plays; *Oedipus* and *Antigone* came out as volumes I and II. There is fragmentary evidence of his continuing work on *Oedipus at Colonus* and *Ajax*. He promised, but it seems never delivered, an introduction to stand at the head of all the volumes; and he entertained the – as it must now seem – far-fetched idea of getting Goethe to stage one or other play at the court theatre in Weimar.

Editors have distinguished four phases of work on *Oedipus* and *Antigone*, which are in fact four distinct modes of translation. Only the last two need concern us here. The first of these, in which the bulk of both plays was done, doubtless in 1801-02, is that of the great Pindar translations, slightly moderated: keeping close to the syntax and word-order of the original and often also to the literal sense of individual words. The resultant German has a luminous strangeness. And the last phase, as Hölderlin revised his work in the winter of 1803-04, is one in which translation and interpretation combine. He warped the original to fit his own idiosyncratic under-standing not only of it but also of his obligation in translating it. The literal and the interpretative modes co-exist in both plays; *Oedipus* though is a more consistent product of the former, and *Antigone* underwent more of the latter.

Hölderlin completed these translations under the approaching shadow of mental illness. In the summer of 1802 he returned from his last employment, as a house tutor in Bordeaux, crossed France in the burning heat, and came home to the news that his beloved Susette Gontard was dead. He was thought by friends who saw him then to be already raving mad, and he said himself that Apollo had smitten him. But he recovered, quietened, and despite terrible fatigue and agitation and in the ruin of all hopes of personal happ-iness, he wrote such poems as 'Patmos', 'Remembrance' and 'Mnem-osyne', which are among his best. This was also a time of an almost compulsive revision of earlier work, an undertaking very like trans-lation. He took finished poems and line by line 'translated' them into a radical other language. Several of the so-called 'Night Songs', among them 'Ganymede' and 'Chiron', were produced in this way (see pages 73, 79, 381). His work on Sophocles, not just the translations but also the accompanying notes, is very much a part of a whole, coherent and desperate creative endeavour, the essence of which was to make sense of and somehow hold himself steady against the destructive pull of the times and of insanity. He could not resist, he was overwhelmed, but left the poems and his Sophocles behind in safety.

When Hölderlin's *Oedipus* and *Antigone* appeared in spring 1804, the learnèd said at once that they must be the work of a madman, and by the time all the reviews came out Hölderlin had indeed passed through the clinic and was beginning the long latter half of his life in alienation in the tower in Tübingen. It is true that the translations are strange, but in their most consistent method at least, the cleaving very close to a Greek original, they were not unprecedented. Johann Heinrich Voß had done the *Iliad* and the *Odyssey* like that, radically estranging the German tongue, and published them in 1793. Yet eleven years later it was his own son Heinrich, also a translator, who wrote the harshest and the most ridiculing review of Hölderlin's Sophocles.

Modern scholars have found more than a thousand errors in Hölderlin's *Oedipus* and *Antigone*. Of course, many of these so-called errors are in practice contributions to the plays' coherent poetry. Nevertheless, the philological inaccuracy of the translations is striking. There are three reasons for it. First, though it has not been entirely established which editions of Sophocles Hölderlin worked from, it is pretty certain that he did not use the most recent and the best available in his day. His chief text for *Antigone* was published in Frankfurt in 1555, and is notably corrupt. Thus many of his errors derive from his faulty sources. Secondly, the two volumes published by Wilmans in 1804 were riddled with misprints. Hölderlin sent him a list, doubtless not exhaustive, of more than 40 in *Oedipus*. This list has survived (the manuscripts of the translations themselves have not) and modern editors have corrected the text accordingly. But no such list exists for *Antigone*, so we can only guess at what might be printer's errors there. To the end of his life, through nearly 30 years of mental alienation, Hölderlin still bore a grudge against Wilmans for the mangling and disfigurement of his text. Finally though, it has to be acknowledged that Hölderlin, who had more insight into the heart of Ancient Greek culture than anybody else in his generation, was not very sound in the grammar of the language, and in translating made basic mistakes. And he seems not to have turned for help to Latin cribs and commentaries as professional and traditional translators surely would have done. That trusting his own judgement, overriding his philological weaknesses, is very characteristic of the whole endeavour. He worked according to his lights, in a state of mind already verging on collapse, towards something very beautiful, strange and troubling.

Hölderlin's Sophocles translations, like most of the rest of his poetry, only came into the mainstream of German consciousness around the time of the First World War. His *Antigone* was first performed in 1913, *Oedipus* in 1921. Since then, being recognised as an integral part of his entire poetic achievement, they have never been lost sight of. Carl Orff set both texts to music, *Antigone* in 1949, *Oedipus* ten years later. Brecht's *Antigone* (1948), and Heiner Müller's *Oedipus der Tyrann* (1967) derive immediately from Hölderlin's.

One thing I only came to realise as I translated Hölderlin's Sophocles is that the language of *Oedipus* is, all in all, odder and more difficult than that of *Antigone*. I had half expected it to be the other way round, since Hölderlin told Wilmans in December 1803 that he was still working at the the latter play, because its language did not seem to him 'lively enough'. The Choruses and even more so Antigone's own speeches in Acts III and IV are of course extraordinarily 'lively', they have a burning compacted intensity; still, much of *Oedipus* is stranger, and seems to be coming from somewhere yet further off, yet more foreign. The reason may be that in *Oedipus* language itself, speech, utterance, is the very issue. In Hölderlin's idiosyncratic reading of the play, Oedipus' sin consists less in his murdering his father and marrying his mother than in helplessly, compulsively, manically rooting out and bringing into the light and uttering things too frightful to be seen or said. Jocasta, and the herdsman being interrogated, warn him off: 'If you're chary of life/ Then do not search', 'Unlucky man, why, what do you want to know?'; but he is compelled to continue. In

Hölderlin's words, he is 'tempted towards the *nefas*', into that which is unspeakable. The Messenger, recounting the catastrophe, still cannot utter the things welling forth from Oedipus himself: '[he] speaks / Unholinesses I am not allowed to say'. In the end, blind Tiresias foresees all, and Oedipus sees too much. As Hölderlin remarked elsewhere (see page 227), 'King Oedipus has an eye too many perhaps'; and we likewise see too much when the great doors are opened and he appears with his eyes put out. Then, as Creon says, he is not fit to be seen by the sun.

Antigone, on the other hand, is more the opposition of irreconcilable views. The exchanges between Creon and Antigone are not at all like the forensic interrogations in *Oedipus* in the course of which a lethal truth is dragged out screaming; they are rather the frank, clear, non-negotiable statements of two opponents. Language itself is not the issue or the problem, but serves them well to articulate what the issue and the problem is.

I mentioned earlier Hölderlin's view of translation as risky servitude abroad. He felt powerfully drawn to the culture of Ancient Greece, but always struggled to assert himself, his own identity and the needs of his own times against the supreme excellence of an age so long in the past. In translating Sophocles it was his wish to serve his contemporaries, and that wish materially affected the way he translated. In Hölderlin's view – rather anticipating Nietzsche's – the renowned clarity, shapeliness and balance of Attic tragedy had been achieved through a determined struggle against a quite contrary tendency, one innate in the Greeks, towards wildness, ecstasy and anarchy; which tendency or principle he termed 'Oriental'. Thus what in Hölderlin's day the Greeks were thought to have excelled at, a quality he called 'sobriety', far from being 'in their nature', was the product of a struggle 'against their nature'. He took an opposite view of his German contemporaries. Natural to them, he thought, was not passion but sobriety, far too much of it. They needed enlivening. Accordingly, he translated Sophocles in such a way as to bring out that underlying counter-tendency of Oriental wildness which Sophocles himself had overcome to arrive at Attic sobriety. That is the chief interpretative tendency in Hölderlin's translations: to bring the ancient texts home in such a fashion that they will quicken hearts and minds in the torpid present.

In translating like that, serving, as he thought, the present needs of his own countrymen, Hölderlin put himself ever more at risk. Always choosing the more violent word, so that the texts are stitched through with the vocabulary of excess, of madness, rage, he was also voicing those forces in his own psychology which, very soon, would carry him over the edge. And in uttering them did he not aid and abet them? It is the old paradox: the better the poet says these things, and none has ever said them better than he did, the better he arms them against himself. So well put, are they not irresistible? His characterisation of *Oedipus*' compulsive quest and utterance as 'idiot-frenetic', as that of 'a sick mind', is unbearably close to himself and the way that he was going.

In Hölderlin's understanding of tragedy, as he expounds it in his very difficult Notes on the two plays, there is an unhappy coming together of personal and cultural predicament. Tragedy, he says, occurs at times of thorough revolution in human thinking and feeling, of 'total reversal'. He sees such a moment in Antigone's revolt against Creon. She is the agent of an ideology wholly irreconcilable with his, and perishes in asserting it. She, and Oedipus also, in the crises of their tragedies, are taken up out of an organised and familiar world into the 'eccentricity' of disintegration, holy madness and death. Again, when he describes the pull of that eccentric zone, its ecstatic temptation, he does so as someone more and more at the mercy of such forces in his personal life. Writing of Antigone and Creon, and translating the classsic account of their combat, he had his eye on the 'total reversal' brought about in his own times by the French Revolution and the ensuing wars; and seems himself to be the tragic vehicle of those times, the locus in which an inevitable process must reach its tragic end.

Two or three years before completing these translations, Hölderlin had struggled with and failed to finish a tragedy of his own, on the suicide of the Ancient Greek philosopher, poet and radical critic of organised religion, Empedocles. His Notes on *Oedipus* and *Antigone* are a continuation of his thinking, in 1800, on the nature of tragedy in general and on Empedocles' tragedy in particular. Likewise in the Notes, when he enquires into the 'mechanics' of tragedy and seeks to trace the 'calculable law' of each of the plays, this is a continuation, still cryptic but more concrete, of the obsessive and solitary deliberations on the spirit and the practice of poetry he had pursued in that same year. Hölderlin is among the most passionate of poets, but also among the most calculating. Hence his insistence, in the Notes, on the value of craft and schooling.

Translation, especially translation out of the past, keeps us in touch with works we cannot do without. I said that Hölderlin's versions of Sophocles are generally recognised and admired nowadays, but that does not in any way lessen their essential strangeness and their power to illuminate and unsettle. They are strange erratics still, all the more fascinating and disorientating for being versions of plays so classical and familiar. They give us Sophocles again, in a radical modernity. You might see Creon, for example, as the obstinate perpetrator of something that no one should ever do; and Antigone as the champion of values more fundamental than his and the state's. In two hair-raising speeches in Act IV Tiresias 'sees' a society stricken by the consequences of offending against fundamental laws. It must sound to us, in our world now, like what has already happened and will surely happen again and again until there is no world left for it to happen in, when we do things, against Nature, for example, that must on no account ever be done. Antigone, a woman against a man, a female ideology against that of the state of men, lives in the wisdom of an old taboo, and dies asserting it. She – or Hölderlin, in language he strove to make ever 'livelier' – causes us to ask ourselves, is there *anything* we, or the people managing us, would not do?

For my translation I mainly used the *Frankfurter Ausgabe* of Hölderlin's works. There his versions are set out opposite the 1555 text of Sophocles which he is known to have used at least for his *Antigone*. Otherwise I drew on the *Große Stuttgarter Ausgabe*, and on the edition published by the Deutscher Klassiker Verlag, which has good notes and commentaries. My rule was not to correct any of Hölderlin's 'errors', but always to translate his text; and I only departed from this rule on a couple of occasions where a distracting nonsense or inconsistency would otherwise have been produced.

Dialogue in classical Greek tragedy is usually conducted in iambic trimeters, lines of six feet. In translating them Hölderlin moves as it suits him between the trimeter and the line most often employed in German and English tragedy, the pentameter. I have followed him in that, giving myself also the extra licence of some shorter lines. To render the complex Greek metres of the choruses and other lyrical passages he uses free rhythms like those of his own hymns, which I imitated as best I could, for the most part allowing myself only as many lines as he has and always paying attention to his line-breaks.

I kept close to his strange German, in the hope of arriving at an analogous strangeness in English. But his language is beautiful and troubling too, and in the carrying over much of that will have been lost like precious water from a leaky vessel. But I learned the other day that Hölderlin is read and loved in translation in Bangladesh, and that encourages me, here adding more to his stock in English.

DAVID CONSTANTINE
2001

OEDIPUS THE KING

DRAMATIS PERSONAE

OEDIPUS.
A PRIEST.
CREON.
TIRESIAS.
JOCASTA.
A MESSENGER.
A SERVANT *of Laius.*
Another MESSENGER.
CHORUS *of Theban Elders.*

FIRST ACT

FIRST SCENE

OEDIPUS. A PRIEST.

OEDIPUS. O you, old Cadmus' children, new offspring,
    In what posture do you assail me here
    Crowned all around with begging sprigs of tree?
    Also the city is filled up with sacrifices,
    With paeans and sighing prayers. Not wishing,
    Children, from any other messengers
    To hear why, I have come myself, myself
    With fame by all called Oedipus.
    But, old man, speak, for you are suitable
    To speak for them. What way do you stand
    In fear or suffering already? All of it
    I will help with. I would be unfeeling
    Had I before such posture no mercy.

THE PRIEST. O ruler of my country, Oedipus!
    You see us lying down, how many of us
    At your altar, these not yet by far
    Strong enough to fly, the others, the priests,
    Heavy with age. I am Zeus's. They are picked
    From youths. The other branches
    Pile garlanded on public squares at Pallas'
    Double temple and Ismenus's
    Foretelling ash. Because the town you see
    Already totters, greatly, and can lift her head out of
    The pit no more and the red wave. Death
    She spots in beakers of the fruitful earth,
    In herds and flocks and in the unborn births
    Of women, and fire from inside
    The plague god brings and empties Cadmus' house
    And Hell grows rich with sighs and howling.
    Now, though I do not rate you like the gods

Nor do the children here, lying at the altar,
Still I do as the first in happenings
Of the world and oneness with the spirits.
You came and loosed the city of Cadmus
From paying the songstress, her, the cruel,
Her tribute and that not knowing else
A thing of us nor being told; God called you,
We say, and think you raised us up. But now
Again, O head of Oedipus,
Strong over all, we do implore you
Humbly, discover us a protection
If you have heard from gods a voice
Or have done from a man, for I know this:
Even the fated things, them most of all,
It is experienced advice brings them to life.
Therefore, you best of men, lift up the town
Again, therefore be shrewd! The land calls you
Its rescuer from the old wild meaning.
Too little will your rule be thought of though
If we are righted and we fall again.
Erect this city with solidity
For if you rule in the land as you have strength to
Better it be with men full than be empty.
For neither tower nor ship is anything alone
If men within are not dwelling together.

OEDIPUS. O poor children, what you come asking
Is known not unknown. I am well aware
All of you are sick so that of all of you
None sick as I am. For your suffering comes
On one who is alone here by himself
On no one other. And my soul
Grieves for the town at once and me and you.
Nor do you wake me sleeping from a sleep
But know that I have wept greatly and come
Errant on many ways of sorrow.
But searching well what I discovered
I carried out, the one means. Sent

Menoeceus' son, Creon, my brother-in-law,
To Pytho, to Apollo's houses there,
So he might see what I should do,
What I should say to save this city.
And I am anxious, measuring from that time
The day, what he is doing. For more than proper
He stays away above the usual time. But when
He comes I should be bad did I not do
Everything the god discloses to us.

THE PRIEST. You spoke to the good, and these here have
    Told me a moment since Creon has come.

OEDIPUS. O King Apollo! Surely if he has come
    He may appear eyes shining with salvation.

THE PRIEST. He seems content however. Else why come
    So fully crowned with the tree of trees, the laurel?

SECOND SCENE

OEDIPUS. THE PRIEST. CREON.

OEDIPUS. Now we shall know. He is close enough to hear.
    O King, my care, son of Menoeceus,
    What voice do you bring to us from the god?

CREON. The right one. For bad things too it is
    Good over all, I say, when they come out right.

OEDIPUS. What kind of word though is it? Neither bold
    Nor wary either does this speech make me.

CREON. Will you hear it here with these standing around?
    I am prepared to speak or go with you.

OEDIPUS. Say it in front of all. For more for them
    Than my own soul's sake I carry the burden.

CREON. Then let me say what I heard from the god.
    Phoebus has bidden us, the King has, clearly,

We must hunt down the shame our country's ground
Has nourished, not nurture the incurable.

OEDIPUS. Through what cleansing? What ill thing is it?

CREON. Banish, or with a murder answer murder
Is what we must. Such blood excites the town.

OEDIPUS. Which is the man he means who had this fate?

CREON. Lord of us formerly, O King, was Laius
Here in the land before you led the city.

OEDIPUS. I know, have heard it, never saw it though.

CREON. That man having died, clearly he wishes now
That we with hands punish those murderers.

OEDIPUS. But what land are they in? Where will we find
The tracks without a sign of the old guilt?

CREON. Here in this land, he says. What gets looked for
We catch. But overlooked, it gets away.

OEDIPUS. Did Laius fall in the houses or outside?
Fall in a foreign country in this murder?

CREON. He left to look at God, they say,
Did not come home again how he was sent.

OEDIPUS. No messenger or companion who saw it
To hear it from and search into it?

CREON. They are dead. One only, fled in fear,
Of what he knew did say one thing.

OEDIPUS. And what? For one thing does give much to learn
If it conceives by hope a small beginning.

CREON. Robbers fell on him, so he said,
Not one strong hand to kill, but numerous.

OEDIPUS. How could they, if it was not silver
The robbers did it for, do such an outrage?

CREON. Indeed. When Laius died however

Nobody came to help us in the evil.

OEDIPUS. What evil hindered it, when thus the lord
    Had fallen, and kept from searching after?

CREON. The Sphinx, when we heard it, her many songs,
    Drove us to search the dark that wanted solving.

OEDIPUS. From the beginning I will light it up.
    For rightly has Apollo, rightly you have
    Determined the dead man this revenge, so that
    Openly you will see me as a comrade
    In arms, me too, revenger of this land
    And of the god. Not for dear strangers' sake
    But mine do I, my sake, expel such loathsomeness.
    For who killed him well might he also me
    With the same hand murder. Serving him
    I will be useful to myself. But children
    Stand up now quickly from the steps and take
    These begging branches. Someone else
    Gather together Cadmus' people here.
    For I'll do everything. Either we show
    In fortune with the god or we shall fall.

THE PRIEST. O children, let us rise. For that was why
    We came here too, the reason this was said.
    And he who sent the prophecies let him
    As saviour come and sickness-curer, Phoebus.

(*They exit.*)

CHORUS. Sweet-speaking word of Zeus, what kind of word are you
    From Pytho come, the rich in gold,
    To Thebes that shines?
    I am spanned wide in an anxious mind,
    Staggering under fears.
    And you the Delian paean of grief
    All around fearing you,
    Will it be new, the fate, or one that you returning

After the rolling hours complete?
Tell me, child of golden
Hope, you undying tale.

   First you naming I come
Daughter of Zeus, immortal Athene,
And her embracing the earth,
Your sister Artemis, whose are
The famous thrones
Around the agora
And Phoebus, longbowman. Io! Io!
You three death-warders-off! Appear to me
If ever before in past error
That fell upon the city
You drove the flame of the evil out
Come now, you gods, as then.

   For the ills are numberless I carry
And all our people sick.
No one was left the spear of care
To have protection by. Nor do
The shoots grow of the famous land
Nor through the pitiable travails
To birth
Can the women hold out. But one upon
The other you can see them lift
Like well-feathered birds
And stronger than unstoppable fire
Towards the shore of the evening
God, whereby innumerably
The city perishes. The children though
In the fields the poor children are lying mortally
Ungrieved. Indoors however the grey
Women and the mothers
Around the shore of the altar and from elsewhere
Others also
Atoning for the grisly troubles
Sigh
And the paean shines and the sighing voice with it.

Therefore look kindly, O golden
You, the daughter of Zeus, and send
Strength. And Ares, tearing me, who now
Without the shield of bronze
Meets me burning me
Drive him of the bad name, him
The reverser drive
Him from our country without fire into the great
Bed of Amphitrite or into
The inclement harbour
Into the Thracian waves.
For at the end when night goes
Such a day comes in.
Him then, O you who direct the powers
Of kindling lightnings, Jupiter, father, under yours
Destroy him, under the bolts.
Lycian King, yours too of your holy and slanted
Bow I should like to deal out
The arrows, the let-loosest,
Assigning them, like comrades.
Also the kindling shine of Artemis
With which she leaps through Lycian mountains.
And I name him too, named after this land,
Bacchus in the rush of wine, oh Evius
With Maenads in the loneliness; let him come
With the brilliantly shining torch burning
On him who is without honour before the gods, the god!

SECOND ACT

FIRST SCENE

OEDIPUS. THE CHORUS.

OEDIPUS. You beg the way you beg wishing from me to take
    The words into the ear and get clear of the sickness.
    Strength you shall have and lightening of
    The evil. I will search though I am
    Strange in this thing, stranger in what preceded.
    Not far should I have searched had I no sign.
    Now, a late citizen, I come however
    Among the citizens and call to you, all Cadmians,
    Who ever knew the son of Labdacus
    Among you, Laius, by whom he died
    I say to him: tell all of it to me
    And if he fears the charge, telling himself,
    He will not suffer otherwise ungently.
    He leaves the country without harm done him.
    But if a man knows of another of
    Another land let him not hush the doer;
    For I will bring about the gains and thanks
    Will be there too; but if you hush
    And fearing for the loved one or himself
    A person pushes it away what I'll do then
    Hear that from me. For this man's sake
    I curse (whoever it may be here in the land
    Which I command the power of and the thrones)
    Let nobody invite or speak to him
    Nor to the holy oaths nor to
    The sacrifices take nor wash his hands,
    But drive him everywhere from home for such a one is
    A spot of shame on us. The utterance
    Of God at Pytho shows me this clearly.
    So I with that daimon and with the dead man have

Become a comrade in the fight. I wish
The one who did it, be he one alone
Hidden, or did with several he may
Badly use up a badly unfit life;
Wish too if he of my own house
Is table fellow and I know it
To suffer what I here have cursed him with.
But you I order do all this
For my sake and the god's and country's
Thus passing fruitlessly and godlessly away.
It was, even were the thing not set by God,
Not right to leave you so unclean
Since he has died who was the prince and best man
But search into it. Now however I
Have got the governance he had before
And got the bed and common
Spouse and children too, had his line not
Ill-lucked, we should have had
In common; but fate struck that head. For it
As though it were my father I will fight
My uttermost if I once seize the murderer
For Labdacus's son and Polydorus's
And Cadmus's, the ancient ruler.
And those who don't do this I pray on them
To gods they do not have a land to plough
Nor children granted them from women
And pass away by such a fate and worse.
But us the other Cadmians whom this
Pleases, being comrades in the case,
Always be kindly with us all the gods.

CHORUS. Since in the curse you seize me, King, I speak
　　Like this: I did not murder, no! Nor can
　　I show the murderer. But if we search
　　The message Phoebus sent must say who did it.

OEDIPUS. You said what's right. But force the gods where they
　　Don't want, no man can do it, not one.

CHORUS. Shall I say secondly what seems to me?

OEDIPUS. And thirdly, don't neglect to, keeping quiet.

CHORUS. The most in this about King Phoebus King
    Tiresias knows. One who asked him,
    O King, could hear it clearest.

OEDIPUS. I haven't not, like slothful men, tried this
    As well. Creon advised it. I sent twice.
    It puzzles people why he has not come.

CHORUS. Also the other words are long since vain.

OEDIPUS. What are they, those? For I look into all words.

CHORUS. They say that he was killed by wanderers.

OEDIPUS. I heard it too but no one sees who saw it.

CHORUS. But if he has a part of fear with him
    And hears your such a curse, he will not bear it.

OEDIPUS. The man the deed did not the word won't frighten.

CHORUS. But there is one to test him. These are bringing
    God's seer this way now who has
    The truth in him alone of people.

SECOND SCENE

OEDIPUS. THE CHORUS. TIRESIAS.

OEDIPUS. O you who think all things, Tiresias
    The said, the unsaid, the heavenly and what
    Wanders on earth, you do not see the town
    But nonetheless know what a sickness she
    Is seized in. As her first saviour
    You are the one alone, King, we find out.
    For Phoebus, though you have not heard the messengers,
    Answered our mission with this missive:
    Salvation from this sickness will come only

If we, enquiring into, kill
The murderers of Laius or banish them.
But you: heed what the birds have said and so
Release yourself, the town, release me also,
Also release the whole shame of the dead man.
For we are yours. And that a man uses
Whatever he has and can, that is the best labour.

TIRESIAS. How heavy knowledge is when useless to
The one who knows. Because I know full well
I am lost. Would I had never come.

OEDIPUS. Why is it you step up with such small courage?

TIRESIAS. Let me go home. The best is you mind your
Affairs, I mine, till you have followed me.

OEDIPUS. You have not spoken right nor kindly for the town
That nurtured you, if you keep back this saying.

TIRESIAS. Because I see what you are saying go
Badly for you, and not to suffer likewise.

CHORUS. By gods no! Even with reason no! Do not
Turn away. We all entreat you, kneeling.

TIRESIAS. Then you are all senseless. But let me not
Say mine, not broadcast your evil.

OEDIPUS. What are you saying? Know it and not speak?
Will you betray us and destroy the town?

TIRESIAS. I care for me, not you. You cannot blame
That ground. For did you follow me? You did not.

OEDIPUS. Will you not finally, worst of the bad
(For you are built like cliffs), speak out?
Why show so colourless, so implacable?

TIRESIAS. You've blamed my anger. Yours, that sleeps with you,
You do not see, but me you scold.

OEDIPUS. But whom would not a word like that anger
With which you are dishonouring this town?

TIRESIAS. It will still come though I depart with silence.

OEDIPUS. It will not, never! You must tell it me.

TIRESIAS. I'll not speak further. Be angry, if you like,
  At that with anger wildly as you will.

OEDIPUS. Oh yes, however the anger is I'll not
  Leave anything out I know. For I suspect you were
  Co-planner and the worker of the work
  Only not murdering with hands. If you were sighted
  The work itself I'd say was yours alone.

TIRESIAS. Truly! I do confirm you will abide in
  The tone you started in, still speak upon
  That day neither to these nor me but speak
  With him who is a spot upon our land.

OEDIPUS. So shamelessly you throw this word out?
  And think no doubt now you secure yourself?

TIRESIAS. I am secured, I nurture a strong truth.

OEDIPUS. Told you by whom? Not from your art, it isn't.

TIRESIAS. By you. You made me speak against my will.

OEDIPUS. What word? Repeat it so I'll know it better.

TIRESIAS. Not known it long since? Is our speech a test?

OEDIPUS. Nothing we've known long since. Repeat it!

TIRESIAS. The man's murder you seek I say it falls on you there.

OEDIPUS. No joy in that, you speak doubly askew.

TIRESIAS. Some I'll say else now, to anger you the more.

OEDIPUS. Much as you like. It will be said in vain.

TIRESIAS. I say you live disgracefully with your best loved,
  In secret, ignorant how far unhappy.

OEDIPUS. You think to say this and be always joyful?

TIRESIAS. If power of truth does count for anything.

OEDIPUS. It does, but not for you, this is not yours,
 Blind in the ears you are and heart and eyes.

TIRESIAS. But you are wretched, how you scold
 Soon nobody will not scold thus against you.

OEDIPUS. The last night nourished you, not me nor
 Anyone else who sees the light do you see.

TIRESIAS. To fall by you is not my fate Apollo,
 Minded to end the matter, vouches.

OEDIPUS. Are these Creon's or are they words of yours?

TIRESIAS. Creon is not a harm to you, but you are.

OEDIPUS. O riches, power, art, outdoing
 Art in life so rich in jealousies!
 How large the envy is that you watch over!
 If for this power which the city gave me
 Unasked, entrusted to me, Creon
 The faithful, always loving, from it
 Stealthily falling on me seeks to drive me,
 Commissioning this sly magician, this
 Deceitful mendicant who only looks
 To profit but born blind in arts?
 For see, tell me, are you a wise seer?
 Why when the songstress bitch was here did you
 Not sing the citizens a solving song?
 Although the riddle wasn't for every man
 To solve and needed seer's arts
 That neither as a present you from birds
 Fetched down nor of the gods from one.
 But I, untutored Oedipus,
 When I came to it I hushed her up,
 Hitting it by nous, not taught
 By birds. You have a mind to expel
 That man and think to come near Creon's throne.
 With tears, it seems to me, you will and who

Span with you, pay for it. Were you not old
You would by suffering feel the way you think.

CHORUS. His seem to us and your words equally
Spoken in anger, Oedipus, but this
Is not what's needed but to see
How best to solve the utterance of the god.

TIRESIAS. Though you have power of yours I must reply
In kind. I have power in this too.
I do not live a serf to you, but Loxias.
I am not listed under Creon.
But I say this, since you have called me blind,
You, having seen, don't see what you are at
In evil, where you live, with what you house.
Do you know where you are from? You are in secret
Detestable to your own kind below
The earth and here above and hitting all around
The mother's and the father's curse
Vastly developing will drive you from the land
Now seeing well but afterwards in darkness
And of your screams what harbour will not be
Full and what Cithaeron soon not shout with you?
Do you feel the marriage as you landed
Voyaging well? It has no shore. Not of
The other evils either do you feel the host
That strike you with your children equally.
But scold at Creon still and also
Into my face for worse than you there is
No mortal man who ever will be fathered.

OEDIPUS. To hear from him this is it tolerable?
Will you not suddenly founder? Show
This house your back and turn away and go?

TIRESIAS. I'd not have come had you not called me here.

OEDIPUS. I did not know that you would utter mad things.
Would not have fetched you to the house here had I.

TIRESIAS. So we are born, as you think, mad. But of

272

One mind with the parents who got you.

OEDIPUS. And which? Stay! Who among humans got me?

TIRESIAS. Day, the day will get you and undo you.

OEDIPUS. How you say everything riddling and dark.

TIRESIAS. But you have small success in solving such.

OEDIPUS. Blame what you will discover me great in.

TIRESIAS. This fate, I grant you, has undone you.

OEDIPUS. But if I saved the town I would not mind it.

TIRESIAS. Then I will go. Boy, lead me, will you.

OEDIPUS. Let him lead you. Being here like this
Seems you will heap the misery up fully.

TIRESIAS. I have said it. I go because of what
I came for, not fearing your face. You have no thing
To undo me with but I tell you the man
You seek with threats and broadcasting the murder
Of Laius, he is here, he lives, it is said,
With us as stranger, but as native soon,
As Theban, will be shown and not be glad
Of the accident. Blind from seeing
And poor instead of rich abroad
Divining with the sceptre he will have to wander.
He will be shown up living with his children
As brother and as father and the woman's who
Bore him, her son and husband, in *one* bed with
The father, his murderer. Go in, think on it
And if you find me for a liar say
I do the seer's work senselessly.

(*They exit.*)

CHORUS. Who is it whom the prophesying
Delphic rock has spoken of
As though he had achieved with bloody hands

What most may not be uttered?
The hour is coming when more powerfully
Than horses moving like the stormwinds he
Must move his feet to flight.
For weaponed on him falls
With fire and lightning
Zeus's son and also in their violence come
The implacable Parcae.

For it has shone from the snows of,
Just shown the utterance has,
From white Parnassus that
Everywhere the hidden man is to be searched out.
For he is erring in the wild wood
In caves and rocks like the bull
The bad-luck man with bad-luck feet, orphaned,
Fleeing the prophecies which from
The midpoint of the earth
Always alive are flying around.

He stirs enormities, stirs up enormities,
The wise birdscrier
That are not clear nor are to be denied
And what I ought to say I do not know
But fly up in hopes
Not looking here nor back.
For what a quarrel is between
The Labdacids and Polybus's son
I never formerly
Have known and also now do not know
In what proof
I meet
The strange story of Oedipus
A helper to the Labdacids
In the hidden death?

But Zeus and Apollo
Are wise and know humans.
But that among men

A seer is more esteemed than I
Is not a true judgement.
With wisdom let the man
Answer wisdom.
But I should never wish, before I saw
An upright word, to show myself
Among the blamers. For over him
Came manifest the winged maid
Once and she seemed wise
But the test was friendly to the town. Therefore
As I think never
Will he pay for it, that bad thing.

THIRD ACT

FIRST SCENE

CREON. THE CHORUS.

CREON. You men, you citizens, I undergo hard words:
　　That Oedipus, the lord, accuses me.
　　So I come, suffering. For if he thinks
　　That he by me has undergone in this case
　　With words or works some thing that harms him
　　Then I have no joy in my further life
　　If I support the shame. It is not simple,
　　The punishment this word strikes me with, but
　　Extremest, if the name I have in this town
　　Is bad to you and to my loved ones bad.

CHORUS. This insult came forced out by rage perhaps
　　More than from counsel of the mind.

CREON. How was it shown that when the seer spoke,
　　Following my counsel, his words were lies?

CHORUS. It is said. What tone in I don't know.

CREON. Was the accusation broadcast over me
　　Rightmindedly, from level eyes?

CHORUS. I do not know. The things the great do I
　　Don't see. But he is here himself.

SECOND SCENE

OEDIPUS. CREON. THE CHORUS.

OEDIPUS. You! How could you come here? Is your face
　　So brazen that you enter into my house
　　As the evident murderer of me

276

And robber, clearly, of my rule? Now by
The gods, tell me have you seen cowardice
On me or foolishness that you should think
To do this and that this your work creeping
Deceitfully I would not recognise and not
Ward off when I did recognise it? Is
Your bid not stupid without men and friends
To hunt the throne that's won with men and money?

CREON. Do you know what you're starting? Hear
For your word like. Judge when you have.

OEDIPUS. You're strong in speech, I poor if I must learn from you.
I find you difficult and falsely minded.

CREON. On that precisely first hear what I say.

OEDIPUS. Precisely do not say you are not wicked.

CREON. If you think self-regard is good without
Temper you do not think aright.

OEDIPUS. If you think anyone mishandles kin
Unpunished your thinking is not good.

CREON. I say so too, that this is rightly said,
But tell me what the suffering is you suffer.

OEDIPUS. Did you advise or not that it was needed
A man be dispatched to the holy seer?

CREON. I am the same in that opinion even now.

OEDIPUS. How long a time ago is it that Laius – ?

CREON. Did work of what kind? I don't know.

OEDIPUS. He grew invisible through a deadly ill.

CREON. Distant the measured time is, long ago.

OEDIPUS. In the art in those days was the seer so?

CREON. He was both wise and rightly well regarded.

OEDIPUS. At that time did he ever think of me?

CREON. Not that I ever stood there when he did.

OEDIPUS. But did you not search after the dead man?

CREON. We did. How should we not? And heard nothing.

OEDIPUS. Why did he not speak then as now, the wise man?

CREON. I do not know. Not knowing, I say nothing.

OEDIPUS. So many things you do know. Say them kindly.

CREON. What then? Knowing, I will not say I don't.

OEDIPUS. This, that he would not, were he not in league
    With you, have called the killing of Laius mine.

CREON. Whether he called it that, you know yourself.
    I wish to hear from you what you want from me.

OEDIPUS. Hear it. I'll not be found a murderer.

CREON. What then? Are you not married to my sister?

OEDIPUS. What you have said is not to be denied.

CREON. You rule as she does, governing the ground.

OEDIPUS. What she desires I see to all of it.

CREON. Am I not joined to you pair as the third?

OEDIPUS. In this now you appear to be a bad friend.

CREON. Not if you do me right as I do you.
    Firstly consider this: whether you think
    That one would rather want to rule, in fear,
    Than sleep sweetly when he has power the same.
    I am not made that I should more desire
    To be a lord than do what's lordly
    Nor any man would who can tame himself.
    Now I have all things without fear from you.
    Ruled I myself, much I must do ungladly.
    How then should being lord be dearer to me
    Than honour without trouble is and power?
    I am not yet so foolish as to want

Anything but what's good and profits me.
Now all delights me, everyone salutes me,
Now those call to me who have need of you.
For therein lies it that all prospers for them.
Why should I go from this and grasp for that?
A man who thinks aright will not turn bad.
Now I am not of such a mind and never,
If someone else did it, would risk it with him.
Take your reproach and go with it to Pytho,
Ask did I make the word known to you clearly.
And if you find that I with the sign-diviner
Dealt, then kill me not on one man's word
But doubly damned, on yours and mine.
Only don't charge me on a dim opinion. For
It is not right to hold in an idle fashion
The bad for excellent, the excellent for bad.
For when a noble man throws off a friend
My own and dearest life feels touched by it.
In time though surely you will learn this.
For time alone reveals the just man but
The bad you recognise on one day.

CHORUS. He spoke well, so that good may come of it.
For thinking quickly is not safe, King.

OEDIPUS. If one laying traps will get away quickly
Myself I must advise myself quickly.
If I am easygoing and wait for him
He'll bring forth his and mine will fail.

CREON. What do you want then but to drive me from the land?

OEDIPUS. No, that you die or run is what I want.

CREON. If you will show me what your ill will is.

OEDIPUS. Do you speak giving way to or believing me?

CREON. If I saw sense in you...

OEDIPUS. My business now!

CREON. Called mine as well.

OEDIPUS. Would be were you not bad.

CREON. But what if you don't know?

OEDIPUS. A man must rule.

CREON. But not the bad rulers.

OEDIPUS. Oh city! City!

CREON. Concerns me too, not you alone, the city.

CHORUS. Give over, lords. I see the woman coming
     To you here from the house, Jocasta.
     With her the quarrel must be straightened out.

THIRD SCENE

JOCASTA. CREON. OEDIPUS. CHORUS.

JOCASTA. Why have you roused this witless war of tongues,
  Poor men, and are you not ashamed, the land
  So sick, to wake your own misfortune?
  Come in the palace and you in the house, Creon,
  And not make little burdens big.

CREON. Oh sister, much your husband Oedipus is minded
  To do to me and chooses two evils.
  He will evict me from the land or kill me.

OEDIPUS. I say so too. I found him working ill
  At my own body, wife, with wicked arts.

CREON. I want no profit now, but let me die
  With curses if I did the thing
  That you accuse me that I did.

JOCASTA. Oh by the gods believe it, Oedipus.
  Honour the gods' oath over all others
  And me and also these here present.

CHORUS. Be trusting, want it, think it,
  I beg you, King.

OEDIPUS. How do you wish I should give way to you?

CHORUS. This man who never before was foolish
  And now big in his oath
  Honour him.

OEDIPUS. D'you know what you are asking?

CHORUS. I do.

OEDIPUS. Say what your mind is.

CHORUS. That you should hold this man in holy love
  Never in blame
  With an uncertain word

Dishonourably expel him.

OEDIPUS. Be told, if you seek this you seek
My ruin or my fleeing the land.

CHORUS. Not so, by all the gods'
Forerunner Helios!
For godless, friendless
In the uttermost let me founder
If I have such a thought.
But my unhappy soul
By the withering land is wearied
When they arrive as well, troubles to troubles,
To the old now yours.

OEDIPUS. He goes, even if I die indeed forthwith,
He is dishonourably banished from the land by force.
Not yours nor his mouth's yammering moves me
To mercy. Through and through let me loathe him.

CREON. You are a coward when you give way glumly
And when you overleap your temper heavily.
It irks such souls to bear themselves rightly.

OEDIPUS. Will you not leave me and go out?

CREON. I go
Misknown by you but likeminded with these.

(*Exit* CREON.)

CHORUS. Woman, will you not bring in
This man into the house?

JOCASTA. Once I know what it is.

CHORUS. An unknown look has come over
The words but also
Unjust things rile.

JOCASTA. Of both of them?

CHORUS. Indeed.

JOCASTA. And what word was it?

CHORUS. My land enough, enough being tired already
    Might it not well be left the way it stands?

OEDIPUS. See where you get with good opinion
    If you desert and turn away your heart.

CHORUS. King, I have said it
    Not only once, but you already know
    I would appear without a thought, astray
    In wisdom, if
    I parted company with you
    Who have led my land, my beloved land,
    Wandering in troubles,
    Right with a fair wind.
    Still now fare happily if you can.

JOCASTA. By gods, tell me it also, King
    Why you have raised up such an anger.

OEDIPUS. I will, because I honour you the most
    Of these here, say what Creon works against me.

JOCASTA. Say it, if you bring a clear charge in the quarrel.

OEDIPUS. They say I am the murderer of Laius.

JOCASTA. Yourself you know this or learned it from others?

OEDIPUS. He sent the seer, the troublemaker, here
    Because he, all he can, looses the tongues.

JOCASTA. Leave your thing be now you are speaking of.
    Obey me and learn this: there is
    No mortal man who has the seer's art.
    I'll show that to you with a striking sign.
    A word came once to Laius, I'll not say from
    Phoebus himself but from the god's servants,
    That him the fate was waiting for to die
    By the son that came from him and me.
    But, so the story speaks it, he was killed
    By foreign murderers on a triple highway.

However, when the child was born to him
Not three days after that he fastened
The joints of his feet up and with strangers' hands
He threw him in the mountains where we cannot go.
And not fulfilled there by Apollo was it that
He was his father's murderer nor did he die,
Who feared that terrible thing, by Laius' son.
Thus did the seers' sayings explain themselves.
Do not mind them. For what a god
Sees needful he will open easily himself.

OEDIPUS. How, hearing this, confusion grips my soul,
Woman, tumult my senses.

JOCASTA. What worry troubles you that you say this?

OEDIPUS. It seems to me I heard from you that Laius
Died on a triple highway.

JOCASTA. So it was said, nor has it ceased to be.

OEDIPUS. Where is the place this fate occurred?

JOCASTA. They call the land Phocis. A split way comes
From Delphi to it and from Daulia.

OEDIPUS. And how much time has since gone over this?

JOCASTA. Closely prior, before you took the land's
Lordship, the news was given to the city.

OEDIPUS. Oh Zeus what do you wish to happen by me?

JOCASTA. Oh Oedipus why is this in your mind?

OEDIPUS. Don't ask me, only say of Laius
How was the man, at what height of his age?

JOCASTA. Big, like wool his white hair flowering,
And yours the form of him was not unlike.

OEDIPUS. Pity me. Truly just now when I broke out
Violently in curses I knew nothing.

JOCASTA. What are you saying, King? Your look makes me afraid.

OEDIPUS. I have a powerful fear the seer can see.
Say one thing else and you will clear it more up.

JOCASTA. I am afraid. But ask me. What I know I'll say.

OEDIPUS. Did he go out alone or, like an overlord,
Did he have with him many pugnacious men?

JOCASTA. Five were all. There was a herald with them.
A mule-cart carried only Laius.

OEDIPUS. Grief! Grief! Now it is manifest. Who was
It, wife, who spoke the words out then?

JOCASTA. A servant who had run away alone.

OEDIPUS. Is he still present in the houses?

JOCASTA. No, not. Since he came here and learned
You had the power and Laius had been killed
He begged me hard, touching my hands, to send him
Into the country, to the sheep pastures,
Where he was farthest from the city's face.
And I did so, for he was fit, this man,
The servant, to have greater grace than that.

OEDIPUS. How might he now come quickly back to us?

JOCASTA. He can attend. Why do you want this?

OEDIPUS. I am in fear of myself, woman, that I
Have said too much why I desire to see him.

JOCASTA. He will come. But I am worthy also, am
I not, to hear what the ill you have is, King?

OEDIPUS. Do not abase yourself too much on the account
Of how I am. To greater than you are
I'd tell how such a lot has been dealt me.
My father Polybus was from Corinth,
The mother Merope from Doris. There
I was esteemed the greatest of the citizens
Until this fate came over me and it,
But not my zeal, may well be wondered at.

A man feasting and full of drunkenness
Told me in wine I was falsely my father's
And I, enraged, hardly held out
The present day but went the following
To mother and to father, asked about it.
Crossly they bore the insult off the man
This word had slipped from. That cheered me
In them. But still it stabbed at me
For there were many things behind it. Unbeknownst
To father and to mother I went away
To Pytho. Phoebus scanted me the thing
I had come for, sent me away and showed me
Other troubling gross unhappy things
And said that with the mother I must be
Mixed and get a brood unbearable
To human beings to look upon and be
The murderer of my father who had planted me.
When I heard this, beneath the stars I measured
All the ground of Corinth, fleeing so
That never there of my bad question to
The oracle I would behold the shame.
But wandering I came into the district
Where, as you say, the lord was killed.
Also to you, woman, and truly I say that
I did approach upon the triple highway where
The herald and a man, as you report,
Riding in a wagon pulled by foals, met me
And violently out of the way
The leader and the old man drove me.
As he steered on at me I struck the driver
In rage, and standing by the wagon when the old man
Saw me he aimed at the middle of my head
And struck me with the double goad. He paid
For it unequally. For swiftly smitten he
By these hands with their staff was toppled
Backwards suddenly out of the cart.
I killed them all. But if that stranger has

With Laius anything in common
Who is so unblessed as the man I am
And who more hateful to the spirits than him
Whom nobody abroad may and no citizen
Invite into the house and no one speak to
But must drive from the house, which curse
Nobody did to me but I myself.
Also the dead man's marriage bed I soil
With the hands he died by. Am I bad?
Am I not quite unclean? And must I flee
As fugitive I may not see my own
Nor go to home, or shall I be
Together with the mother yoked for marriage
And shall I kill the father Polybus
Begetter of me and who nourished me up?
Would anyone who judged the man I am
Not say this doing was a brutal spirit's?
No, by the holy sunlight of the gods
Let me not see that day but rather
Disappear from people and not see
The insult of such a chance encounter me.

CHORUS. To us, King, it is terrible but till you
    Learn it from someone who was present, hope.

OEDIPUS. But now this much remains to me of hope
    Only to await the man, the shepherd.

JOCASTA. When he appears what is it you desire?

OEDIPUS. I'll tell you. If it is found that he
    Says that to you, then I may flee the suffering.

JOCASTA. What word especially did you hear from me?

OEDIPUS. He spoke of robbers, so you say,
    That they killed him. If now he still
    Utters the same number it was not I
    Killed him. One cannot equal many.
    If he names one man having no companions
    Clearly upon me now this deed comes.

JOCASTA. Be assured, the word is very manifest
     And he is not allowed to topple it.
     The city heard it, not myself alone.
     If now somewhat he shifts from the former word
     Still he will not, King, make known Laius'
     Murder right and straight as Loxias
     Uttered it, that he'd die by my child.
     That poor unfortunate was not his killer then
     Of course, but perished earlier itself.
     So in the prophecies I'm not inclined
     Now nor the first time to see anything.

OEDIPUS. You mean it well. But send a messenger
     To the countryman, do not neglect to.

JOCASTA. I will send quickly. But let us go indoors.
     I should not like to do what you don't wish.

(*They exit.*)

CHORUS. Would that it were my part
     To have holiness in words exactly
     And in all the works whose laws
     Are before our eyes and have been shaped and born
     Of the heavenly ether and have
     For father Olympus alone. No mortal nature
     Of men begot them
     Nor will they ever sleep and be forgotten
     But in those laws the god is great
     And never ages.

          Boldness plants tyrants, over-
     Boldness filling up vainly overfull with many things
     Not timely and not healthy
     It climbs to the highest, it topples
     Into abrupt necessity
     Not using its feet aright.
     But I pray the god will never undo
     The city's old good standing. God

I will never leave but as
One set before me keep him.

    But if a man looks beyond and wanders with hands or
With words and does not fear what is right and
Does not honour the thrones of the daimons
Let a bad fate have him
For his unseemly showing
If his winnings are not won right
If he shuts up what is manifest
And seizes what is untouchable, the fool.
How may a man in his heart and mind then
Shut up the arrows and not
Defend his soul? For are
Such doings proper?
What shall I sing?

    Never again shall I go to the earth's
Untouchable navel with awe
Nor to the temple in Abae
If this is not right
Manifestly to all mortal men.
But in your power, Zeus,
Ruling all things if you
Hear the upright truth
Let it not be hidden from you and your
Immortally lasting rule.
For Laius' old
Words from the gods are coming to nothing and no longer
Is Apollo manifest in honour.
God's matters are going unhappily.

FOURTH ACT

FIRST SCENE

JOCASTA. A MESSENGER. CHORUS. *Later*, OEDIPUS.

JOCASTA. O you my country's kings, the thought came to me
    To go into the temples of the daimons, here
    To take up incense in my hand and crowns.
    For upwards Oedipus lifts his spirit
    In manifold torment not like a man
    Calmly, he reads new things from old.
    His word however is, though he speaks fear,
    That I, to the end, should not do any more
    But should to you, O Lycian Apollo, since you
    Are very near, come on my knees with this
    Worship that you might send us
    Some means speedily saving. For we
    Are all afraid now seeing him
    Struck like the steersman of the ship.

MESSENGER. Can I hear from you, strangers, where
    The houses of the ruler are, of Oedipus?
    You are the best to tell me where he lives.

CHORUS. The house is here and he is in it, stranger,
    And this lady is mother of his children.

MESSENGER. May she be rich and always with the rich
    And always be the wedded wife of him.

JOCASTA. Riches to you too, stranger, you deserve them
    For that kind word. But tell me
    What plea you come with or what news.

MESSENGER. With good into the house and to the husband, lady.

JOCASTA. What is it and who is it you have come from?

MESSENGER. I come from Corinth. My word will gladden you

Perhaps. How not? Or sadden you, it might.

JOCASTA. What is it that has double power in this way?

MESSENGER. As lord the natives of the Isthmus want
To set him up and have the throne in that place.

JOCASTA. How so? Old Polybus no longer rules?

MESSENGER. No more. Not now Death holds him in the grave.

JOCASTA. What are you saying? Polybus is dead?

MESSENGER. If I'm not speaking truth let me die too.

JOCASTA. Oh maid won't you go to the lord at once
And say it? O you prophecies
Of the gods, where are you? Long has Oedipus
Fled from the man so that he would not kill him
Who dies off now by chance not by his doing.

OEDIPUS. Most loved, o you, my wife's, Jocasta's head
Why did you call me here out of the houses?

JOCASTA. Hear him, this man, enquire and hear where are
The high, the seer's sayings of the god.

OEDIPUS. But who is this and what does he tell me?

JOCASTA. He comes from Corinth, says that Polybus
Your father is no more, says he is dead.

OEDIPUS. You say what, stranger? Enlighten me yourself.

MESSENGER. If I must make this known clearly the first
Then hear me: he has gone away with Death.

OEDIPUS. Died secretly? Drew sickness on himself?

MESSENGER. A small occurrence makes old bodies still.

OEDIPUS. The old man was wilting, so it seems, with sickness.

MESSENGER. And with the large enough measure of time.

OEDIPUS. Well then. Who now another time would question, wife,
The prophesying hearth or from

Above, screaming, the birds, whose sense it was
I was to kill my father who has died
And in the earth is sleeping; here however
Am I and clean my lance unless
He lost his life in a dream by me. In that way
Let him have died by me. He takes with him
The seer's sayings today and lies now
In Hades, Polybus, no longer valid.

JOCASTA. Did I not tell you long ago this would be?

OEDIPUS. You did. I was seduced by fear.

JOCASTA. Take nothing further now to heart from that man.

OEDIPUS. Shall I not fear my mother's bed either?

JOCASTA. What shall a man fear who is close
With luck? Nothing is there clear inkling of.
To live ahead the way one can
That is the best. Do not fear marriage with
Your mother for often a mortal man
In dreams has lain down before now
With his own mother. But whoever counts
This nothing he bears life the lightest.

OEDIPUS. All this would be well said by you were not
The mother living still but while she lives
There is great need, well though you speak, to fear.

JOCASTA. And yet a great light is your father's grave to you.

OEDIPUS. A great. Indeed! I only fear the living woman.

MESSENGER. What woman are you fearful on account of?

OEDIPUS. Old man, it is Merope, wife of Polybus.

MESSENGER. What is it making you afraid of her?

OEDIPUS. Power of a god-made prophecy, O stranger.

MESSENGER. May or may not another man know it?

OEDIPUS. He may. It is that Loxias once told me

I must mix with my mother
And tear my father's blood out with my hand.
On that account long since and far away
I fled from Corinth with good luck but it
Is lovely too to see our parents' eyes.

MESSENGER. For fear of that did you estrange yourself?

OEDIPUS. So not, old man, to be my father's murderer.

MESSENGER. Have I not now from this your fear
By my kind coming set you free, O King?

OEDIPUS. And thanks too, worthy of me, you will get.

MESSENGER. But mostly this is why I came here: that
If you come home it will be well with me.

OEDIPUS. I'll never live near those who planted me.

MESSENGER. You show you don't know what you are doing, child.

OEDIPUS. How do I, by the god, old man? Speak something.

MESSENGER. Is it on their account you won't go home?

OEDIPUS. I fear that Phoebus will come clear to me.

MESSENGER. That you will get some shame from parents?

OEDIPUS. Just so, old man, this thing still frightens me.

MESSENGER. Do you not know that you are fearful wrongly?

OEDIPUS. How? Then am I not that mother's child?

MESSENGER. No. Polybus was not of your stock.

OEDIPUS. What are you saying? Polybus did not plant me?

MESSENGER. About as much as I'm the one who did.

OEDIPUS. But how? A father who is like nobody?

MESSENGER. A father, yes. Not Polybus, not me.

OEDIPUS. Why then does that man call me child?

MESSENGER. From my hand he received you as a gift.

OEDIPUS. Why, from another hand, did he so love me?

MESSENGER. It was his childlessness moved him.

OEDIPUS. Had you bought me or as the father gave me?

MESSENGER. I found you in Cithaeron's green ravine.

OEDIPUS. Do you go about for something in those places?

MESSENGER. I minded the animals of the mountains there.

OEDIPUS. Herdsman, or did you wander for day wages?

MESSENGER. I was your rescuer in that time, child.

OEDIPUS. What did I have to make you count me poor?

MESSENGER. The flexings of your feet are your informers.

OEDIPUS. Oh me, why do you name that old evil?

MESSENGER. I undid you. The ends of your feet were stitched.

OEDIPUS. Out of my swaddling clothes I brought a violent shame.

MESSENGER. And after that thing you are named.

OEDIPUS. That, gods, oh that, by mother, father, speak!

MESSENGER. I do not know. Who gave it, he knows better.

OEDIPUS. Got me from others or found me yourself?

MESSENGER. No, for another herdsman gave you me.

OEDIPUS. Who is he? Can you tell me that much clearly?

MESSENGER. Yes: that he called himself of Laius' people.

OEDIPUS. Who had been formerly the lord of this land?

MESSENGER. Mostly he was the herdsman of that man.

OEDIPUS. Is he still living so that I can see him?

MESSENGER. You know that best who are the natives here.

OEDIPUS. Is there among you present anyone
　　　　Who knows the herdsman he has named

And who has seen him in the fields or here?
Report it me. The time has come to find it.

CHORUS. I know of no one but him in the country
Whom you before already asked to see.
Jocasta may however say it best.

OEDIPUS. Do you not think, wife? Him, to whom we sent
The messenger, is meant by this man?

JOCASTA. Who spoke of which one? What is it to you?
And what was said don't think on it too much.

OEDIPUS. It must not be that I, on signs like these,
Should not uncover what blood I am of.

JOCASTA. By gods, do not. If you're chary of life
Then do not search. I have sickened enough.

OEDIPUS. Be cheerful. If I from three mothers
Were three times serf it would not lower you.

JOCASTA. But follow me, I beg you, do not do it.

OEDIPUS. I cannot, must still find it out exactly.

JOCASTA. I mean it well. I'm telling you what's best.

OEDIPUS. This best though has tormented me a long time.

JOCASTA. Poor you, may you know never who you are.

OEDIPUS. Will someone go and fetch the herdsman to me?
Let her take pleasure in rich stem and stock.

JOCASTA. Alas, alas, unhappy man. This one thing
I can still say to you. Now nothing else, ever.

(*She exits.*)

CHORUS. Why did the wife of Oedipus depart
On that spring of wild pain? I am afraid
Out of this quiet an evil thing will break.

OEDIPUS. Let break what must. I want my kith and kin

However base, I want to learn it. She
Is rightly – women have high ideas –
Ashamed my birth is lowly. I however
Holding myself to be the child of fortune,
Goddess of gifts, will not go without honour
With her for mother. Small and large
The moons born at my time surrounded me
And so produced I will not exit so
But will uncover wholly whose I am.

CHORUS. If I am a soothsayer
And knowing in meaning
By Olympus you
Will not be shy, Cithaeron
At full moon tomorrow
But will allow us to extol you
As country kin
Of Oedipus and nurse
And mother and to say of you
You have done our princes
Kindness, but to you
Dark Phoebus may this be pleasing.

Who had you, child
Who of the blessed, did one
Approach herself to Pan the wanderer on mountains or
Were you brought by a daughter of Loxias
To whom are sweet
All the country's lowlands, or Cyllene's
King or the bacchic god
Who lives on high mountains
Did he receive you as a find from one of the nymphs
Of Helicon who are often his playfellows?

SECOND SCENE

OEDIPUS. CHORUS. THE MESSENGER. A SERVANT.

OEDIPUS. May I also, although I was not present,
    Elders, say something? I think
    I see the herdsman we have long looked for.
    This man's appearance is of long old age
    Like his here. Also I know my servants,
    The escort. But with your knowledge you may
    Help me, having seen the man before perhaps?

CHORUS. Be told then: yes, I know him. If one ever
    Was true with Laius, he was, this herdsman.

OEDIPUS. I ask you first, stranger of Corinth,
    Do you mean him?

MESSENGER. Him you are looking at.

OEDIPUS. Old man, look at me, answer me
    What I ask you: were you once Laius's?

SERVANT. His servant, not a bought one, raised in the house.

OEDIPUS. Doing what sort of work, having what life?

SERVANT. Mostly I spent my life among the herds.

OEDIPUS. What region did you live in for the most part?

SERVANT. It was Cithaeron and the land around.

OEDIPUS. The man here, do you not know where you found him?

SERVANT. What did he do? Of which man are you speaking?

OEDIPUS. Of that man there. Were you together once?

SERVANT. Not that by thinking quickly I can say so.

MESSENGER. It is no wonder, but I do remember
    The unknown man myself, know very well
    He knows how in the regions of Cithaeron
    He came with two herds, I with one

Together from the spring until the time
Of Arcturus, the time of three whole moons.
In winter then I herded back into
My byres away, and he to Laius' courts.
Do I not speak or do I real and true?

SERVANT. You speak the truth although a long time since.

MESSENGER. Come now and say you know you gave to me
    A child that I should care for it and raise it.

SERVANT. What are you speaking of the story for?

MESSENGER. He is the one, oh him there, who was young then.

SERVANT. Will you not perish? Will you not be silent?

OEDIPUS. Old man, oh do not scold him, your words more
    Deserve a scolding than do those of him.

SERVANT. Have I done wrong in anything, best lord?

OEDIPUS. Say what it's called, the child he speaks of, him here.

SERVANT. His speech is witless, him here he is elsewhere.

OEDIPUS. You will not speak for thanks but will in tears.

SERVANT. Don't scourge an old man for it, by the gods.

OEDIPUS. Will you not fasten him his hands at once?

SERVANT. Unlucky man, why, what do you want to know?

OEDIPUS. Did you give this man here the child he speaks of?

SERVANT. I did. Would I had passed away that day.

OEDIPUS. You will now if you do not speak aright.

SERVANT. Much more still if I do speak I am lost.

OEDIPUS. The man, it seems, is driving to postponement.

SERVANT. Not so. I said long since that I did it.

OEDIPUS. Where did you get it? Was it yours or others'?

SERVANT. It was not mine, I had it from another.

OEDIPUS. What citizen was that, out of what house?

SERVANT. No, by the gods, do not ask further, lord.

OEDIPUS. If I ask this one more time you are lost.

SERVANT. Then it was someone of the house of Laius.

OEDIPUS. A servant or related to that house?

SERVANT. Oh now I am saying the evil thing itself.

OEDIPUS. And I am hearing it. But hear I must.

SERVANT. He was named son of that house but inside
Your wife may be the best to say it to you.

OEDIPUS. She gave it you then?

SERVANT. Yes, my king, she did.

OEDIPUS. To do what with?

SERVANT. So that I should destroy it.

OEDIPUS. Because she bore unluckily?

SERVANT. For fear of bad things said.

OEDIPUS. What things?

SERVANT. That it would kill the parents was the word.

OEDIPUS. Where did you meet then, you and the old man?

SERVANT. He lived, lord, as though wishing to depart
Into a far land, there. But he saved you
For grossest things. Because if you are he
Whom this man names then you are wretched.

OEDIPUS. Howl! Howl! The lot comes out exactly.
O light, I see you for the last time now.
They say that I am got where I should not
Have been and sleep with what I shouldn't and there
Where I was not allowed to I have killed.

(*He exits.*)

CHORUS. Oh broods of mortal men
  How like and as nothing
  I count your lives.
  For whoever, any man
  Who carries more of happiness
  Further than it seems he might
  He lives in seeming and he falls away.
  Now I have your example
  And your unlucky daimon
  I call no one of mortal men happy.

    Over the measure you had hit it
  And won wealth of good fortune through and through,
  Oh Zeus, and her with the crooked nails,
  The prophesying virgin, you undid her
  Upstanding like a tower among my country's deaths
  On which account you were called my king
  And honoured highest
  In great Thebes ruling.
  But where do we hear now of a man
  Wearier in the changes of life
  Dwelling in travail, wild with pains?

    Oh Oedipus, Oh lofty head
  You had a matrimonial harbour large enough
  As son
  To go in with the father.
  How could, how ever could
  The father's tracks, Oh you unhappy man
  Mutely fetch you hither?
  Unwilling, time found you out
  Who sees all things
  And set up the marriage that was always not
  A marriage because
  It coupled with itself.
  Oh child of Laius
  Would I had, would I had never seen you
  Who am howling now who once

Exulted from the mouth.
The truth is that I had my waking breath from you
And lulled my eyes to sleep.

FIFTH ACT

FIRST SCENE

A MESSENGER. CHORUS.

MESSENGER. O you having always been in the country here
  The most revered, what works must you
  Now listen to and see and what lament
  Now raise if you being native here still grant
  The houses of Labdacus solicitude.
  I think neither the Ister nor the Phasis will
  Wash clean this house again so much does it
  Harbour. The bad is coming to light now,
  Guiltless or guilty. But of evils that
  Hurts worst that shows as self-elected.

CHORUS. It wanted nothing more than what we know
  Already for sighing, what do you know else?

MESSENGER. It is the swiftest word to say and hear:
  Jocasta's godly head has lost its life.

CHORUS. Unlucky woman, on account of what?

MESSENGER. Of herself by herself. Of that though
  The saddest is far off. The sight is missing.
  However you shall learn, as much as I
  Have memory, that struggler's suffering.
  For when she came in rage and tumbled into
  The inner court she ran fast to the marriage bed
  And tore her hair out with her fingerpoints.
  And having closed the door behind her
  She called for Laius who is long since dead
  Remembering the old seed on account of which
  He's dead and left the mother over
  Who childless after him is got with children
  And wails over her bed where she unluckily
  Two husbands made of one and children of the child.

And how thereupon she died I do not know
For Oedipus came tumbling in with screams
And her ill fate we could not see for him.
At him, how he went here and there, we looked.
He wanders, wishing we'll hand him a spear,
That he will find his wife, his not-wife, and the field
That is mother of him and of his children.
One of the daimons showed it him raging
And not a man of any present there.
With violence then, as though under a drover,
He hurled at both the doors and burst
The foundings of the hollow locks and broke
Into the chamber where we saw the woman hanging.
You would have seen her strung and strangling.
Seeing her, he bellowed, he, the poor man, loosed
The hanging rope and down on the earth he fell,
The sufferer. Thereupon the sight was terrible.
The golden needles ornamenting her
He tore them from her dress and opened them
And stabbed into the bright of his eyes and said
This thereabouts: it was to not see her,
And not what he was suffering and what bad he had done
So that in darkness in the future that would be
How he saw others whom he must not see
And those that he was known to, unbeknownst.
And so in glee he stabbed often, not one time,
Holding the lids up, and the bloody apples
Of the eyes dyed him his beard and not in drops
As though spilled from a murder ran but blackly
Spilled the blood was, pelted down.
It issued from a couple, not a sole evil,
An evil got together by man and wife.
Their former wealth before this truly was
A wealth. But now this day there is
Sighing and error, death and shame as many as
Of all the evils there are names, none lacking.

CHORUS.   How does the poor man rest in the evil now?

MESSENGER. He howls that they should draw the bolts and to all
    The Cadmians reveal that man,
    The father-killer, him, the mother's, speaks
    Unholinesses I am not allowed to say.
    Banish himself he wishes from the land
    Cursed, as he cursed, and not rest in the house.
    Strength he will need and one to lead him now
    For it is too big to be borne by him,
    His sickness, but he'll show it you.
    The bolts are slid, the doors are opening
    And you will see a sight of such a kind
    Even an enemy would have mercy surely.

SECOND SCENE

CHORUS. OEDIPUS. *Later*, CREON

CHORUS. Oh terrible to see, a grief for people,
    Oh of them all most terrible, of all the many
    I have met. What is it, pitiable thing,
    What madness has come on you, what daimon
    Conducted you, the highest there is,
    Into your lethal fate?
    Pitiable you, alas, alas, but look at you
    I cannot, things to say,
    Things to advise you do and things to think
    I have in any number, such
    A shudder you cause me.

OEDIPUS. Pain! Pain! Pain! Pain!
    Oh I am sorrow. Where to on earth
    Am I being carried suffering thus?
    And where does the voice extend and where will it bring me?
    Where are you pulling, daimon?

CHORUS. Into a weight of things, unheard of, can't be seen.

OEDIPUS. Night, my own cloud of it, oh frightful

Foaming around me and cannot be said
Or tamed or overcome, oh me, oh me
How with these stabs
There enters into me
At once a working and a memory of the evils.

CHORUS. Such being the misery it is no wonder
You howl for two and bear the evils twice.

OEDIPUS. Oh friend
Conductor biding near to me
For you still suffer me
And tend me, blind. Alas, alas
For you are not concealed from me and though
Going dark I do still know your voice.

CHORUS. Vast things already done, how could you
So soil your eyes, what daimon drove you?

OEDIPUS. Apollo, it was Apollo, friends
Achieved a misery of this size,
Here, these sorrows, mine.
No death I do myself apes his done me
But suffering I
What should I look upon
To whom, sighted, nothing was sweet to look upon?

CHORUS. It was so as you say.

OEDIPUS. What have I still to see and still to love
Or hear, my dear ones, any friendly thing?
Lead me swiftly from this place
Dear friends, lead me no longer fit for anything
And more accursed than anyone and also
Hateful to the gods the most among mankind.

CHORUS. Small in spirit and one with the event
My wish is I had never known you.

OEDIPUS. Founder whoever it was
Who from the wild
And wandered moor redeemed

My feet and from the murder
Saved and sheltered me. No thanks
For doing it. For dead then
Not to my loved ones nor to myself would I have been such
        a grief.

CHORUS.   My wish this would have been as well.

OEDIPUS. Then should I not have come as murderer
    Of him and groom of her
    Whose young I was.
    Travailed I am. Son of unholy beings
    And mixed in sex with those
    I stem from, wretched. Whatever ancient
    Evil there ever was
    Oedipus got it.

CHORUS. I cannot say that you have come out well
    For you were better not alive than blind.

OEDIPUS. This being accomplished now not for the best
    Give no opinion and advise me nothing.
    It was because I did not know what eyes
    I'd see my father with, coming to Hades,
    And my poor mother too. For both of them
    I've fashioned troubles worse than torture.
    There were the children's faces, lifted day by day,
    As lifted, never to be seen by me now
    With the eyes of my old age, the towers, the town
    And the sacred likenesses of the gods,
    For of them all one single man upheld
    In Thebes deprives me and he is
    Myself, the vilest. For I said myself
    That all hate him, godless as he is,
    Who is revealed as somebody unholy
    By gods and as the flesh of Laius.
    Thus having published my disgrace should I
    Still look at these things with straight eyes?
    Never. No. But if for the fount of sound
    In the ear there was a bolt I would not hold it

Open but shut my troubled body
And make me blind and deaf. For sweet
Is a dwelling place of thought away from evils.
Cithaeron, oh why did you harbour me and not,
Receiving me, kill me at once
So I should never tell men who I was?
O Polybus and Corinth, fatherly
And celebrated homes, how well
You brought me up, well hidden from evils.
Now I'm found bad and son of bad creatures.
O you three roads and you the hidden grove
And wood and cranny where three roads meet where
You drank blood from my hands, my blood,
My father's, do you think of me, what works
I did among you and when I came here
What I did then? Oh marriage, marriage!
You planted me. And when you planted me
So doing you sent the same seed out
And showed forth fathers, brothers, children, one
Related blood, and virgins, women, mothers
And what worst shame can spring up among humans.
But things not fit to do one must not say.
Quickly as possible, by the gods, entomb
Me outside somewhere, kill or fling
Me in the sea where I'll be out of sight for ever.
Do it! Believe it worth your pains to touch
The man of troubles. Follow me and be
Fearless. For my evil is such
That no man, never, carried it before.

(*Enter* CREON.)

CHORUS. For what you want Creon himself is here
　　　　To do and to advise. For he alone
　　　　Instead of you is left to watch the land.

OEDIPUS. O me, what can I say to what you say?
　　　　What mark of proper loyalty will I have?

For long since in his eyes I have been found bad.

CREON. I don't come as a mocker, Oedipus,
Nor saying in blame one of the old evils.
But if you people do not shy from being seen
By mortal breeds, honour at least
The flame that pastures all things of King Helios.
Ill like this cannot be shown uncovered
For the earth will not nor will the light
Nor will the holy rain address it.
Quickly now bear him in inside the house.
They are the fittest who are of the breed itself
To see and listen to an inbred evil.

OEDIPUS. By gods, since you have stopped me in my longing
And as the best have come to the worst man
Do what I ask. I speak for you, not me.

CREON. What is it that you beg so hard to gain?

OEDIPUS. Fling me quickest you can out of the country
Where I will not have any talk with people.

CREON. I should already have, believe me, did I
Not wish to learn from God first what to do.

OEDIPUS. The utterance is all done by him already:
Destroy the godless father-killer, me.

CREON. So it was said, but in the case we stand in
To listen what to do is better still.

OEDIPUS. So you will ask about this travailed man still?

CREON. Perhaps you'll give the god your credence now.

OEDIPUS. So I prescribe it you and bid you.
Her in the houses raise the way you will
Her hill, for rightly you do that for yours.
But for myself don't deem it worth the pain
That I should be a fellow-dweller in
The fatherly town alive. But let me dwell
Upon the mountains where my famous

Cithaeron is that, still alive, my mother
And father chose to be my burial mound
So I may die through those who have destroyed me
Though I know this, not sickness could undo me
Nor anything else, for I was saved from death
Only for this colossal evil.
But this my fate let it go where it will.
For them, the children, for the males, and me,
You need not care, Creon. They are men
And will not suffer want wherever
They are in life. But my troubled girls
Who never did go hungry at my table nor
Sit without me and everything I touched
They shared, they do deserve mercy.
Always in all things take good care of them.
And surely you permit that I touch them
With hands and weep over the misery.
Go, my king
Of noble stock will you not go? If I touch them
It will seem I am holding them as when I saw.
What am I saying?
By gods do I not hear my darlings as
They weep for me and Creon in his mercy
Sends them to me, the dearest of my children.
Am I not right?

CREON. You are. I have this minute brought them you.
    I know they always were your joy.

OEDIPUS. May you be blessed and may some spirit
    Conduct you better on the way than me.
    Oh children where are you, come here, come now
    Into my brotherly hands, oh you who once
    When he was raising up the plants
    Were such a pasture for his then bright eyes,
    Children to me who ignorant, untaught,
    Became a father there where he was ploughed from.
    I weep for you, I cannot look at you

The dreary rest of life imagining
And how from people you must suffer violence.
Where in what city gatherings will you go?
To what festivity from which you will not
Go home in tears and not as joyous dancers?
But when you come to the peak of marriage
Who will it be who throws his sons away
And takes the shame and what upon my parents
And you will come, the insults?
For no evil is wanting. Your father
Murdered the father, he ploughed the childbearer
In whom he was himself seeded and with
The same he had you, with the ones from whom
He had issued himself. So they will jibe
And who will want to court you? Nobody,
Children, but it is certain you must pass away
Dry and without weddings. But you
Son of Menoeceus, being the only one
Left them as father for the ones who had them
We, the pair, have perished
Do not despise these poor unmanned
Related strays. You will not, will you,
Equate them with my evils but will show them
Mercy, seeing this their age.
They are deserted utterly. It rests with you.
Give me your word on it, give me your hand.
Children, if you already had the senses
There's much I'd warn you of. Now promise me
The things life has to have and that you'll live
Lighter than he who got you did, the father.

CREON. Enough, where are you getting to, weeping?
Now go indoors.

OEDIPUS. A man must follow though it gives no joy.

CREON. Everything in its proper time is good.

OEDIPUS. Do you know what I want now?

CREON. Say it. I will know if I hear it.

OEDIPUS. Send me away out of my homeland.

CREON. That which the god gives you ask me for.

OEDIPUS. I come as one gods hate.

CREON. And so will soon receive it.

OEDIPUS. You'll say it now?

CREON. I will not say twice what I do not think.

OEDIPUS. Lead me yourself hence now.

CREON. Go. But leave the children.

OEDIPUS. Don't take them off me, ever.

CREON. Presume nothing.
    Not even what was yours will follow you in life.

CHORUS. Dwellers in Thebes' land see this Oedipus,
    Solver of famous riddles and above all men a man.
    Paying no heed to others' envy nor to fortune
    Into the weather of a great doom he has come.
    Therefore look to the last appearing day
    Whoever is mortal and call no man fortunate until
    He has got through to his life's end without grief.

Notes to *Oedipus*

1

It will be a good thing, giving poets even in our country a secure social existence, if poetry, even in our country and notwithstanding the differences of the times and of the political systems, is raised to the μηχανη of the Ancients.

Other works of art too, compared with the Greek, lack reliability; at least, until now they have always been judged more by the impression they make than according to their calculable laws and other procedures by which beauty is brought into being. But modern poetry is especially lacking in schooling and craft which would enable its procedures to be calculated and taught and once learned be always reliably repeated in the practice. Most important for humankind is to see with respect to every thing that it *is something*, in other words that it is knowable in the medium (*moyen*) of its appearance, that the conditions of its existence may be determined and taught. For that and for higher reasons poetry needs especially certain and characteristic principles and limits.

Therein belongs precisely the aforementioned calculable law.

We have to see then in what way the content of a work differs from this law, through what procedure, and how in an infinite but thoroughly determined interconnection the particular content relates to the general calculation, and how the onward march of the work, the things it has to bring into shape, the living sense which cannot be achieved by calculation, how all that is related to the calculable law.

The law, the calculation, the way in which a sensibility, the whole person, under an elemental influence develops, and ideas, feelings, reasonings, in different sequences, but always according to a sure and certain rule, are produced one after the other, in the tragic poem this is more a matter of weighting and balance than of pure sequence.

For the *transport* in tragedy is of itself empty, and the most unbounded.

For that reason in the rhythmical succession of scenes in which the transport is made manifest, it becomes necessary to have what in prosody is known as a caesura; the pure word, the counter-rhythmical interruption, is needed, so as to confront the pull of the succession of scenes at its height and in such a fashion that instead of facets of a manifestation there comes manifestation itself.

In that way a division is made in the calculated sequence and in the rhythm, and the two halves are so related that they appear of equal weight.

If the rhythm of the scenes is such that, in eccentric rapidity, the earlier ones are more carried away by those following then the caesura or counter-rhythmic interruption must lie towards the front so that the first half is, as we might say, protected against the second, and, because the second half is originally faster and seems to weigh more, the balance, because of the counter-working of the caesura, must incline from the back towards the beginning.

If the rhythm of the scenes is such that the later ones are more under pressure from those at the beginning then the caesura will lie more towards the end because it is the ending which must, as we might say, be protected against the beginning, and the balance will as a consequence incline more towards the end since the first half extends itself further and thus the balance comes later. So much concerning the calculable law.

The first of the laws of tragedy indicated above is that of *Oedipus*. *Antigone* proceeds according to the second law.

In both plays the caesura is constituted by Tiresias's speeches.

He enters the process of fate as overseer of the natural order which, in tragedy, removes man from his own zone of life, from the midpoint of his own inner life, and carries him into the eccentric zone of the dead.

2

To understand the whole we must above all look closely at the scene in which Oedipus interprets the message from the oracle too infinitely, and is tempted towards the *nefas*.

For the oracle says:

> Phoebus has bidden us, the King has, clearly,
> We must hunt down the shame our country's ground
> Has nourished, not nurture the incurable.

It was possible that meant: Judge, in a general way, with strict and pure judgements, keep good civic order. But Oedipus at once responds to it in priestly language:

> Through what cleansing etc

And goes into the particular,

> Which is the man he means who had this fate?

And so brings Creon's thoughts to the terrible utterance:

> Lord of us formerly, O King, was Laius
> Here in the land before you led the city.

In this way the words of the oracle are brought into a connection they do not necessarily have with the story of Laius' death. Then in the very next scene Oedipus' spirit, in an angry presentiment, knowing everything, actually utters the *nefas*, as he suspectingly points the general commandment into the particular and applies it to a murderer of Laius and takes the sin then too for an infinite one:

> Who ever knew the son of Labdacus
> Among you, Laius, by whom he died
> I say to him: tell all of it to me etc
>
> For this man's sake
> I curse (whoever it might be here in the land
> Which I command the power of and the thrones)
> Let nobody invite or speak to him
> Nor to the holy oaths nor to
> The sacrifices take...
>
> The utterance
> Of God at Pytho shows me this clearly etc

Thus, in the exchanges that follow with Tiresias, the wondrous angry curiosity of a knowledge that has torn through its barriers and now, as though drunk in its lordly harmonious form (which may remain intact, for a while at least), incites itself to know more than it can bear or comprehend.

Thus later in the scene with Creon the suspiciousness of thoughts that, all unbridled and burdened with sad secrets, are now becoming unsure, and the true and certain intelligence suffers in an angry excess that revels in destruction and lets itself go down the rapids of the times.

Thus, in the middle of the play, in the speeches with Jocasta, the sad tranquillity, the foolishness, the pitiable naïve error of the powerful man, when he tells Jocasta of his supposed birthplace and of Polybus, whom he fears he will kill, supposing him his father, and Merope, whom he will flee from, supposing her his mother, so as not to marry her, after the words of Tiresias, who has told him he is the murderer of Laius and that Laius was his father. For in the already mentioned quarrel between him and Oedipus, Tiresias says:

> The man
> You seek with threats and broadcasting the murder
> Of Laius, he is here, he lives, it is said,
> With us as stranger, but as native soon,
> As Theban, will be shown and not be glad
> Of the accident.
>
> He will be shown up living with his children
> As brother and as father and the woman's who
> Bore him, the son and the husband, in *one* bed with
> The father, his murderer.

Thus at the beginning of the second half of the play in the scene with the messenger from Corinth, when he is tempted again towards life, the despairing struggle to come to himself, the trampling and almost shameless striving to be master of himself, the idiot-frentic pursuit of a consciousness.

> JOCASTA. For upwards Oedipus lifts his spirit
> In manifold torment not like a man
> Calmly, he reads new things from old.
>
> OEDIPUS. Most loved, o you, my wife's, Jocasta's head
> Why did you call me here out of the houses?
>
> OEDIPUS. The old man was wilting, so it seems, with sickness.
> MESSENGER. And with the large enough measure of time.

It should be noted how at this point Oedipus' spirit raises itself up on the good words; so that the following speeches may appear as proceeding from a nobler motive. Here, not by any means bearing things on Herculean shoulders, in fact in a lofty weakness, now to become master of himself he flings the cares of his kingship away:

> OEDIPUS. Well then. Who now another time would question, wife,
> The prophesying hearth or from
> Above, screaming, the birds, whose sense it was
> I was to kill my father who has died
> And in the earth is sleeping; here however
> Am I and clean my lance unless

315

He lost his life in a dream by me. In that way
Let him have died by me. He takes with him
The seer's sayings today and lies now
In Hades, Polybus, no longer valid.

Finally what dominates in the speeches is a sick mind's questing after consciousness.

MESSENGER. You show you don't know what you are doing, child.
OEDIPUS. How do I, by the god, old man? Speak something.

OEDIPUS. What are you saying? Polybus did not plant me?
MESSENGER. About as much as I'm the one who did.
OEDIPUS. But how? A father who is like nobody?
MESSENGER. A father, yes. Not Polybus, not me.
OEDIPUS. Why then does that man call me child?

MESSENGER. I undid you. The ends of your feet were stitched.
OEDIPUS. Out of my swaddling clothes I brought a violent shame.
MESSENGER. And after that thing you are named.
OEDIPUS. That, gods, oh that, by mother, father, speak!

JOCASTA. By gods, do not. If you're chary of life
    Then do not search. I have sickened enough.
OEDIPUS. Be cheerful. If I from three mothers
    Were three times serf it would not lower you

OEDIPUS. Let break what must. I want my kith and kin
    However base, I want to learn it. She
    Is rightly – women have high ideas –
    Ashamed my birth is lowly. I however
    Holding myself to be the child of fortune,
    Goddess of gifts, will not go without honour
    With her for mother. Small and large
    The moons born at my time surrounded me
    And so produced I will not exit so
    But will discover wholly what I am.

And precisely this questing after everything, this interpreting of everything, is the reason why in the end his spirit is defeated by the rough and simple language of his servants.

Because such people stand in violent circumstances their language too, almost in the manner of the Furies, speaks in a nexus of more violent connections.

3

Tragedy consists chiefly in this: that the monstrousness of the pairing of God and Man and the boundless coming together in anger of the powers of Nature and the innermost heart of a man, is grasped in the catharsis of that boundless union through boundless separation. Της φυσεως γραμματευς ην τον καλαμον αποβρεχων ευνουν.

Hence the constant to and fro of the dialogue, hence the chorus as its antithesis. Hence the all too chaste, all too mechanical interplay (ending in facts) of the different parts, in the dialogue, and between chorus and dialogue and the large passages or dramas made up of chorus and dialogue. It is all speech against speech, and the speeches cancelling each other out.

Thus in the choruses of *Oedipus*: sorrow, tranquillity, religion and the pious lie ('If I am a soothsayer' etc), and pity to the point of complete exhaustion towards a dialogue that in its angry hypersensitivity will rend the hearts of precisely those listeners; the terrifying ceremoniousness of the scenes; drama like an inquisition, as right language for a world in which, amid plague and confusion of the senses and the spirit of prophecy flaring up everywhere, in an idle time God and Man, so that the course of the world shall have no gap in it and the Immortals shall not fade from memory, participate in one another in the all-forgetting form of an infidelity; for divine infidelity can be retained the best.

At such a moment Man forgets himself and the God and, like a traitor, but in the way of holiness, he turns about. – For at the furthest frontier of suffering nothing else stands but the conditions of time and of place.

At that frontier Man forgets himself because he is wholly in the moment; and the God forgets himself because he is nothing but time; and both are unfaithful, time because in such a moment it is a categorical turning-point in which beginning and end cannot at all be made to fit; and Man because at that moment of categorical turning he must follow but in what follows he cannot at all match what was there in the beginning.

Haemon stands thus in *Antigone*, and Oedipus himself thus at the centre of the tragedy of *Oedipus*.

ANTIGONE

DRAMATIS PERSONAE

ANTIGONE.
ISMENE.
CHORUS *of Theban Elders.*
CREON.
A GUARD.
HAEMON.
TIRESIAS.
A MESSENGER.
EURYDICE.
A SERVANT.

FIRST ACT

FIRST SCENE

ANTIGONE. ISMENE.

ANTIGONE. O common sisterly Ismene's head
    Do you know any thing the Earth's Father has not
    Gone through with us who have lived up to here,
    Any nameable thing, since Oedipus was snatched?
    Not one sad work nor any error and no
    Disgrace and no dishonour anywhere is there
    That I in your and my unhappiness have not seen.
    But now have you an inkling what the General
    A minute since has told us in the open town?
    Have you heard it, or do you not yet know
    That on the loved ones the enemy's evil comes?

ISMENE. No word, Antigone, came to me of loved ones,
    No loving word nor sad either since we,
    The both of us, lost both brothers
    Who died on one day by two hands;
    But now that gone the Argive army is
    Last night, further than that I know nothing
    And am not happier and not sadder.

ANTIGONE. That's as I thought and called you out of doors
    For this, that you particularly could hear it.

ISMENE. What is it? You seem to dye your words with red.

ANTIGONE. For has not Creon with the last rites wreathed
    One of our brothers and the other one insulted?
    Eteocles, it's true, they say he treats
    Justly with justice, by the law, and hides
    Him in the earth, pious to the dead down there.
    Of the other's though, who has died wretchedly,
    Of Polynices' corpse they say they have
    Broadcast it in the city he shall not

Be hidden in any grave and not lamented.
He shall be left unwept without a grave,
Sweet dish for the birds that look and lust for food.
Some such they say kind Creon has told you
And me, for I mean myself too,
And comes here now to tell it clearly to
Them not knowing it. And that the matter is
Not one that does not matter. Who does something
Will die the death by stoning in the place.
So it stands for you. And you will prove now whether
You are well born or the bad one of the good?

ISMENE. What then, unhappy girl, if it stands so?
Am I to leave it be or go to the grave?

ANTIGONE. Are you with me, to do and help? Ask that.

ISMENE. You reckon recklessly. What do you mean?

ANTIGONE. Will you with this hand here carry the dead man?

ISMENE. His grave will you go to whom the town abjures?

ANTIGONE. Of you and me, I think, whether you will or no,
The brother. I won't be caught faithless.

ISMENE. You have run wild. Does Creon not forbid it?

ANTIGONE. What's mine has not at all to do with him.

ISMENE. Oh me, remember, sister, how the father
Of us hated and infamous went under
After the errors he had brought upon himself
Stabbing his pair of eyes with his own hand.
And then the mother, wife also, a sorrow
Doubled, how she with twisted cords
Defaced her life. And third the brothers
Who both of them on one day with the hands
Of enemies worked a related death.
And now we two who are alone remaining
Perish the worst of all if we
Violently evade the ruler's force

And orders. Think of this too: we are women
And must not make a quarrel against men.
Then too, because those ruling us are stronger
We have to listen, even to worse things still.
Therefore I beg them who are underground
Forgive me that this has befallen me
And let the rulers rule remote from us.
There is no sense in doing what goes beyond.

ANTIGONE. I won't demand it. Even if you now wished
To do it after all, your help would be no joy.
No, you think as you like; but I
Will bury him. To die after is good then
And lovely to lie by him then, my loved one,
When I've done what is holy. Then a longer time
I shall be liked by those down there than here
For there I'll dwell for ever. You, if you like,
Give things before the gods deserving honour none.

ISMENE. I don't give none. But I was not born right
To take the step of citizens in revolt.

ANTIGONE. Make that your excuse. But I will go
And heap a grave up for my dearest brother.

ISMENE. Alas for me, oh how I fear for you.

ANTIGONE. Don't counsel me. Come out with your own life.

ISMENE. Very well. But let nobody hear the deed.
Keep silent now. Then I can be there with you.

ANTIGONE. I say cry it out loud. I hate you even more
If you keep quiet and won't speak out before all.

ISMENE. How warm your soul feels towards the chilly dead.

ANTIGONE. I know who I must try to please the most.

ISMENE. Yes, if. But what you're trying can't be done.

ANTIGONE. True, if I cannot I must leave it be.

ISMENE. No one need chase what from the start no one can do.

ANTIGONE. If you can say that and the like, I hate you,
    Also the dead man hates you and is right to.
    Let me however and my errant counsel
    Suffer the violence. For I am not at all
    So delicate that I may not die well.

ISMENE. If it seems so to you, go then. But listen:
    Your speech is senseless, though to kindred kind.

CHORUS. O glance of the sun, the loveliest shone
    On Thebes for a long time
    The seven-gated, now you shine
    O light, O glimpse
    Of the eye of the golden day
    Rising over Dirce's streams
    And over the White Shield, him from Argos,
    The man come here in his weaponry
    Fled at full tilt
    You curbed him sharply and move him along
    With whom Polynices
    Swung himself over our land
    From a double quarrel and sharp as an eagle
    He screamed and flew
    Snow white his wings
    Terrible, with weapons, with many,
    And helmets swish with horsetails,

      And stood up over the palaces and pointed at
    The seven mouths in a ring
    Full of bloody spears
    But left, not having
    Filled his cheeks with our blood and before
    Hephaestus' torch
    Had taken the crown of the towers.
    So the rumble of Mars
    Was on the enemy's back
    And baulked the dragon.
    For Zeus detests
    A big tongue boasting and when he sees

Their long strides coming and looks into
Their gold and vain anticipation
Swinging fire
He topples them from where
On steep steps
Too soon they were singing the gleeful victory.

  They hit the hard ground, tumbling down,
Who had snorted hither
In passion, drunk,
The bacchantic mob
In a rage
On the throw of unlucky winds
But found something else;
For the battle wraith deals
This to him, that to him
When he comes at him hard with his just deserts
And smashes his hands.
Seven princes, set up
At seven gates, equal to equal, they lost
Their weapons of bronze to triumphant Zeus
Except the abominable
Got by one father, born of one mother, against one another
They levelled the doubled spears and received
The lot of a death in common, that pair.

  But the big name of victory has come
And favoured the numerous chariots of Thebes.
Now after the war
Let there be forgetting.
To all the gods' temples
With choirs through the night
Come and shake Thebes
With the stamp and dancing of Bacchus.
But Creon, king
Of the territory, son of Menoeceus, new from
The new dispensations of the gods
Is coming to speak
His counsel since he has called

And commanded here the gathering of elders
And sent public word.

SECOND SCENE

CREON. CHORUS.

CREON. Citizens, our one city, after shaking it
    With a great flood our gods
    Now once again have given it back its shape.
    But you for two reasons of all the men
    I have summoned, for one because I know
    You honour properly the rule of Laius' throne
    Then also, when Oedipus set up the city
    And afterwards went under, you remained
    True-minded to the children of those parents.
    Since they now in a double dispensation
    On one day perished striking and
    Struck down in a shame of their own hands
    I have the power totally and the throne
    Ensuing from the family of the dead.
    But only with such who are used to right and orders
    Can we in soul and cast of mind and thinking
    Get on in understanding, with others hardly.
    For it seems to me a man pre-eminent
    Who does not hold himself in the highest thinking
    But in a fearfulness keeps his tongue locked
    A bad life that, is now and always was.
    And who rates higher than his motherland
    Some dearest thing of his own, I count him nothing.
    For I, Zeus knows, who sees all things, always,
    I will not keep it quiet if I see error
    Coming to the citizens against their welfare, nor
    If on the ground here there's a sulking man
    Make him my friend, for that ground, I know,
    Holds us together and if our conduct
    Thereon is right, that way we may win friends.

By such prescription I'll advance the city.
And meanwhile likewise I have informed the citizens
Concerning the progeny of Oedipus.
Eteocles, of course, who fighting for the city
Died, aligning all things with his spear,
Cover him with the grave and bless
With everything fit, the best of the dead below.
But he who is his relative in blood
Him, Polynices, the returning fugitive
Who wished to topple his father's land and the gods
Of home with fire from the crown downwards
And pasture on related blood and these here
Lead them away captive, I say of him
And in the city it has been proclaimed
That no one bury him, no one mourn him,
That he be left unburied and on show,
A meal, a meat torn up by birds and dogs.
This is my mind and never will the bad
Be more in honour with me than the good.
Who means the city well though, dead or alive,
Equally for ever he has my esteem.

CHORUS. Son of Menoeceus, Creon, you think thus
    Concerning the city's enemy and her friend
    And over all you make use of the law
    Concerning the dead, likewise the living.

CREON. You, oversee the aforesaid matter now.

CHORUS. Fill such like posts with younger men.

CREON. Not that. The corpse already has a watch out there.

CHORUS. But in the duty you are taking us up too.

CREON. Yes. There are certain people this displeases.

CHORUS. There's no such fool here who will gladly die.

CREON. That is the wages. But with hopes often
    Of profiting a man has come to grief.

THIRD SCENE

CREON. CHORUS. MESSENGER.

MESSENGER. My King, this time I don't come telling you
    That I am fetched here by a breathless hurry
    And lifted my feet lightly. Often
    Worry held me back and turned me on the way
    Towards retreat. My soul was singing me
    Her many dreams. Poor you, where are you going,
    Where are you answerable when you arrive?
    Unlucky you, don't go, but if you don't
    Creon will hear it from another person.
    How will you not be still in trouble then?
    Thinking such things, slowly I took my time
    And so a little way became a long one.
    Finally of course this won that I
    Had to come here, and though I speak for nothing
    I'll say it nonetheless. For I come in hopes
    Only what has to be will follow on what I did.

CREON. Why is it that you come with such small courage?

MESSENGER. I'll tell you everything in this that's mine
    For neither did I do it nor know who did
    And shall not fairly suffer punishment.

CREON. You make provision, all about encircle
    The deed, and seem to point to something new.

MESSENGER. Heavyweight things are very difficult.

CREON. Speak, will you, finally, then go again.

MESSENGER. I'll tell you. Just now someone who escaped
    Has buried the dead man, twice sprinkled the skin
    With dust, and in the fit way honoured him.

CREON. What do you mean? Who was it dared do this?

MESSENGER. Not thinkable. Nowhere had any mattock
    Gone in or any shovel thrust, the land

Was solid, the earth nowhere dug up,
Not ridden over by wheels. The master had left
No mark and when the day's first glimpse denounced
It to us, it had an eerie feel, like a miracle.
Not ceremonial. Not a burial mound.
Only a gentle dust as though someone had shied
Before the ban. And nowhere any footsteps
Of wild beasts, or dogs that had come and torn.
And dire words went crossing to and fro.
One guard accused another, and almost
It would have come to blows. For nobody
Had stopped it, everyone seemed he might
Have done it but no one evident and each
Had something he could say on his account.
But we were ready to handle redhot iron
And go through fires and swear by the gods
That we had done nothing and that we
Knew nothing of whoever had deliberated
Or carried out the happening. At last
When there was nothing left to ask one said,
And all of us our heads by what he said
Were sunk down to the ground, for fear, for nothing
Against it occurred to us nor how we might
Manage to do it well: we said we must
Report the deed not hide it from you.
And this triumphed: my spirits left me and the lot
Fell on me that I should be the conscience
And here I am now present, against my will
And not in the presence of welcomers, I know,
For nobody loves the bearer of dire words.

CHORUS. My king, my conscience is advising me
   It may be gods who are the workers here.

CREON. Leave that, before you talk me into judgment
   In rage and you be found senile and foolish.
   For it falls all too heavily that you say
   The spirits in the country over there might be
   Thoughtful on account of this dead man.

Honour so tenderly and shade a man who came
To burn the clusters of their temple columns
And sacrifices and to burst asunder
Their land and laws? Or have you seen
Bad men being honoured by the heavenly gods?
Never. Some in the city have however
Taken this thing amiss a long time now
And mutter secretly, shaking their heads
And in the harness will not bow their necks
The necessary way for human beings.
From them have come some gifts to these here,
I'm sure of that, to put them up to this.
For among all things ever stamped for use
None is so bad as silver. Whole towns
It leads astray, and goads men from their houses.
It can deform and alter honest minds
Until they think the bad works men do good.
It shows men many ways of moneymaking
And the knack of any and every godless work.
However many did this, for reward,
In time the reckoning will come for what they did.
But if the Lord of the Earth lives in me too
I do know this and, put on oath, I say
It to you now: you must deliver up
Who did the shovelling of the dead, bring him
Before my eyes or, hung on the cross alive,
Betray the whole luxuriant scheme to me.
Then make yourselves prepared for Hell.
Then see where you can draw your winnings from,
With one another share the plunder and find out
Not everything is made for making money.
Then you will know that by bad profiting
More have been disappointed than preserved.

MESSENGER. Do you give something I must do, or shall I go?

CREON. Do you know what pain there is now in your words?

MESSENGER. Does it stab the ear or stab the life inside?

CREON. Where do you think what's grieving me resides?

MESSENGER. The doer plagues your mind, I plague your ears.

CREON. Such terrible talk is in your nature, is it?

MESSENGER. Because I'm not a party in this business.

CREON. You are! For money you are the traitor of your soul.

MESSENGER. Knowledge is terrible without the truth.

CREON. Mull the law how you like. But if you do not
　　Denounce the ones who did it you may say
　　That profit wrongly got is bad for you.

(*Exit* CREON.)

MESSENGER. They can be sought after, that's true enough.
　　But hit as well? I wonder. Such things
　　Happen the way they happen to. It does not seem
　　You will be seeing me come here again.
　　Being beyond my hopes, and not as I expected,
　　Preserved, I give the gods much thanks now.

(*Exit* MESSENGER.)

SECOND ACT

CHORUS. Monstrous, a lot. But nothing
    More monstrous than man.
    For he, across the night
    Of the sea, when into the winter the
    Southerlies blow, he puts out
    In winged and whirring houses.
    And the noble earth of the gods in heaven
    The unspoilable tireless earth,
    He rubs out; with the striving plough
    From year to year
    He does his trade, with the race of horses,
    And the world of the gaily dreaming birds
    He ensnares, and hunts them;
    And the train of wild beasts
    And Pontus' nature that thrives in salt
    With spun nets
    This knowing man.
    And catches the game with his arts
    That sleeps and roams on the mountains.
    And over the rough-maned horse he flings
    The yoke on its neck, and over the mountain –
    Wandering and untamed bull.

      And speech and airy
    Thought and the pride for governing cities
    He has learned and to flee the damp airs
    Of ill-dwelling hills and their
    Unlucky arrows. All-travelled
    Untravelled. He comes to nothing.
    Only the future place of the dead
    He does not know how to flee
    Nor to think of a way
    Of flight from clumsy plagues.
    Possessing something
    More than he hopes of wisdom and the skills of art
    He comes to grief one time and to good another.

He offends the laws and the sworn conscience
Of earth and the rulers of nature.
In high civility uncivil he comes
To nothing where beauty is
With him and thuggish pride.
May no one doing these things
Be by the hearth with me
Nor my companion in thinking.
But it stands before me now like God's temptation
That I see her and yet shall say
This is not the child Antigone.
O unhappy girl of the unhappy
Father Oedipus what is bearing over you and to where
Seizing hold of you
In disobedience to the King's laws
And in unreason?

FIRST SCENE

MESSENGER. CHORUS. CREON. ANTIGONE.

MESSENGER. She did it. She did. We seized her
    Making the grave. But where is Creon?

CHORUS. He comes, even as you ask, back from the house.

CREON. What thing and I occur together here?

MESSENGER. My king, humans should swear to nothing.
    For when they know, it mocks what they supposed.
    I never thought I'd come back here lightly
    After the threats that pelted me before.
    No other pleasure equals anywhere near
    That of a joy that takes us by surprise.
    I come on oath although I swore I would not,
    Bringing the girl. She was discovered
    As she dressed up the grave. Then nobody
    Threw lots, for the find is mine and nobody
    Else's. So take her now, King, her

As you will, and do what's right and punish.
My right is to be rid of this ill luck.

CREON. How is it you fetch her here? Where did you seize her?

MESSENGER. She buried the man. Now you know everything.

CREON. Do you know what you have said? Have you said it right?

MESSENGER. I saw her burying the dead man which you have
    Forbidden. Is that not clear as can be?

CREON. How was she seen and how was she found guilty?

MESSENGER. The affair was so. When we had gone away
    From you, from under your colossal threats
    We wiped off all the dust the dead man had
    On him, so laying bare the damp body
    And sat up in the air high on a hill
    Because of the smell he gave off, frightened.
    One man prompted another and threatened him
    If he would not pay attention to the work.
    And so it stayed a long time till the sun
    Broke from its arc and stooped down straight
    From the ether, throbbing hot. Then suddenly
    A warm and twisting storm rose from the ground
    Troubling heaven, filling the fields and tearing
    The hair out from the valley's trees and all the vast
    Ether was full of it. We shut
    Our eyes and suffered pains from God and when
    We were free of it, a good while after,
    The child was seen and she was weeping loudly
    With a sharp voice the way a bird will grieve
    When in an empty nest orphaned of young
    She sees the sleeping place. So she when she
    Espied the dead man bare, she howled
    And cursed whoever had done it with bad curses
    And in both hands brought dust, quickly,
    And from the jug of hammered iron three times
    With waterings she wreathed the dead man.
    We, seeing it, we came, seized hold of her,

Unabashed, and charged her with the present
And with the already happened. But she
Denied nothing and was at once a sweet
And an unhappy thing in my view.
For to escape yourself from evils is
The pleasantest but bringing friends into
Misfortune is unhappy. But still all that
Is smaller than the gain of my own safety.

CREON. You with your head down, bowing to the earth,
Do you say or deny it that you did it?

ANTIGONE. I say I did it and do not deny it.

CREON. Go where you like, you, go away,
Set free of heavy guilt. But you, tell me,
Not lengthily but briefly, did you know
How it was given out not to do that?

ANTIGONE. I knew. How shouldn't I? Was it not clear?

CREON. Why did you dare to break a law like that?

ANTIGONE. Because. *My* Zeus did not dictate that law
Nor did the justice of the gods of death
Here in the house who limit human laws,
Nor did I think your word so very much
That humans, who must die, should break for it
The unwritten fixed decrees in heaven.
Not only today and yesterday, they live for ever
And nobody can tell where they have come from.
So among them in heaven I did not wish to risk
Punishment for fear of what a man thought.
I knew however I should have to die.
Why not? I should even had you not said so.
But if I die before my time I say
That is a gain. Who lives like me with many ills
Surely receives some small advantage, dying.
So meeting such a fate is not for me
A sadness. If I had left
My mother's dead son when he died without a grave

That would have saddened me. But the other
Saddens me not at all. But if to you,
Having done that, I come and seem a fool
Perhaps I owed the fool some foolishness.

CHORUS. You see the wild spawn of the wild father in
The child. She cannot pass an evil by.

CREON. Surely you know that those too pure in speech
Fall easiest. And even the strongest iron,
Cooked in the furnace, still its obstinacy
Will break and fail. You see this every day.
And horses, fearfully far-stretched,
No sooner bridled they are stayed and stalled.
He has no business thinking big who is
The servant of those surrounding him.
But she discovers a delight in muddying
The laws prescribed. And having done it
Her second impudence is to boast and laugh
That she did it. Now I am not a man
But she is a man if power of that kind
Comes to her unpunished. What if she is
Stuff of my sister and my closest kin
And of the whole god of my hearth
No matter all of that, she'll not evade
A bad death. Nor will her sister. Just as dear
I charge that one as I charge this one here
That she provided for the earthing over.
Call her out. I saw her in there raging
Not mastering her senses. It is never long
Before a secret mind is apprehended
When something wrong has been done in the dark.
Surely I hate it when a person caught in the wrong
Makes out the thing is something beautiful.

ANTIGONE. What more d'you want, now that you have me, than
to kill me?

CREON. Nothing. If I have this I have it all.

ANTIGONE. Well then. Not one of all your words

Is pleasant to me and never will be pleasant.
Mine therefore likewise are unpleasant to you.
But where should I get sweeter sounding fame
Than if I lay my brother in his grave.
And that it pleases sweetly all these here
The tongue, if fear didn't stop it, would admit.
The cunning kingdom though is everywhere
And does and says whatever things it likes.

CREON. Are you the only Cadmian who sees this?

ANTIGONE. These see it too, but keep their mouths shut for you.

CREON. Aren't you ashamed to interpret them unasked?

ANTIGONE. Surely we honour humans of one flesh?

CREON. He's also of one blood who died for the land.

ANTIGONE. One blood. Child of the selfsame man and wife.

CREON. But you bring thank-you's to the godless one?

ANTIGONE. That sleeper surely would not count himself that.

CREON. Not if you count all one godless and godly.

ANTIGONE. It was not serf-work, he is still my brother.

CREON. One ruined the land, the other stood for it.

ANTIGONE. Even so, the world of the dead loves such a law.

CREON. But the bad are not to be taken like the good.

ANTIGONE. Who knows? Perhaps down there the custom's different.

CREON. The enemy, even dead, is never a friend.

ANTIGONE. One thing is sure: I am for love not hatred.

CREON. Go down below then if you want to love
         And love down there. In life no woman will rule me.

SECOND SCENE

CHORUS. CREON. ANTIGONE. ISMENE.

337

CHORUS. Ismene is coming from indoors
    The peaceable girl, weeping for her sister.
    Over her eyebrows a ghostliness
    Covers her bloodshot sight
    And cheeks and temples streaming.

CREON. Yes you, squatting in there at home like snakes
    Safely and sucking me out, have I not had
    Warning of two conceits against me
    And enemies of the throne? Say, did you share
    The deed at the grave or are you thick with innocence?

ISMENE. I did the work if she agrees I did,
    And take my part. I take the blame on me.

ANTIGONE. Justice however will not let that happen.
    You would not do it, I did not take you with me.

ISMENE. I'm not ashamed of being in your trouble,
    And make myself your fellow-traveller in it.

ANTIGONE. By those who have gone through with it
    And talk with one another down below
    I don't like anyone who loves with words.

ISMENE. Sister, don't bring me so into suspicion, as though
    I could not die with you and make the grave amends.

ANTIGONE. Don't die in common. What's no concern of yours
    Don't make it yours. My death will be enough.

ISMENE. Have I, when you are gone, a love left in my life?

ANTIGONE. Creon, love him. Haven't you shown him the way?

ISMENE. Why are you grieving me? What does it help?

ANTIGONE. We are at odds. I laugh you out of court.

ISMENE. What help can I be to you even now?

ANTIGONE. Some to yourself. Leave me and good riddance.

ISMENE. Alas for me. You die, am I to blame?

ANTIGONE. You know your part is life and mine is death.

ISMENE. But what I said to you is also part.

ANTIGONE. And that was good. But I wanted my own mind.

ISMENE. Equally both of us have failed.

ANTIGONE. You are alive, be cheerful, but my soul
Long since is dead and so I serve the dead.

CREON. These women, I say, one has become witless
Just now, in the other it always housed.

ISMENE. Not even the homely heart stays quiet, King,
Where it feels ill, but gets beside itself.

CREON. Yours has, by doing wrong with wrongdoers.

ISMENE. No thing lives, I am alone, unless she does.

CREON. The talk is not of her now. She is done with.

ISMENE. The girl you're killing is your son's bride-to-be.

CREON. Others than her will please him among women.

ISMENE. But none belonged like him and her together.

CREON. I warn my sons: beware of evil women.

ANTIGONE. Oh dearest Haemon, how he dishonours you!

CREON. And how you burden me, you and your bed.

ISMENE. You take her from him who is part of you.

CREON. Such growing together Hell will put asunder.

ISMENE. It seems decided that she is to die.

CREON. For you and me! And no more dallying. Maids,
Take them indoors. The need from now on
Is not to let these women loose. For flight
Is something even the strong will try when they
See the realm of Hell open on the rim of life.

(ANTIGONE *and* ISMENE *are led away.*)

THIRD ACT

CHORUS. Lucky who live in a time not tasting evil, for
     Should gods ever be stirring in a house
     It will not be short of madness in what follows when
     It has increase. Like that down there
     The night under the salt
     When the Thracian winds
     Blow evilly on the sea
     Befalls a little dwelling
     And turns the dark sand inside out and upside down
     Dishevelling it
     And all the thrashed coast groans.

      Ageing in the houses of Labdacus
     On the foundered house I see more ruin fall
     On ruin, nor does one generation
     Hand on to the next but a god
     Strikes it down. And never has release.
     For now upon the last
     Root left the light is trained
     In Oedipus' houses
     And the killing dust, the dust
     Of the gods of death, is eating them and their
     Unbridled speech and the raging of their senses.

      Father of the Earth, your power
     Who among men can reach it by over-reaching?
     Sleep, to whom everything sinks, cannot remove it nor
     Can the months and stormy moons of the Spirits
     But in an ageless time, in riches, you
     Retain the marble
     Shine of Olympus
     And now and the future
     And past you oversee.
     But madness also samples
     As mortals live their lives
     The fixity of your thinking.

Hope lives, errant and restless,
Helps many men
And fools the light minds of many
And a man who is thinking of nothing
Hope stays with him till fire is burning his soles.
From one man's wisdom
One famous word has come:
Bad things often seem noble
So soon as a god
Has driven the mind to delusion.
But rarely does he bring it
Home without madness.
Now Haemon is coming,
Your lastborn son
Troubled the young Antigone should perish
The wedding woman
Sick that their bed will evade him.

FIRST SCENE

CREON. HAEMON. CHORUS.

CREON. Soon, more than seers, my son, we'll have, it seems,
Decision at last. Do you close your ears to me for love
Of her, the young woman, and come furious to me
Or are you with me still in all my actions? Speak.

HAEMON. Father, I'm yours. The way you think is mild,
You rule me right. I follow willingly.
For so much worth I lay on no wedding that I
Would hold it dearer than your happiness in ruling.

CREON. Indeed, my son. In the heart it must be so
That all else falls in with the father's thinking.
For which reason a man wants first and foremost
Pious offspring, to accustom them at home
To hold an enemy off and damage him,
Honour a friend however like the father.

But when a man gets fit-for-nothing children
What can you say about him except this:
That all he gets is trouble for himself
And much derision among his enemies.
Don't therefore now, my son, for the woman's sake
For lust throw away your sense, but think
That it becomes a chill embrace having
As dweller-with a bad woman in the house.
On earth what is there that deals uglier bruises
Than bad friends? But you, esteem her as
You do the godless, let her go and court
A boy in Hell, for openly I found her
Of all the city being her alone
Disloyal and cannot now as a liar
Stand before the city, and must kill her.
Sing that away, if she likes, where her brother is.
If family goes bad I succour strangers.
A man who's good in what belongs to him
Appears a just man in the city too.
But anyone overstepping and doing harm
To the laws or mastering a ruler
Praise cannot very likely come his way from me.
But whomsoever the city appoints, what he says,
Right talk or small or nonsense, must be listened to.
And such a man, so I believe, he will
Rule well and also want good ruling
And when he's set up in the storm of spears
He'll be a proper helper and stay brave.
There's no worse evil than unruliness:
It spoils cities, it enrages
The houses, it tears holes in spear-fighting.
Those who are ruled aright however
The overlord preserves their many bodies.
Therefore secure the ones who build your world
And never in anything give way to women.
Better, if it has to be, fall with a man
So we shall never be named behind the women.

CHORUS. To us, unless the times hold us in darkness,
　　　What you have spoken of seems said with sense.

HAEMON. Father, as though from God the coming of sense
　　　Is heavenly and is of all good best.
　　　My own life cannot say however
　　　And does not know if what you've said is right.
　　　Let beauty move to others from now on.
　　　I had my life for you, to be the watcher
　　　Of all that people say and do and censure.
　　　Are not your eyes too terrible for them
　　　To let you hear what you don't wish to hear?
　　　But I am given to hear things on the quiet
　　　And know the town is full of sadness for the girl.
　　　'Shall she more innocent than any woman
　　　End badly for a thing done famously?
　　　Who did not want her brother, fallen killing,
　　　Without a grave left to be eaten by
　　　Merciless dogs or a bird among the birds.
　　　Shouldn't such a one be worthy of golden fame?'
　　　Darkly and secretly these murmurs come to us.
　　　But if what you are doing goes well, than that,
　　　Father, for me there is no greater good.
　　　For if the father flourishes what thing better
　　　Behoves children and what fame is there godlier
　　　Than piety in conduct with the father?
　　　But don't now hoard in you your own custom
　　　And don't say you are right and no one else.
　　　For anyone who thinks alone he has
　　　No thoughts and speech and soul like any other
　　　If such a man were ever opened up
　　　He would appear empty. It is no shame,
　　　If somewhere there is someone wise, to learn
　　　A lot and not push anything too far.
　　　See by the stream in spate that's hurtling past
　　　The trees give way, and all of those
　　　Leaf up warmly but the strugglers against
　　　Are gone at once. Likewise a prospering ship

343

That throws its weight around and will give way to nothing
All falling backwards from the banks of rowers
Its certain course is wreck. Give way
Where your mind is, allow us change.
There may be in this speech something of mine,
The opinion of youth, whereas the grown man's mind
Is old and fully filled with knowledge:
But if not quite so filled, and rarely will it be,
Words that are good may still be good teachers.

CHORUS. King, it is right if what he speaks is timely
To learn from it yourself even from him.
For right was spoken here with two voices.

CREON. Since I'm so old I will for my part then
Learn how to think in the manner he does here.

HAEMON. Without offence. I may be young but more
Than looking at the years look at the deed.

CREON. Do homage to what affronts the world, is that your deed?

HAEMON. I don't say we show piety to the wicked.

CREON. Was she not caught in sickness of that sort?

HAEMON. In Thebes neighbour to neighbour does not say so.

CREON. The place tells me then what to do and not do?

HAEMON. Listen to that! How over-boldly young it sounds.

CREON. And someone else be master in the land?

HAEMON. No place is right and proper that's only one man's.

CREON. Is it not said a city is its ruler's?

HAEMON. You'd rule the truest in the desert all alone.

CREON. He seems to be the woman's fellow-fighter.

HAEMON. If you are the woman. My concern is you.

CREON. Oh bad, bad! In court against the father.

HAEMON. Because I will not see you lying at justice.

CREON. If I stand by my first beginning am I lying?

HAEMON. You are not doing that not holding God's name holy.

CREON. Oh shameless thing, worse even than the woman!

HAEMON. I doubt you'll find me going after evil.

CREON. You lay yourself this far open for her sake?

HAEMON. For hers and yours and mine and for the deathgods'.

CREON. The time's already gone that you could have her living.

HAEMON. So she will die and dying kill someone else.

CREON. Now it is out: rage and then impudence.

HAEMON. To an empty mind it might seem so, I grant you.

CREON. Weep and mind out. Your own mind might be empty.

HAEMON. If you were someone else I'd say you'd strayed.

CREON. You come for favours like a winsome woman, in vain.

HAEMON. You want to say things, never want to hear things.

CREON. Just so. But by the heaven of my fathers
You shan't peeve me with censure as you like.
Fetch out the creature, now, before his eyes
Let her die hard against her bridegroom here.

HAEMON. Not me. Truly, don't let yourself think that.
It will not be near me she perishes.
And never will you have my head before your eyes
So you can stay untroubled among your own.

(*Exit* HAEMON.)

CHORUS. He went away in anger quickly, King,
But such a soul is heavy when it suffers.

CREON. Let him do it. Let him think bigger than a man,
He'll nonetheless not save the girls from death.

CHORUS. Do you have a mind even to kill them both?

CREON. Not her who didn't touch it. There you are right.

CHORUS. The other then: how will you do the killing?

CREON. I'll lead her where the tracks of men are lonely
       And keep her living in the pit of rock,
       Reach in such nourishment to her as is fit
       So that the city will not wholly be disgraced.
       There no doubt she will pray to the god of death,
       The only one she honours of all the gods,
       And it may be that she will never die.
       So she will understand, but as the ghosts do,
       Honouring dead things is a mere excess.

(CREON *goes in.*)

SECOND SCENE

CHORUS. *Later* ANTIGONE.

CHORUS. O Love, nobody bests you
       In a quarrel, you bow the trades
       Under your peace, you overnight
       On the girl's soft cheeks, you
       Move on the waters
       And over houses in the open spaces.
       Even the hearts of the immortals almost
       Break for you and the hearts
       Of humans do who will go to sleep and whoever
       Has you in him is not himself. For
       Even of the just you cause the less just senses
       To shy and bolt away
       Into disgrace, even here, in this quarrel of men,
       Blood-related, you linger and fling it to and fro.
       And the powerful plea
       In the lids of a bridal girl
       Will not be defeated, it joins
       Foremost in the making of great

346

Ends. For in them unwarlike
Heavenly beauty plays her part.
But now I come, myself, by law,
To witness this and can no longer
Contain the spring of tears
Seeing Antigone walk her way
To a bed where all is hushed.

ANTIGONE. See, citizens of my mother country,
    Me going the final way
    And seeing the sun's
    Last light.
    That never again? The god
    Of death who hushes everything
    Is leading me living
    To the banks of Acheron, I am not called
    To Hymen, no wedding song,
    No song of praise sings me but I
    Am married to Acheron.

CHORUS. But you go famous and accompanied by praise
    Off to this chamber of the dead.
    No sickness strikes you and spoils you
    No sword puts paid to you
    But living the life of your own among
    Mortals unique
    You go down into the world of the dead.

ANTIGONE. I have heard she turned to a wasteland
    That Phrygian so full of life
    Whom Tantalus dangled, on Sipylus' peaks
    She is crouched and shrunk
    To a slow stone, they put her in chains
    Of ivy and winter is with her
    Always people say, and washes her throat
    With snow-bright tears
    From under her lids. Like her exactly
    A ghost brings me to bed.

CHORUS. But she was named sacred and she

Was engendered sacred but we
Are earth and engendered earthly.
Though you perish now still something great will be heard:
That you have, like those like God, received your lot
Living and then you died.

ANTIGONE. Oh, I am their fool! Oh why do you
By all the spirits that protect our land
Raise yourself above me who have not yet gone below
But am in the daylight still?
Oh city, and from the city
You men of plenty
And oh you springs of Dirce
And ringing Thebes, where the chariots
Rise up, you woods
You must be my witnesses one day
How I unwept by loved ones and in accordance with
What sort of laws
Must enter the opening dug for me
The unheard of grave
Poor woman that I am alas
Not among mortals, not among the dead.

CHORUS. A dweller neither with
The living nor the having died.
Pushing boldness to the parting place
On to the heights of justice
So deep you have fallen, child
Like father, like daughter, in the fight with death.

ANTIGONE. You have quickened the angriest
Of my beloved griefs
The manifold lamenting of the father
And of all
Our fate besides
Us famous Labdacids.
Oh in the beds
The unlucky mother in delusion with her arms around
My father, her

Own birth,
And from them with a darkened mind I came
And to them I am coming cursed
To live with them without a man.
Alas, alas, my brother
Fallen in a dangerous wedding
Me too who was still here
You drag down with you dying.

CHORUS. Piety is good
Somewhat. But power
When power is the issue
Never gives. In the angry
Knowing yourself
You have destroyed yourself.

ANTIGONE. Unwept, without a friend, unwed
Dark in the mind I am conducted
This readied way. It no longer is
My usage to see the holy eyes
Of this light, poor girl, and for this
My fate there are no tears and no one
Loves it or laments it.

THIRD SCENE

CREON. ANTIGONE. CHORUS.

CREON. Singing and howling at the point of death
Will never stop if you talk to and fro.
Lead her away at once and with the crypt, with darkness
Overshadow her, as said. Let her rest there
Lonely alone and die if she must die
Or wither living under such a roof.
For we are pure in what concerns this girl
But here above she has no domicile.

ANTIGONE. O grave, O bridal bed and housing

Underground, always awake. There I will journey
To kith and kin of whom the most when they
Had gone ahead a light has welcomed in
Among the dead, angrily, pityingly.
Of them the last and in the worst way I
Must perish in the wide world now before
The edge of my life arrives. But when I come,
I nourish this with hopes exceedingly,
My coming will be welcome to the father
And welcome to you, mother, welcome also,
Brotherly head, to you. For when you died
I took you all of you with my own hand
And decked you out and brought over your grave
The sacrificial potions. Polynices
Covering your corpse now I have come to this
Though in well-minded eyes I honoured you.
For never had I either been a mother
Of children or if in death a husband
Had lain rotting would I with force,
As though wanting revolt, have brought this off.
And what law do I say thanks to for this?
A husband dying there would be other husbands
And even children by another man
If I embraced that man. But when the mother
And father sleep both in the place of death
It cannot be another brother will grow.
According to that law I honoured you.
To Creon however it seemed a sin
And great temerity, O my brother's head.
And now he leads me, handling me, away,
Me without bed and wedding, not the marriage part
Have I received nor nourishing a child
But lonely so from loved ones sad in soul
Living into the desert of the dead
I am descending, overstepping what
Law of the Spirits? Poor girl, why look henceforth
To heavenly powers? What comrade sing for help?

Since I from piety got godlessness.
But if this thing is lovely to the gods
We suffer it and beg forgiveness for
How we have sinned. But if the fault is theirs
May they not suffer greater misery
Then what they evidently have done to me.

CHORUS. Still from the same tempests she has
  The same assaults in her soul.

CREON. Therefore to those who are conducting her
  Tears will come because of the delay.

ANTIGONE. Oh me, straight before death
  This is the word.

CREON. I warn you, venture nothing
  And speak her nothing for her comfort of that kind.

(*Exit* CREON.)

FOURTH ACT

FIRST SCENE

ANTIGONE. CHORUS.

ANTIGONE. O fatherly city of the land of Thebes,
  All you good Spirits who are with the fathers
  Am I to be led thus and stay no longer?
  O lords of Thebes, look what dues
  Are laid on me,
  The only queenly one remaining, by these dutiful men
  Because they caught me in an act of piety.

CHORUS. Danaë too she had to have
  On her body instead of the light of the sky
  An iron grid, and bear it.
  She lay in the dark in a room
  With Death, in chains.
  Oh child, though her birth was high
  She counted the strokes of the hours,
  The golden strokes, for the Father of Time.

  But Fate is terrible, it falls
  Like rain on the fighting men and on
  The tower and catches
  Even the black and ocean-splitting ships
  And Dryas' son, the Edonian king,
  Whose mouth ran over with insults, him
  The furious rapid Dionysus apprehended
  And buried under mounds of stones.

  He wept out almost all his madness so
  And his luxuriant rage and groping in madness
  With insults on his tongue
  He got to know the god
  For he vexed the women full of the god
  And the flute-loving Muses

And fed the exultant fires.

    By skyblue rocks
Where at both ends sea is
There are the Bosporus shores
And the lap of Salmydessus
Belonging to Thracians; and there
Close to the city the butcher god
Spectated whilst the wild wife
Struck the two sons of Phineus a blinding wound
And it grew dark in the bold orbs of their eyes

    With spear pricks, under bloody hands
And needle points
And thinning to nothing, poor things, they wept
Their poor pain to their mother; they had
An unmarried beginning, but hers
Was the seed of Erechtheus
Begun long ago.
In wandering caves
She was reared, in her father's storms, a girl
Of the North Wind, the sheer hills
Running with horses,
But on her too
A daughter of the gods
A massive fate rested, child.

(ANTIGONE *is led away.*)

SECOND SCENE

TIRESIAS. CREON.

TIRESIAS (*led by a boy*).
    Princes of Thebes, we come our way together
    Both seeing by one. So we, the blind,
    Fare on our way with pathfinders.

CREON. What is there new, old man Tiresias?

TIRESIAS. I will say it. You, listen to the seer.

CREON. In past times too I was not far from your sense.

TIRESIAS. And steer straight with the city because of that.

CREON. I am the proof I have learned useful things.

TIRESIAS. Now on the delicate moment likewise: think.

CREON. What is it then? Horrors are on your tongue.

TIRESIAS. You know it, you hear the signings of my art.
    I sat in the ancient chair, scrying the birds
    And had before me a haven of all the birds
    And heard an unknown screaming out of them,
    Wildly in an evil raging they were screaming
    And tearing at one another with their claws
    In murder, I marked that, the rush of the wings
    Being intelligible. At once afraid
    I made a test of all the flames on all
    The lit altars but from the sacrifices
    Hephaestus did not shine but from the ash
    The clammy smell devoured the thighs
    And smoked and writhed and a high anger
    Was sown around and the sprinkled thighs
    Looked open from the fat that covered them.
    I learned it from this boy, these signless orgies'
    Deadly interpretation, for he is
    The guide to me and I am guide to others.
    And this. The city sickens from your mind
    Because the altars are and fire places
    Full of the eats of birds and dogs, full of
    The unseemly fallen son of Oedipus.
    And now the gods will not take up from us
    Prayers at sacrifices nor the flames of thighs
    Nor will the birds' well-meaning crying
    Come rushing here for it has eaten
    The fat of dead human blood. Consider, child

Erring is common to all humankind
But when one errs that man precisely
Is not a fool nor an unfortunate
If he, fallen into evil, lets himself
Be healed and does not stay immovable.
For self-conceit is a stupidity.
Yield to the dead man, do not persecute
One who has gone. What sort of strength is that
To kill the killed? Meaning you well
I say it well. It is a joy to learn
If one speaks well and useful what he says.

CREON. Old man, as though we were an archer's target
    You aim all this at us. I am not unschooled
    In the arts of prophecy the way you do it.
    Sold and betrayed I was a long time since.
    Make money. Buy electrum, if you like,
    From Sardes and buy gold from India
    But in the grave you won't stow that man there
    Not even if the bird of thunder tugged at him
    To carry him to the throne of God for food.
    That disregarding, I who am not afraid
    Of sicknesses of heaven won't let the man a grave.
    No human touches God, I know that much.
    But among mortal men, old man Tiresias,
    Even some very mighty fall
    A very grievous fall if they speak sweetly
    Words that desolate, for their own profit.

TIRESIAS. Alas, does no one know and nowhere say it?

CREON. Know what? Say what? You talk too far and wide.

TIRESIAS. Sweet temper is needed now much more than wealth.

CREON. But needed least, I think, is thoughtlessness.

TIRESIAS. Of that particular sickness you are full.

CREON. It is not my wish to answer the seer back.

TIRESIAS. But did so, calling me a false prophet.

CREON. Because the breed of seers all love silver.

TIRESIAS. The breed of tyrants loves disgraceful gain.

CREON. You know you are addressing a commander?

TIRESIAS. I do. It was through me you got the city.

CREON. You are a wise seer but you love injustice.

TIRESIAS. You work me up to say out loud some things
  My thoughts have not disturbed yet.

CREON. Disturb them! Only do not speak for profit.

TIRESIAS. Do I not seem allotted to you still?

CREON. You will not fool my mind. Be aware of that.

TIRESIAS. Be aware yourself, you will not brood much longer
  In the jealous sun from now on. Soon
  Out of your own bowels it will cost you
  A dead man for the dead, for her
  Whom from above you have flung down
  And scandalously sent her soul to dwell
  In the tomb. And from down there you still have one
  Up here, without a fate, the dead man
  Unburied, unholy, the God of Death's
  And no business of yours nor of the gods
  Above. But thus you use your power and so
  In the beyond are lying in wait for you
  And wonderfully harmful God's
  Own crones, to sentence you and laugh
  That you are stricken in the same
  Ills yourself. Think then whether
  I say these things for stupid silver. There is coming,
  In not much more time now, of men and women
  A lamentation in your houses.
  For every city will go down in error
  Whose corpses dogs and wild animals
  Bring to rest and when on wings
  A bird comes to the city's settled hearth

With a defiling stench. That is your state:
In dudgeon certainly. And like an archer
My temper has sent forth the heart's arrows
Steadily and you will not evade
Their warmth. Oh child! And now lead me
Away into my house so this man here can vent
His temper on younger men. And let him learn
To make his tongue more used to being quieter
And better disposed his mind than it is now.

(*Exit* TIRESIAS.)

THIRD SCENE

CHORUS. CREON.

CHORUS. My king, the man left prophesying
    Many things, but we know since we swapped
    Black hair for white, as you can see,
    That in the city he never has used lies.

CREON. I know it too. My mind is in confusion.
    It is a big thing to give way. But when someone
    Treads on my spirit with madness, that is hard.

CHORUS. Creon, Menoeceus' son, it needs good counsel.

CREON. What shall we do? Say it. I'll follow you.

CHORUS. Come, let the girl free from the house of stone
    And make a grave for him lying out there.

CREON. You speak for this and seem to think it right.

CHORUS. As fast, my king, as it is possible.
    God's retribution runs on speedy feet
    To abbreviate the man whose mind is wrong.

CREON. Alas, I hardly will, I lack the heart for it,
    But there's no arguing with necessity.

CHORUS. Do this now. Come. Do nothing else but this.

CREON. So I will go, just as I am. Servants,
    Absent and present here, take axes in your hands
    And hurry to the place that you will see.
    But I, since now opinion turns for her,
    And since I fastened her myself, I will release her.
    I fear the best is to uphold
    The law that is, and in that fashion end.

FIFTH ACT

CHORUS. Creator of names, pride of the waters
    That Cadmus loved, and a part of him
    Who echoes in the thunder
    Earth's Father
    And over famous Italy
    You rove far and wide
    In growth. But common to all
    Is something impenetrable. For you
    Govern also at Eleusis, in the womb.
    But here, O God of Joy,
    In the mother city, in bacchantic
    Thebes you are at home, at the cold beck of Ismenus
    At the hedges where the mouth
    Of the dragon snaps its breath.

      By the smoke of sacrifices sweetly shaped
    Over the shoulders of the rocks you have been seen on
    Cocytus where the waters
    Tumble drunkenly and by
    Castalia's forest also.
    And under the hills of Nysa
    Listening from far away
    The wellsprings
    And the green banks hung with grapes
    Excite you to come to Thebes
    To her undying words
    Into the streets where they were rejoicing.
    For above all others you honour her
    As highest of the towns
    With the mother the lightning struck.

      But now, the town
    All caught in a violent sickness,
    We must walk the steps of penance over
    Parnassus hill or through
    The sighing ford.

O you walker in fire
Leader of the dance of the stars and keeper
Of secret speech
Son born of Zeus
Be manifest with the wakeful madded
Naxian Thyades
Who sing you choruses
Their revelling lord.

FIRST SCENE

MESSENGER. CHORUS. *Later* EURYDICE.

MESSENGER. O you neighbours of Cadmus and Amphion
    It is not that I wish to praise or blame
    The life of man whatever shape it has.
    The unthinkable lifts, the unthinkable flings down
    Again and again the happy and the unhappy.
    No seer's mind can reach what's there.
    So Creon always I thought enviable
    Since he from enemies saved the land
    Of Cadmus and won sole lordship
    Hereabouts and rules and flourishes
    Amid a wellborn seed of children. Now
    All that vanishes. I hold good things
    Unworthy of the man when they turn faithless.
    Rich, if you will, he is at home, very:
    The shape he lives in is a king's;
    But when the joy goes away from him not even
    For smoke, for the shadow of smoke,
    Could you sell all the rest as pleasant for a man.

CHORUS. Why is it you bewail the Prince like this?

MESSENGER. They have died. The ones who live are guilty.

CHORUS. And who has killed? Who is laid out? Say it.

MESSENGER. Haemon has gone, by hands of his own blood.

CHORUS. What? By his father's hand or by his own?

MESSENGER. Himself. In anger at the father in his murder.

CHORUS. Oh seer! How right the words you brought us were!

MESSENGER. So things stand now. Others want thinking on.

CHORUS. I see Eurydice, the unhappy wife
    Of Creon coming. Whether in the house she has
    Heard it or she is here by chance.

EURYDICE. Oh citizens I heard something being said
    When I was going to the gate of Pallas
    To come and speak to her with prayers, the goddess.
    No sooner had I slid the bolts of the door
    And it had opened than a voice telling
    Of bad misfortune in the house hit through my ears.
    In dread I fell back on my maids
    Senseless. But what rumour this was
    Tell it me again. I will hear it
    As one not inexperienced in ills.

MESSENGER. Dear lady, I will say it as the eyewitness,
    I will not leave a word of the truth unsaid
    Because what reason would I have to soothe you
    And afterwards appear a liar to you?
    The truth is always upright. I followed
    Your lord as his companion to
    The high field where, its flesh being torn by dogs,
    The poor dead body of Polynices lay.
    We begged Enodia, the goddess, her
    And Pluto, they would hold their wellmeant rage,
    Prepared a sacramental bath and laid him,
    What was left, among fresh branches
    And raised a mound up like a lifted head
    Of the homeland's earth and went then to
    The stone and hollow bed of the virgin girl
    Where she had married in the manner of the dead.

But one among us heard a voice and loud
Lament and crying in the chamber
And he went near and hearkened Creon to it,
The master, and that dark and troubled voice
The nearer he came the more he felt it in
And all around him till, up close, he screamed
And in a terrible lamentation said these words,
These poor lamenting words, 'Am I
Soothsayer to myself? Am I treading
The real unhappiest road of all the roads there are?
My child's voice touches me. Servants, you
Go in to the grave now quickly, mark
Exactly where the bolt has left the wall,
Go in there at the door itself and find
Whether the voice I hear is Haemon's or
A god is deceiving me.' We searched after
The frightened master's words. Thereupon
Back furthest in the tombs we saw hanging
Her, by the neck, by the belt of her linen dress,
And him entangled in her, stretching out, and wailing
Over the bridal bed, over the abyss below,
His father's work, the unhappy sleeping place.
He, seeing this, screams hideously and goes
In to him and moans and cries, 'Oh my
Poor boy what have you done? What had
You in your thoughts? What fate is killing you?
Come out my child, I beg you on my knees.'
With baleful eyes and saying nothing in return
Wildly the son stared back at him
And drew his two-edged sword against him first.
But when the father, frightened into flight,
Turned, it failed. Then savage-mindedly,
Outstretched, standing there, the unhappy man
Thrust with the point of it full in his side.
Before his senses went he kissed the girl's
Moist arm, on her white cheek he frothed
Sharp breaths of bloody droplets out.

Death lies with death now, shyly they came to
Their wedding's consummation in the houses in
The world of the dead and show how lost for counsel
Humans are and greatest this man's ill is.

(*Exit* EURYDICE.)

CHORUS. What do you say to that? The woman left
Without saying a good word or a bad.

MESSENGER. I wonder too, but feed myself with hope
That for her child's bad fate she could not wail
In public view with decency
And in the rooms within will tell the maids
To cry the house lament, for she has not
So lost her sense that she would fail in that.

CHORUS. I do not know. For all too big a silence
Seems meaningful when screaming is in vain.

MESSENGER. Then let us see if there are things held down
In secret hiding in her swelling heart.
Indoors! For you are right to say
Too big a silence may be meaningful.

CHORUS. But now the King is coming himself.
He bears a large memorial in his hands,
If it is right to say this, not from another's
Error, but he has erred himself.

SECOND SCENE

CHORUS. CREON.

CREON. Senseless senses, oh
My hard, my deadly
Goings wrong! Oh see
Killing and killed
Friends of the blood!

Oh me, oh my
Sad counsels, oh
My child, too early dead
Alas, alas, alas
Dead and separated
By my not your folly.

CHORUS. Oh me, why must you be so late to see what's right?

CREON. I have learned it in fear. But by my head
In there a god
Heavily seized hold of me
And beat and shook me on the wild ways.
Alas, alas
The troubles of humans, oh the travail!

THIRD SCENE

MESSENGER. CREON. CHORUS.

MESSENGER. Oh sir, what you have got and do you own already!
That there you carry in your arms. And that indoors
That misery too you must come in and see.

CREON. What worse thing is there than a thing so bad?

MESSENGER. The lady is dead, all mother of this dead child.
She twists and turns still on the hurts just dealt.

CREON. No, oh no, oh filthy harbour of the underworld
What now? Me now? Are you undoing me?
Reporting ills
And hither sending misery.
Oh no, oh no, you bring in such a scream
You have foundered the man.
What are you saying, child? What is your news?
Alas, alas, alas
That butchered lies
For her part in my general collapse
The woman on the ground?

MESSENGER. You can see it. She is not in her room still.

CREON. Oh me, oh wretch
     That misery too, the second, shall I see?
     What else? What fate is still in waiting?
     Here I am holding in my arms my child,
     Oh wretch, and look upon the dead boy here
     And, oh, the troubled mother, oh my child.

CHORUS. So much had smitten her. The killing all around.

CREON. She widened her dark eyes. What did she weep for?

MESSENGER. The already dead Megareus' famous bed.
     Then cried for him there, lastly raised a paean
     To your bad deeds, the murderer of children.

CREON. Aiee! Aiee! Aiee! Aiee!
     Now I am winged with fear. Why has
     Nobody raised a sword against
     And slaughtered me?
     Coward that I am, alas, alas
     Mixed in cowardly straits.

MESSENGER. Of one and the other since you bear the guilt
     Give the order too concerning the dead lady.

CREON. What way in murdering was she delivered by?

MESSENGER. She stabbed her liver when the loud lament
     Came to her for the passion of her child.

CREON. Oh me, oh me, no other human does
     This all belong to. Mine is the guilt in this.
     I killed you. I did. Oh! You servants
     Lead me from here fast. Lead step by step
     Me who am nothing other now than no one.

CHORUS. If the ill has some good in it you will find it.
     Great evils at our feet are brief.

CREON. Oh come, oh come
     Appear, O loveliest of all my fates
     Bringing me the day at last

The last. Oh, come, come
That I no longer have to see the day after.

MESSENGER. It will. But what to do in this here now?
Our care must be the things concerning us.

CREON. I wish the thing I said, precisely that.

MESSENGER. You need not wish. Nobody mortal
Can have release from his determined fate.

CREON. Lead me step by step, the unneeded man. For I
Who killed you, child, not wanting to, and her, her,
I do not know whom I should look at now,
Poor wretch, nor where to go.
Bleak fate has heaped
Here in my hands, here on this head of mine
The sum of all wrong things.

CHORUS. Thinking is more, much more
Than happiness. Things of the gods must not
Be desecrated. For they reward
Great looks
With great blows on the lofty shoulders.
In old age they have taught us to think.

Notes to *Antigone*

1

The rule, the calculable law of *Antigone* stands to that of *Oedipus* as does __/__ to ____, so that the balance inclines more from the beginning towards the end than from the end towards the beginning.

The rule is one of the various sequences in which imagination and feeling and reasoning develop according to poetic logic. For whereas philosophy only ever treats one of the soul's capacities, so that the presentation of this one capacity makes up a whole and the mere hanging together of the parts of this one capacity is called logic, poetry treats the various capacities of the human being so that the presentation of these various capacities makes up a whole, and the hanging together of the – more autonomous – parts of these different capacities may be called the rhythm (in a higher sense) or the calculable law.

But if the rhythm of the scenes is such that in the rapidity of the inspiration the earlier ones are more carried away by those following, then the caesura (A) or counter-rhythmic interruption must lie towards the front so that the first half is, as we might say, protected against the second and, because the second half is originally faster and seems to weigh more, the balance, because of the counter-working of the caesura, must incline more from the back (B) towards the beginning (C).

Thus: C $\overset{\text{A}}{\diagdown}$ B.

But if the rhythm of the scenes is such that the later ones are more under pressure from those at the beginning then the caesura (A) will lie more towards the end because it is the ending which must, as we might say, be protected against the beginning and the balance will as a consequence incline more towards the end (B) since the first half (C) extends itself further but the balance comes later.

Thus: C $\overset{\text{A}}{\diagup}$ B.

2

Why did you dare to break a law like that?

> Because. *My* Zeus did not dictate that law
>   Nor did the justice of the gods of death etc

The boldest moment in the course of a day or a work of art comes when the spirit of the times and of nature, the divine that is seizing hold of a human being, and the object in which he is interested are at their most wildly opposed because the sensuous object of his interest only reaches half way but the *spirit* wakes to its greatest power *beyond that half.* At that moment the human being must keep the firmest hold on himself, for which reason he stands most open in his character.

The tragically moderate weariness of the times, whose object is of no real interest to the heart, follows the pull of the spirit of the times without the least moderation and this spirit appears then as something wild and not, like a ghost in daylight, sparing man at all, but quite pitiless, as the spirit of the always alive unwritten wilderness and the world of the dead.

> CREON. But the bad are not to be taken like the good.
>
> ANTIGONE. Who knows? Perhaps down there the custom's different.

Lovable and intelligent in misfortune. Dreamily naïve. The real language of Sophocles, whereas Aeschylus and Euripides are better able to objectify suffering and anger but less the mind of man going on its way under the unthinkable.

> CREON. If I stand by my first beginning am I lying?
>
> HAEMON. You are not doing that not holding God's name holy.

Instead of: 'treading underfoot the honour of the gods'. It was, I think, necessary to alter the sacred wording here because of its high significance, here at the midpoint, in its seriousness and as an autonomous utterance against which everything else is objectified and made clear.

The manner in which at the midpoint time turns can, I think, not be altered nor how a character categorically follows the categorical times, nor how the Greek shifts to the Hesperian, but the sacred name under which supreme things are made palpable or occur, that may be altered. The speech refers to Creon's oath.

> You will not brood much longer
> In the jealous sun from now on.

On earth, among human beings, since the sun may bear physically upon us, in the moral sphere too it may actually have such a bearing.

> I have heard she turned to a wasteland etc.

Perhaps Antigone's highest trait. Such lofty mockery, in so far as holy madness is the highest human manifestation and is at this moment more soul than speech, outdoes all her other utterances; and it is moreover necessary to speak of beauty thus in the superlative because the demeanour itself rests upon, among other things, a superlative of human spirit and heroic virtuosity.

It is a great resource of the soul in its secret workings that in the state of highest consciousness it evades consciousness and before being actually seized by the god there present it confronts him with bold, often indeed with blasphemous words, and in this way upholds the sacred living possibilities of the spirit.

In the state of high consciousness the soul then will liken itself to objects that have no consciousness but which in their fates have taken on the forms of consciousness. One such is a countryside that has become a wasteland through having in its original abundant fruitfulness too greatly increased the effects of the sun's light, and so become arid. Niobe's fate in Phrygia; as it is everywhere the fate of innocent Nature, who, in her virtuosity, everywhere runs in precisely the same degree into the excessively organic as human beings, in more heroic circumstances and emotions, do into the aorgic. And Niobe is thus a quite peculiarly apt image of early genius.

> She counted the strokes of the hours,
> The golden strokes, for the Father of Time.

Instead of: 'managed for Zeus the coming of the streams of gold'. To bring it closer to our way of seeing things. To be more definite, or indeed less definite, we should have to say 'Zeus'. But for the full seriousness: 'Father of Time' or 'Father of the Earth' because his character, countering an eternal tendency, has been to convert *the striving out of this world into another into a striving out of another world into this*. We must everywhere present the myths more demonstrably. 'The coming of the streams of gold' doubtless means the rays of light, which also belong to Zeus in the sense that time, thus denoted, is more able to be measured by such rays. And it always is when time is measured in suffering because then body and soul follow the passage of time with a greater empathy and so comprehend the simple march of the hours without the mind making assumptions from the present about the future.

But since this steadfast abiding in the passage of time, this heroic life of a hermit, is really the highest consciousness the following chorus takes on a sense of purest generality and truest point of view from which the whole must be apprehended.

For, as a counter to the excessive passion of the preceding passage, it contains in the highest impartiality both the characteristic dispositions in which the different *dramatis personae* act.

First in what characterises the *antitheos* where one, after God's own mind, acts, as it seems, against God and recognises His supreme spirit through lawlessness. Then the pious fear in the face of Fate, and with it the honouring of God as something set in law. This is the spirit of the antitheses placed impartially against one another in the chorus. In the first sense acting as Antigone more. In the second as Creon. The two in their opposition, not as national and anti-national (or, in that instance, cultured) like Ajax and Ulysses, nor like Oedipus against the Greek country people and Nature in her ancient and original shape, as a free-thinking man against loyal simplicity, but weighing equally one against the other and different only in relation to the times, so that the one loses pre-eminently because it is beginning, and the other wins because it is following on behind. In that way the strange chorus being discussed here fits the whole in the most apt fashion and its cold impartiality is a kind of warmth because it is so peculiarly fitting.

3

Tragedy, as the notes on *Oedipus* have already indicated, resides in this: that the immediate God, wholly one with man (for the god of an apostle is less immediate but is the highest the understanding is capable of, in the highest spirit), that an infinite enthusiasm infinitely, which is to say in antitheses, in consciousness that cancels out consciousness, and sacramentally departing from itself, apprehends itself, and the god, in the shape of death, is present.

Hence, as already touched upon in the notes on *Oedipus*, the dialogic form and the chorus as its antithesis, hence also the dangerous form in the scenes, which, in a way more characteristic of the Greeks, has a necessarily factive outcome in this sense that the word becomes more mediatedly factive and seizes rather the body's senses; but in our times and according to our conception of things, it becomes more immediate and seizes rather the body's spirit. The language of tragedy for the Greeks is lethally factive, because the body it seizes hold of does literally kill. For us, standing as we do under a Zeus more our own, who not only pauses between this world and the wild world of the dead but also forces the natural course of things (which is always hostile to man) on its way into the other world more decidedly back to earth, and because this greatly alters our essential and our national conceptions, and because our poetry must be proper to our homeland, its subject-matter chosen in accordance with our view of the world and its conceptions those of our homeland – for us then Greek conceptions alter because the chief striving of the Greeks is to compose themselves, that being where their weakness lay, whereas our chief striving in the way our times see things is to hit upon something, to have a fate, because having no fate, being δυσμορον, is our weakness. For that reason the Greeks have more skill and greater virtue as athletes, and however paradoxical the heroes of the *Iliad* may seem to us that is indeed what they have as their true excellence and serious virtue. Those qualities are in our world more subordinated to propriety. And so also Greek conceptions and poetic forms are more subordinated to those of our homeland.

Thus the lethally factive, the real murder by language, is doubtless to be viewed rather as a peculiarly Greek form and so as one now subordinated to an art form more characteristic of our homeland. Such an art of our homeland, as we could doubtless show, may be a language that of itself works killingly rather than one which causes things to happen that will result in death; so not actually ending with murder or death as that through which tragedy must be apprehended, but more in the manner of *Oedipus at Colonus*, where the words spoken by a mouth inspired are terrible, and kill, but not in a graspable Greek way, in an athletic and plastic spirit, where the words seize the body so that it kills.

371

Thus, either more Greek or more Hesperian, tragedy resides in more violent or more unstoppable dialogue, and in choruses which are a stay or an interpretation for the dialogue and which give the unending quarrel its direction or its force, as the suffering organs of the body in divine struggle, which cannot be dispensed with because even in the shape of infinite tragedy the God cannot communicate itself to the body absolutely unmediatedly but must be grasped by the mind or appropriated into the life; but most of all tragedy consists in factive words that, more a context than an utterance, move in the manner of Fate from the beginning to the end; in how the plot proceeds, in the grouping of the characters against one another, and in the form that reason takes in the terrible interlude of a tragic age, which, having presented itself then, in its wild genesis, in antitheses, later, in a humane age, will count as an established opinion, born of a divine fate.

The plot in *Antigone* has the form of an unrest in which, so far as it is a matter for the nation, the essential thing is that every character, caught up in an infinite reversal and shaken through and through by it, apprehends herself or himself in the infinite form in which he or she is so shaken. For reversal in the mother country is the reversal of all ways of perceiving things and of all forms. Total reversal in these however, like any total reversal with no restraint, is forbidden to Man as a thinking being. And in a reversal in the mother country, where the whole shape of things alters and Nature and Necessity, which are always there, incline to another shape, going over either into wilderness or into some new shape, in such a change everything merely necessary is on the side of change, for which reason, in the possibility of such change, even a neutral person, not only one taken up *against* the form of the mother country, will be forced by a violence of the spirit of the times to be patriotic, to be present to an infinite degree in the religious, political and moral forms of his or her country. (προφανηθι θεος). Such serious remarks are necessary for the understanding of the works of art of the Greeks as for all genuine works of art. The actual procedure or conduct in a time of unrest (which is admittedly only one kind of national reversal, one having a more definite character) has just been indicated.

When such a phenomenon is a tragic one it happens through reaction, and formlessness takes fire at the all too formal. Typically then the people caught up in such a fate do not stand like those in *Oedipus* in the shape of ideas in a conflict over the truth and like a man defending his reason, nor like one defending his life, his property or his honour like the characters in *Ajax*, but they confront one another like persons in a narrow sense, as persons of rank, they become formalised.

The grouping of such characters is, in *Antigone*, comparable to a contest between two runners where the first to get out of breath and stumble against his opponent has lost, whereas the struggle in *Oedipus* may be compared to a fist-fight, that in *Ajax* to a fencing match.

The rational form here developing tragically is political, indeed republican, because between Creon and Antigone, the formal and the anti-formal, the balance is held too equally. This is most apparent towards the end when Creon is almost manhandled by his servants.

Sophocles is right. This is the fate of his times and the form of his country. We may perhaps idealise, for example choose the best moment, but the ways a country has of perceiving things, in their hierarchy at least, must not be altered by the poet, whose job it is to present the world on a reduced scale. For us such a form may still just about be used because infinite things like the spirit of states and of the world can in any case only be grasped from some off-centre point of view. However, the national forms of our poets, where such forms exist, are preferable because they exist not just in order to learn to understand the spirit of the times but once that spirit is grasped and learned to hold it steady and to feel it.

TRANSLATOR'S NOTES

In brackets are the poem's opening words if other poems have the same title; the title and where necessary the opening words, in German; the volume and page reference in the Stuttgart edition of Hölderlin's complete works, *Grosse Stuttgarter Ausgabe* [GStA].

.

19. **Greece [Griechenland; 1, 179]**: Written 1794, published 1795. The addressee is Gotthold Friedrich Stäudlin, editor and political activist and the first influential encourager of Hölderlin's poetic career. For his revolutionary views he was exiled from Württemberg in 1793 and committed suicide three years later, having struggled to make a living outside his homeland.

21. **The oak trees [Die Eichbäume; 1, 201]**: First published 1797, probably written the year before. One of many expressions of Hölderlin's love of trees.

22. **To Diotima ('Come and look at the happiness ...') [An Diotima (Komm und siehe die Freude...); 1, 210]**: Unfinished. Probably written 1797 as one of the first of the poems to Susette Gontard; not published until 1908. The phrase 'a loving quarrel' is a key to much of Hölderlin's poetic philosophy.

23. **Diotima ('Heavenly Muse of Delight...') [Diotima (Komm und besänftige mir...); 1, 231]**: Probably written in 1797, first published 1826.

24. **'The peoples were silent...' [Die Völker schwiegen, schlummerten...; 1, 238]**: Unfinished, seems to have been written in the autumn of 1797, first published 1921. The subject is the Wars of the First Coalition (1792-97) against Revolutionary France

25. **Empedocles [Empedokles; 1, 240]**: Drafted in 1797, perhaps not completed till 1800, first published the following year. Also in 1797 Hölderlin made a plan for a tragedy on the subject of Empedocles, worked at it 1798-9, but could not complete it to his satisfaction.

26. **To the Fates [An die Parzen; 1, 241]**: Written 1798, first published 1799. This was one of the very few poems Hölderlin's mother showed an interest in. She was worried by it, understandably. In fact he was given more than one summer, but not many more.

27. **To her good angel [An ihren Genius; 1, 243]**: Written 1798, first published 1799.

28. **Plea for forgiveness [Abbitte; 1, 244]**: Written 1798, published 1799. The poignancy of the poem lies in the fact that the woman cannot, unlike the moon, resume a former tranquil radiance.

29. **To the Sun God [Dem Sonnengott; 1, 258]:** Written 1798, first published 1846.

30. **Hyperion's Song of Fate [Hyperions Schiksaalslied; 1, 265]:** The poem occurs in the second volume, published 1799, of Hölderlin's novel *Hyperion*. The hero sings it as the ruin of his life is becoming clear.

31. **'When I was a boy...' [Da ich ein Knabe war...; 1, 266]:** Written towards the end of Hölderlin's time in Frankfurt, 1797-98; first published 1826. To earn a living, he was four times the tutor of young children.

33. **Achilles [Achill; 1, 271]:** first published in 1846, the poem was probably written at the end of September 1798, soon after Hölderlin's abrupt departure from the Gontard household. He went to live in nearby Homburg vor der Höhe and saw Susette rarely and only with great difficulty. They separated for good in May 1800. Here he expresses his distress through the figure of Achilles who, robbed of the girl Briseis, complains to his mother, the sea-goddess Thetis (*Iliad* 1, 384-430).

34. **'Once there were gods...' [Götter wandelten einst...; 1, 274]:** Fragments – the end of the third and the beginning of the fourth section – of a substantial elegy, written in the spring of 1799, first published 1909. The rest of the poem, if it was finished, has not survived. Addressed to Susette Gontard the lines celebrate and affirm their alliance in times that are hostile to the spirit.

35. **'If I heeded them warning me now ...' [Hört ich die Warnenden izt...; 1, 275]:** Unfinished, written 1799, first published 1922.

36. **Parting [Abschied; 1, 276]:** Unfinished, written 1799, first published 1846.

37. **The Zeitgeist [Der Zeitgeist; 1, 300]:** Written 1799, first published 1800.

38. **Evening fantasy [Abendphantasie; 1, 301]:** Written 1799, first published 1800. One of several poems struggling, in the absence of Susette Gontard, to make the best of an incurable loneliness.

39. **Morning [Des Morgens; 1, 302]:** Written 1799, first published 1800.

40. **The Main [Der Main; 1, 303]**: Written 1799, first published 1800. The first of Hölderlin's river poems, all of which more or less consequentially connect Germany with the Ancient World. 'The Main' shares half a dozen of its stanzas with 'The Neckar' (p. 51).

42. **That which is mine [Mein Eigentum; 1, 306]**: Autumn 1799, first published 1846. The writer, restless and essentially homeless, looks for an abiding stay in the poem itself.

44. **'Another day…' [Wohl geh ich täglich…'; 1, 313]**: Unfinished. Written perhaps as late as spring 1800; first published 1846. The elegy 'Menon's lament for Diotima' (p. 83) is a large expansion of this topic.

45. **'The sun goes down…' [Geh unter, schöne Sonne…'; 1, 314]**: Written whilst Hölderlin was still in Homburg; that is, before May 1800. First published 1846. It ends (in German at least) with one of those realisations of love and fulfilment that Hölderlin's verse is peculiarly capable of. There is another in 'The Rhine' (p. 135, ll. 10-23).

46. **Peace [Der Frieden; 2, 6]**: Written 1799, first published 1846. Lines 1-2, Hölderlin did not fill in the gap he left between 'the' and 'transformed'. The poem addresses and longs for peace in a time of widespread and seemingly endless war.

48. **Heidelberg [Heidelberg; 2, 14]**: The poem was begun in 1798, finished in 1800, first published in 1801. Heidelberg is on the Neckar. Hölderlin was first there in June 1788 and wrote an account of the visit for his mother. He particularly noted the ancient castle and the new bridge.

50. **The Gods [Die Götter; 2, 16]**: June 1800 at the latest, first published 1801. Characteristically, when addressing or imagining the gods Hölderlin has his mind on human strife, anxiety and sadness.

51. **The Neckar [Der Nekar; 2, 17]**: Early 1800, first published 1801. Compare this poem with 'The Main' (p. 40).

53. **Home [Die Heimath; 2, 19]**: Expansion, in 1800, of a two-strophe poem composed in 1798. First published in 1806. Here Hölderlin, like John Clare after his return from the asylum in Epping Forest, finds himself 'homeless at home'.

54. **Love [Die Liebe; 2, 20]**: Expansion, in 1800, of a single-strophe poem composed in 1798 and entitled 'The unforgiveable thing' [Das Unverzeihliche, 1, 254]. 'Love' was first published in 1826.

55. **Course of life [Lebenslauf; 2, 22]**: Expansion, in 1800, of a single-strophe poem composed in 1798. First published in 1826.

56. **The Parting, *second version* [Der Abschied; 2, 26]**: Expansion, in 1800, of a single-strophe poem composed in 1798 and entitled 'The Lovers'. 'The Parting' was first published in 1826.

58. **Diotima ('You are silent, you suffer it...') [Diotima (Du schweigst und duldest...); 2, 28]**: Expansion, in 1800, of a two-strophe poem composed in 1798 and published the following year. This longer version was not published till 1826. Diotima belongs among the Greeks. The poem celebrates them, laments their passing and looks forward to a time in which Diotima would be at home again.

59. **Return to the homeland [Rükkehr in die Heimath; 2, 29]**: Written in 1800 and first published the following year.

60. **Encouragement, *second version* [Ermunterung; 2, 35]**: Probably begun in 1799, finished early 1801, first published in 1826.

61. **Sung under the Alps [Unter den Alpen gesungen; 2, 44]**: Hölderlin's only Sapphic ode, written early 1801 when he was in Hauptwil, Switzerland; first published 1802. The proximity of the Alps moved him greatly (see also the elegy 'Homecoming'). He felt himself to be close to innocence. It was in Hauptwil that he learned of the Peace of Lunéville, a brief cessation of hostilities to which he attached large hopes (see 'Celebration of Peace'). In the last lines here his poetic vocation seems clear to him.

62. **The calling of poetry [Dichterberuf; 2, 46]**: Expansion in 1801 of a two-strophe poem written in 1798, published in 1799 and entitled 'To our great poets' [An unsre großen Dichter]. 'The calling of poetry', first published in 1802, considers the upheaval in Europe around the turn of the century and the poet's responsibility in the midst of it.

65. **Voice of the people, *second version* [Stimme des Volks; 2, 51]**: The large expansion, first in 1800 then in 1801, of a two-strophe poem written in 1798 and first published in 1800. This

second version was published in 1802. Again, it is a poem in which Hölderlin tries to make sense of the times and of his responsibilities in them. The opening line alludes to the saying 'vox populi, vox dei' [the voice of the people is the voice of God] but in the images of the rivers and of the citizens of Xanthus Hölderlin anxiously wonders how to counter the helpless drive into dissolution, of which he sees examples in human history and which, he fears, characterises the present times and, increasingly, his own psyche. The story of the Xanthians' suicidal courage is told by Plutarch in his *Life of Brutus* (30-1) and by Herodotus in his *Histories* (1, 176).

68. **The blind singer [Der blinde Sänger; 2, 54]**: Written 1801, first published 1826. The epigraph – meaning 'Ares has loosed the torment from his eyes' – is from Sophocles' *Ajax* (l. 706) and occurs in the third of the three extracts from that play translated by Hölderlin.

70. **Poetic courage,** *first version* **[Dichtermuth; 2, 62]**: This, the first version of the poem, begun around the turn of the century, was finished perhaps a year later. First published 1826.

71. **Poetic courage,** *second version* **[Dichtermuth; 2, 64]**: Probably early in 1801 Hölderlin undertook a thorough revision of all but the opening two strophes of the poem. This version had its first publication in 1885 in the context of preparations for a critical edition of his work. Both versions, especially in the fourth strophe, insist that the poet must be in the midst of people, open to the lives they lead.

72. **The fettered river [Der gefesselte Strom; 2, 67]**: Probably written early in 1801, first published 1826. A poem imagining or enacting one of those 'returns' George Herbert experienced. The primary image is that of the river released from stasis in the ice by the coming of spring. But Ganymede, who will become central in the radical re-writing of this poem, is already waiting in the wings.

73. **Chiron [Chiron; 2, 56]**: This and the following eight poems first appeared in 1805, as a cycle with the title 'Night Songs', in a periodical published by Friedrich Wilmans, who the year before had published Hölderlin's *Oedipus* and *Antigone*. The poems, like the plays, met with derision. It is best to understand the transformation of 'The blind singer' into 'Chiron, 'The fettered river' into 'Gany-

mede' and 'Poetic courage' into 'Timidity' as an act more of translation than of revision. Hölderlin translated his own poems into another language (at the same time as he was translating Sophocles into a language all his own, his own but foreign). To 'The blind singer', as to 'The fettered river', he adds another strand of metaphor: from the myths. So Chiron the Centaur longs for release from suffering. Heracles, who accidentally wounded him with a poisoned arrow, returns now with the promise that, despite being the son of a god, he is to be allowed to die. This news breaks in upon him like daylight.

75. **Tears [Thränen; 2, 58]**: Written in 1802 (from a first draft around 1800) and revised for publication in December 1803. 'Tears', originally called 'Sappho's swansong' [Sapphos Schwanengesang] is full of longing for the islands of Greece. The grief it expresses is nearly overwhelming.

76. **To Hope [An die Hoffnung; 2, 59]**: Revised for publication in December 1803. The last lines suggest that the writer would welcome reanimation at whatever cost.

77. **Vulcan [Vulkan; 2, 60]**: The poem's first title was 'Winter'. The new title 'Vulcan', doubtless preferred during revision in December 1803, is of a piece with 'Chiron' and 'Ganymede'. Love here, like hope in the previous poem, is an active mythic figure, not an abstraction.

78. **Timidity [Blödigkeit; 2, 66]**: The third version of 'Poetic courage' (December 1803) with a new title suggesting the opposite – courage (like hope) being needed rather than already present.

79. **Ganymede [Ganymed; 2, 68]**: Ganymede was carried off by Zeus' eagle to be the gods' cupbearer. In this poem, after a separation, he returns to them as spring comes.

80. **Half of Life [Hälfte des Lebens; 2, 117]**: This poem, probably Hölderlin's best known, seems to have come out of the chance proximity of notes for two or three separate poems on one manuscript page. Written or prepared for publication in December 1803, it is beautifully balanced – before life tilts into winter. When its author was transported to the Tübingen clinic in 1806 he was half way through his life.

81. **Ages of life [Lebensalter; 2, 115]**: Written or prepared for

publication in December 1803. There is an eerie sense of time, destruction and loneliness in this poem.

82. **Hahrdt Nook [Der Winkel von Hahrdt; 2, 116]**: Like all the other 'Night Songs', prepared in December 1803 for publication in 1805. The place is a cave in woodland between Denkendorf and Nürtingen, close to where Hölderlin grew up. Ulrich is the Duke of Württemberg who in 1519 hid from his enemies there.

83. **Menon's lament for Diotima [Menons Klagen um Diotima; 2, 75]**: Written probably in the first half of 1800 'Menon's lament' is an expanded and more thoroughly composed version of a poem in the same metre (elegiac couplets) and on the same subject (separation from Susette Gontard) called simply 'Elegy' [Elegie] written some months earlier. It was first published, very unsatisfactorily, over two issues of the *Musen-Almanach* in 1802 and 1803. The name 'Menon', deriving from Greek, means 'the one who remains or abides'. Really, in the natural rhythm of elegy, palpable in each three-strophe phase, Menon remains just about intact by conjuring up the very condition of present love whose loss is unbearable.

88. **A walk into the country [Der Gang aufs Land; 2, 84]**: The poem, unfinished, was completed thus far, with drafts for its continuation, in the autumn of 1800 when Hölderlin was staying with his close friend Christian Landauer in Stuttgart and to him it is addressed. The first eighteen lines of it were published in 1826. Very typically, it is driven not by a present joyous state but by the will to engender joy, as though the writer might induce the leaden sky to clear by the very force of setting off – for the inauguration of a new *Gasthaus* on the hilltop and by beginning the poem itself. Margarethe von Trotta's 1981 film about the terrorist Gudrun Ensslin took its title, *Die bleierne Zeit* [The Age of Lead], from line 6 of this poem.

90. **Stuttgart [Stutgard; 2, 86]**: Written probably towards the end of 1800, first published in 1807. Siegfried Schmid (1774-1859) was, in his youth at least, a rather unstable would-be poet very drawn to Hölderlin as to a kindred spirit. Schiller and Goethe, discussing the two of them in 1796, decided they epitomised much that was wrong and dangerous in the younger generation. 'Stuttgart', like so many of Hölderlin's poems, is structured by a journey, here

on foot to Lauffen, Hölderlin's birthplace, on the borders of his homeland, to meet the friend and conduct him to the festivities. Barbarossa (1122-90), Conradin (1252-68) and Christoph (1515-68) were all (among other things) Dukes of Württemberg.The words in the last strophe 'oh come, oh make it true!' are the driving injunction of much of Hölderlin's verse.

94. **Bread and Wine [Brod und Wein; 2, 90]**: Begun in the autumn of 1800, finished that winter. The first strophe was published, as though it were a complete poem having the title 'Night' [Die Nacht], in a literary periodical in 1807, without Hölderlin's permission. There was no complete publication until 1894. In Hölderlin's mythology we inhabit the night; that is, we live in the absence of the gods. This poem seeks to make sense of our times and to counter, in poet and reader, the inclination to despair. The poem is dedicated to Wilhelm Heinse (1746-1803) and addresses him directly in the second and seventh strophes. He was a friend of the Gontard family and, as the author of a philhellene novel *Ardinghello, or the blessed isles* [Ardinghello oder die glückseligen Inseln] a lasting inspiration to Hölderlin. In the third strophe the poem shifts to Greece, especially to the area around Delphi, the Isthmus of Corinth, Mount Cithaeron, Thebes, the latter two places being closely associated with the worship of Dionysus, 'the coming god'. Cadmus was the founder of Thebes. In strophes 4, 5, 6 the poem first confronts the fact that from Greece also the gods have now absented themselves. Only their cult sites and monuments remain. Next their first coming into the lives of human beings is recalled or imagined. Then, again, their departure and absence. In the poem's final three strophes Hölderlin, trained for the Lutheran church, offers a very heterodox myth. Christ, already introduced in the last lines of strophe 6, closes the period of divine presence in the Greek daylight and ushers in our age of night. He is twinned or even fused in this capacity with the wine god Dionysus. Indeed, their myths have much in common.

99. **Homecoming [Heimkunft; 2, 96]**: Written soon after Hölderlin's return from Hauptwil in April 1801; almost certainly his last elegy; published 1802. The poem is structured by the literal homecoming: the crossing of Lake Constance to Lindau, the journey from there to Nürtingen, the reunion with family and friends. The mood is one of joy and hope, but an undertow of

personal sadness is also discernible. In Strophe 5, l. 8 alludes to the Peace of Lunéville, 9 February 1801.

103. **The Archipelago [Der Archipelagus; 2, 103]**: This tremendous poem, probably written in the spring of 1800 (first published 1804), opens with an evocation of spring in the Greek archipelago, and its wish throughout is that this literal regeneration should also become a figurative one and that we, in the present, should recover, in our 'Hesperian' mode, the condition of Periclean Athens. The poem re-enacts the rebuilding of the city after the Persians, who had sacked it, were defeated at the Battle of Salamis. That image at the heart of the poem (p.108, ll. 4-24) is immensely encouraging; but the poem also repeatedly faces up to our loss, to the barbarism of our times and to the precariousness of the poet's existence in them (p. 108, l. 4ff.; p. 108, l. 25ff.; p. 109, ll. 32ff.; p. 111, 15ff). Nevertheless, its constant drive is towards fulfilment, amply imagined in p. 110, ll. 10-30. The youth sitting alone (p. 105, l. 15) is Themistocles, preparing to confront the Persians. He persuaded the Athenians to trust themselves to the sea, and in so doing encouraged democracy, since it was from the lower classes that the sailors for the new navy came and after Salamis they wanted their say. Some years before writing 'The Archipelago' Hölderlin had explicitly associated the wars of Athens and Persia with those of France and reactionary Europe, a war of citizens against the kings. The king here (p. 105, l. 28) is Xerxes. After Thermopylae the Greeks withdrew to their last line of defence on the Isthmus of Corinth, and brought back their fleet to Salamis, leaving Athens and the whole of Attica to be sacked. Themistocles forced the outcome then in the narrows of Salamis (480 BC). Hölderlin's account of the battle may be compared with the Messenger's report in Aeschylus' *The Persians*. P. 109, ll. 16-20 name three places famous for prophecy. They are: Dodona, where Zeus spoke through the wind in the oak tree; Delphi, where Apollo spoke through his priestess; and 'the prescient town' of Thebes, home of Tiresias.

112. **Those sleeping now [Die Entschlafenen; 2, 113]**: Written by Hölderlin in the autumn of 1800, the lines were inscribed on a relief in the house of Christian Landauer. They commemorate the deaths of Landauer's father and brother. First published in 1846.

113. **As when on a holiday... [Wie wenn am Feiertage...; 2,**

118]: Written perhaps in the summer of 1800, not published till 1910, this important fragment is Hölderlin's first attempt to write hymnic poetry in the manner of Pindar and his only attempt to reproduce the triadic structure and the metrical patterning of Pindar's odes exactly. He was, probably at the same time, translating, word for word and cleaving very close to the literal sense, at least 2000 lines of Pindar, which extraordinary exercise enabled him then to write the great hymns that follow. For Semele and Dionysus see notes on 'The calling of poetry' and 'From Euripides' *Bacchae*'. Towards the end of my translation I have included some drafted lines (those in italics) that Hölderlin would perhaps have altered or omitted had he finished the poem.

116. **To Mother Earth [Der Mutter Erde; 2, 123]**: Unfinished, probably worked at in the autumn of 1801, first published 1916. The final structure would most likely have been nine strophes disposed triadically (3x3) among the singers. Klopstock, whom Hölderlin greatly admired, had composed odes for three voices in the 1760s. In this poem the singers have no congregation. They sing in an age of absence. Final passage, 5 lines up: the German word 'Horde' [horde] has also been read as 'Herde' [herd] and I prefer that reading.

119. **At the source of the Danube [Am Quell der Donau; 2, 126]**: Written early 1801, first published 1916. The opening two strophes are lost but their sense and function in the whole poem can be deduced from Hölderlin's drafts which I have translated. The poem has a two-way structure. 'The voice that shapes our humanity', coming out of Asia Minor, breaks over us like the tremendous music of the organ over a congregation. The Danube – rising in the Black Forest, flowing into the Black Sea – is a still-living connection with our origins. See also 'The journey'.

123. **Celebration of Peace, *first version* [Versöhnender, der du ...; 2, 130]**: Written in February 1801 after the announcement of the Peace of Lunéville. First published 1916. Not until 1954 and the appearance (in London) of the final version could 'Reconciler, never believed in ...' be understood as its beginnings. By no means all of this first version (nor of the second and third) was taken up into the finished 'Celebration of Peace' and my two translations, of the first and the final version, may give at least some sense of the process of composition.

126. **Celebration of Peace,** *final version* [Friedensfeier; 3, 531]: This final version was probably completed in the winter of 1803-4 to be published, as a single poem, the first in a series, by Friedrich Wilmans. In fact it had to wait for publication till 1954. Many thousands of words have been spent interpreting it, particularly on trying to 'fix' the identity of the 'Prince of the Festival' (Christ or Napoleon or a fusion of the two being the front-runners). Best try to read it with some of the 'negative capability' that Keats thought indispensable for the *writing* of poetry. And to note that Hölderlin's poem, written in celebration of an announcement of peace is, very typically, full of doubt, hesitation and uncertainty. So what we most feel is not peace but the longing for peace, the longing for a peaceful humanity. Passages of the poem realise that condition, imagine it present. Meanwhile the world of nationalisms and politics continues.

131. **The journey [Die Wanderung; 2, 138]:** Probably early 1801, first published 1802. Swabia ('Suevia'), Hölderlin's homeland, is here celebrated in its medieval extent, and thus has Lake Constance ('the long lake in the haze') and the Alps as its southern border. Neckar, Rhine and Danube are its principal rivers. A journey east, to the origins, is an important element or main structuring device in this poem as in 'Bread and Wine' and 'Patmos'. Swallows, peach, cherry, vines, all connect east with west, but the chief link here, as in 'At the source of the Danube', and 'The Ister', is the river. Hölderlin will have known very well that in the eighteenth century Swabians emigrated in great numbers down the Danube and settled in the region now known as the Banat. But for his own mythology he has them travel east in the remote past, to intermarry on the Black Sea with 'children of the sun'. The Greeks called that sea 'kind to strangers' (*pontos euxeinos*). The whole achievement of Greece is represented by famous mountains: Taygetus, for Sparta; Hymettus, for Athens; Parnassus, for Delphi. The Rhine's abrupt change of course (p. 133, ll. 27-29) is remarked upon again in the next poem (p. 36, l. 6). The poet-traveller has come to Greece to invite the Graces (also known as the Charites) back to his own country which, he feels, is badly in need of them.

135. **The Rhine [Der Rhein; 2, 142]:** Written 1801, first published 1808. The poem begins as a meditation on the course and nature of the Rhine and continues among the possibilities engendered by that meditation. It turns to Rousseau, a force like the river in

Hölderlin's view. Generally, the poem may be said to be about the management of energy, its struggle with form, a 'loving quarrel'. The Morea was the name for the Peloponnese in Medieval and Early Modern times. The Ticino and the Rhône both rise, like the Rhine, in the Gotthard massif, the Ticino flows into Italy, the Rhône into France. The Rhine flows east at first, as far as Chur, then bears conclusively north. Rousseau withdrew to the Île St-Pierre, in Lake Biel, for two happy months in 1765. The 'one wise man' is Socrates who in the *Symposium* stays awake all night and his conversation never flags. In the dedication and in the final strophe Hölderlin addresses his close friend Isaak von Sinclair, a combative and politically active man. But 'The Rhine' was first dedicated to Wilhelm Heinse and the final strophe, in its original form, was closely appropriate to him. It read:

> And you say from afar to me
> Out of a soul always serene
> What do you call happiness?
> What unhappiness? My father,
> I well understand the question but the wave
> That took me under
> Still rages in my ear and I dream
> Of the precious pearl on the sea floor.
> But you, connoisseur of the sea
> And of terra firma contemplate the earth
> And the light and think them unalike
> But both holy for sent to you
> Out of the clear blue upper air
> You have always a genial spirit around your brow.

Heinse was the confidant of Hölderlin and Susette Gontard and knew what he suffered losing her – ll. 5-8 describe it, she is the precious pearl. Heinse died 21 June 1803. Doubtless Hölderlin changed the dedicatee after that date.

142. **Germania [Germanien; 2, 149]**: Written, very likely, 1801; first published 1896. Hölderlin, like his early mentor Schiller, wished to define a character and purpose for Germany that would accord with her geographical situation at the heart of Europe. It would be a definition in large part through the negative: not mercantile like Britain nor political like France. He would have loathed the *Reich* that came into being under Bismarck in 1871 by unification, let alone Hitler's hideous fabrication. Note particularly this poem's last four lines. 'Germania' is a bid to make Germany

the new locus of the spirit of Ancient Greece. But that bid is fraught with doubts: about its propriety as much as its feasibility. Also, since the pull of Greece, of the past, is still every bit as strong as it was in that early poem 'Greece' (p. 19), the whole enterprise is risky. So the verses swing continually between faith, fear of transgression, and a sense of personal peril.

146. **The only one,** *first version* **[Der Einzige; 2, 153]**: First published in 1896, this version was begun, most likely, in the autumn of 1801; continued, but never finished, a year later; by which time, after the death of Susette Gontard and another failure to secure a livelihood, Hölderlin was struggling to hold on to his sanity. 'The only one' and 'Patmos' are part of his concerted effort in these years to make a coherent myth of the life of Christ, the ending of Greek civilisation, and European history thereafter. Life in the interim, as he understood it, in the meanwhile, in an age of darkness, hoping for millennial light, being grievously disappointed. This first version, with a limpid grace, puzzles at how to associate the 'worldly men', Heracles and Bacchus, two of many gods in a pantheism, with Christ, whose religion insists that he is the one and only. What Hölderlin wants here is a trefoil.

149. **The only one,** *ll. 50-97 of the second version* **[2, 158]**: This section was first published in 1941. I've translated just these lines because in them Hölderlin's compulsive radical rewriting is most evident. Here and in the third version, and also in the later work on 'Patmos', grace and clarity are near to being abandoned, the lines extend almost helplessly in the welter of material and in the effort to get at a tenable truth. 'The Bard' may be Ossian or Klopstock. 'The African' may be Augustine.

151. **The only one,** *third version* **[2, 249]**: First published 1916. These later versions, overflowing the lines, seem themselves at times to exemplify the unrestraint that Hölderlin felt and feared throughout his life and spoke of here: 'For the world is / Forever ecstatically lifting away from the earth and would / Denude it where there is no hold in humane things.' Huntsman, ploughman, beggar may well be Dionysus, Heracles, Christ.

154. **Patmos [Patmos; 2, 165]**: The poem was finished early in 1803 and first published in 1808. It is addressed to the pious ruler of the little state, near Frankfurt, in which Hölderlin lived after the death of Susette Gontard and until his removal to the Tübingen

clinic in 1806. Like 'The Rhine' it derives a wider meditation out of its particular subject. 'Patmos' treats Christ's Ministry and Passion rather as Pindar treats the myths of his age, and it struggles to hope for the best in times of absence and benightedness. Much of the poem is teased out of the imagery of the opening lines. His prayer answered, the poet-traveller arrives in a compressed landscape of fabulous Asia Minor, the locus of the beginnings of Hellas, but soon turns his back on it and makes for Patmos, one of the Dodecanese, visible from the coast, an island of our time, where St John wrote the Apocalypse. Hölderlin believed him to be the same John who was Christ's disciple and who wrote the Gospel. Between that gospel and Hölderlin's poem there are many points of contact.

161. **Patmos,** *fragments of a later version* [2, 179] and 165. **Patmos,** *ll. 136-195 of work on a final version* [2, 185]: Hölderlin was revising 'Patmos' in the summer and autumn of 1803 whilst in that period also working on the later versions of 'The only one'. In both undertakings there is the same rather hectic inrush of new material, the chief marker of which is greatly extended lines. Working on 'The only one' he was trying to finish a poem he had begun two years previously. 'Patmos', however, is not only finished and in the fair copy given to the *Landgraf* in February 1803 a thing of great physical beauty, it is also the most perfected of Hölderlin's 'Pindaric' hymns and among the very best of all his poems. Yet six months after its completion he broke it up – or we might say it was broken up by new ideas and images forcing an entry. He felt pressed to dwell more on Christ's Ministry – the place-names Nazareth, Jordan, Capernaum, Galilee, Cana are like a list of things that want their due. But so does Peleus, shipwrecked on Cos. Then the Crusades, and Emperor Heinrich IV's penitential journey to Canossa in 1077: more and more presses in, to define the interim age that begins with Christ's death. The rewriting of 'Patmos' is akin to the rewriting (perhaps as late as December 1803) of 'The fettered river' or 'The blind singer'; but with this distressing difference: 'Ganymede' and 'Chiron' are completed poems, born out of, translated out of, completed poems. 'Patmos', perfected in the dedication copy, survives; but the reworking of it entered into the chaos of further creation, into an abundance which in the time allowed him Hölderlin could not manage. The revisions of 'Patmos' were first published in 1916.

167. **Remembrance [Andenken; 2, 188]**: Written 1803, first published 1808, the poem is full of memory-images of Hölderlin's time in Bordeaux. For him now in Swabia, the north-east wind makes the connection. Bellarmin in Hölderlin's novel Hyperion is the recipient of the hero's letters. In this poem Hölderlin may have his own friend Sinclair in mind. India here is the source. The early mariners thought to reach it by sailing west. 'The airy point' will be the Bec d'Ambès, where the Garonne and the Dordogne meet and make for the sea.

169. **The Ister [Der Ister; 2, 190]**: Written 1803, first published 1916. The Danube, in Hölderlin's mythology the great connecting river, was called Ister by the Greeks. Here he dwells particularly on its sluggishness, and contrasts it with the headlong course of the young Rhine. The poem rises against torpor, conjures up animation. According to Pindar (Olympian III) Heracles fetched the olive from the banks of the Ister, for a sprig of it to be the prize at the Olympic Games.

172. **Mnemosyne,** *second version* **[Mnemosyne; 2, 195]** and 174. **Mnemosyne,** *third version* **[2, 197]**: There are wide differences of opinion as to the date (1803 or 1806) of the complex of writing published in *GStA* as 'Mnemosyne' and in D.E. Sattler's Frankfurt edition as 'Die Nymphe' [The nymph], and also as to what would be included where in any final version of the poem. My translations are of versions 2 and 3 as deciphered and arranged by Beissner and printed in *GStA*. Michael Hamburger's are of Beissner's third version and Sattler's 'The Nymph'. The drafts were first published (but very imperfectly) in 1916. Mnemosyne was the mother of the Muses; her name means memory. The ruins of Eleutherae, her city, lie on the western slopes of Mount Cithaeron, facing Mount Helicon, in Boeotia. The poem, like much late Hölderlin, combats the loss of memory and seeks to hold on. Recalling Achilles, Ajax and Patroclus, all dead at Troy, serves that need; but so also, and perhaps better, do the many startlingly sharp images of *present* life strewn through these lines.

176. **As birds slowly pass over...' [Wie Vögel langsam ziehn ...; 2, 204]**: Probably written before 1806, not published until 1916. It is an extended simile wanting the thing it refers to and may be part of a poem never written or lost.

177. **'As upon seacoasts...' [Wie Meeresküsten...; 2, 205]**: Dates

as the last. A complete simile (its two sides running together) and perhaps a complete poem.

178. **Home [Heimath; 2, 206]:** Dates as the last. Unfinished. Here and in the next three poems, all unfinished, the sensuousness is remarkable.

179. **'For when the juice of the vine...'** [Wenn nemlich der Rebe Saft...; 2, 207]: Dates as the last.

180. **'On pale leaves...'** [Auf falbem Laube...; 2, 208]: Dates as the last.

181. **'When over the vineyard...'** [Wenn über dem Weinberg ...; 2, 330]: Perhaps earlier than the last. Not published until 1951. Doubtless belonging in a larger context.

182. **To the Madonna [An die Madonna; 2, 211]:** This substantial draft of a long poem, written perhaps as early as 1802 or as late as 1805, was first published in its entirety in 1959; but a definitive text has not been, nor will be, agreed. It is a part of Hölderlin's large project to (as he put it) 'define the Hesperian *orbis* in opposition to the *orbis* of the Ancients'. The Madonna is a Hesperian goddess, but the Christianity she is most worshipped in is more southern and eastern, so that he, as a Lutheran, feels his approaching her to be a presumption, if not a transgression. The poem is intensified by the personal memory of his journey through Catholic Westphalia in 1796 with Wilhelm Heinse and Susette Gontard. He connects the Knochenberg, ('mountain of bones') through a false etymology to Mount Ossa in Thessaly and also to Calvary ('place of the skulls'). Teutoburg, where the Germanic tribes under Arminius annihilated the legions of Varus in 7 AD, is another connection across the eras. The memory of Susette, by then dead, in that 'mixed' landscape is akin to his calling Frankfurt 'the navel of the earth' (see note on 'Where we began ...'). The story of Elizabeth (Mary's friend), her husband Zacharias and the birth of their son, John the Baptist, is told in the first chapter of Luke's Gospel.

188. **The Titans [Die Titanen; 2, 217]:** Probably 1802; first published 1916. Here again, in the violent disorder of the interim age, remembrance is a responsibility and a strength. And there are passages of grace too: luminous present being, in the real circumstances of common human life.

191. **'Once I asked the Muse...'** [**Einst hab ich die Muse gefragt...; 2, 220**]: This and the following two fragments were composed between 1802 and 1806, first published in 1916, and may in fact belong together with 'Home' as parts of one unfinished poem. The line of poetic argument is hard, or at times impossible, to follow, but in all three parts there are passages of great sensuous beauty and clarity. In the first, for example, the opening lines which allude to Hesiod's fabled encounter with the Nine Muses on Mount Helicon: they gave him leaves of the laurel to eat.

193. **'But when the heavenly powers...'** [**Wenn aber die Himmlischen...; 2, 222**]: Here the image of madness without eyes slinking through the garden, or the Dioscuri going to and fro between heaven and earth, bringing breath: an immanent beauty.

196. **'But formerly, Father Zeus...'** [**Sonst nemlich, Vater Zeus...; 2, 226**]: And here the huntress Diana walking the earth and the Lord angrily lifting up his countenance over us. Such moments make greater 'sense', of course, in the whole context of late Hölderlin, but they come at us with the force of terrible truth even as particles.

197. **The eagle [Der Adler; 2, 229]**: Unfinished, written perhaps 1805-6, first published 1916. The poetic geography is familiar, from the Indus to the Alps. But here, in primeval times, the first eagle looks down on a Flood, an ark, hungry animals. After the first passage Hölderlin left a space and in it wrote the one word 'Reh' [Deer], to be developed later. The poem has the simplicity of language, the clarity of vision, the matter-of-fact self-assurance, of truths worth dwelling on. The fundamental questions: Where shall we stay? Where is our nourishment? The named places are all resonant. Under Mount Haemus, for example, in Thrace, Orpheus was born. The shadow of Mount Athos is said to reach the island of Lemnos, eighty-seven miles to the east, when the sun sets at the solstice. And on that island Philoctetes was marooned by his comrades for ten years, in agony with a putrid foot.

199. **Nearest and best,** *third version* [**Das Nächste Beste; 2, 237**]: Unfinished, worked on – probably – 1802-05; first publications of parts of it: 1916 and in the 1920s. As with several of the drafts in the Homburg *Folioheft*, editors have judged for themselves which pieces of writing should be brought together in any one poem.

This version has the merit of being largely structured by the lovely developing image of the migrating starlings. Following that, Hölderlin, in a slightly laborious fashion, construes the line of some South German hills as he had already, much more persuasively, the courses of the great rivers. The poem is alive with sharp memories of places in France.

201. **Tinian [Tinian; 2, 240]**: Tinian is a Pacific island that Hölderlin first thought of as a poetic subject in 1797. He knew of it from his reading of George Anson's *Voyage around the World in the Years 1740-44* (published 1748, German 1749). In this poem – written in 1803 or later, first published in 1916 – Hölderlin again defines our age as one of wandering. (Chariot-racing for the Greeks, the Circus for the Romans, wandering in the wilderness for us.) The great voyages of discovery, among them Anson's, are an example. Tinian's history since the late seventeenth century is largely atrocious. The arrrangement of some of the poem's lines is my own.

203. **'And to feel the lives…' [Und mitzufühlen das Leben…; 2, 249]**: Written before 1806, first published 1920. Intense and vivid images (in life that is 'humming with heat') but no easily discernible poetic argument. Perhaps the whole fragment seeks to carry out the injunction of its opening words: 'to feel the lives of …'.

204. **'Where we began…' [Vom Abgrund nemlich…; 2, 250]**: Probably written before 1806, not published entirely until 1951. The fragment, very difficult to make whole sense of, is remarkable for the brilliance and sharpness of its memories, particularly those of France; and for its calling Frankfurt, where Susette Gontard lived, the navel of the earth (that being Pindar's term for Delphi). 'Gratitude' [Dankbarkeit] is a lovely word for the memory-feeling of a place. The poem is the gift in return.

206. **…the Vatican… […der Vatikan…; 2, 252]**: First published 1920. As in most of these late fragments there are markers of a proceeding argument: 'here we are' – 'and' – 'but when' – 'because' – 'and since' – 'and meanwhile' – 'but' … In lieu of any argument, however, we read vivid images, which, though coming in a sequence, line by line, actually jostle in a sort of simultaneity. Thus Catholic Rome, Catholic Westphalia, with the Alps and the pilgrim routes between them; Wilhelm Heinse ('my honest master') and with him, as always, the ghost of Susette Gontard; Julius Caesar, John the

Baptist, Apollo, Patmos (John of the Apocalypse), Hellas under Turkish occupation, confusion of tongues, owls in the ruined cities... Abundance or chaos, birth pangs or end game? It is a kaleidoscope that won't hold still because our thinking and feeling continually make different connections. But the fragment ends in an accomplished vision of peace, harmony, proportion, shining beauty.

208. **Greece,** *first version* **[Griechenland; 2, 254]**: The three phases of work on this draft of a poem were first published in the 1920s. Much of the first sketch derives from the opening half-line: 'Ways of the traveller!' One leads south via Avignon and over the Gotthard as far as Virgil's grave at Posillipo outside Naples. There the poet-traveller has reached Magna Graecia, if not yet Greece itself. Again, as in '...the Vatican...', a place has a personal charge. Virgil's tomb was enthusiastically described by Heinse in his *Ardinghello*. Very abruptly then the poem shifts back north, to Windsor, London, the Channel, and opens into one of those luminous autonomous images so frequent in late Hölderlin: '...the level ocean, glowing'.

209. **Greece,** *ll. 13-21 of the second version* **[2, 256]** and 210. **Greece,** *third version* **[2, 257]**: In the second draft, and more in the third which Hölderlin wrote over it, there is a mêlée of conflicting thoughts and images, of confusion, threat of dissolution, terror, remoteness or too much nearness of God, efforts to hold on in homely, earthly circumstances. So the draft finishes in a vicinity that feels close, familiar and safe – but still with the lure of the open road, so that we might rejoin the first draft and set off again south, over the Alps, in among the memorials of the all-too glamorous Ancient World.

212. **'Severed and at a distance now...' [Wenn aus der Ferne ...; 2, 262]**: Probably written after 1806, first published 1921. The poem, unfinished, is associated with very late expansions of the novel *Hyperion* and may be thought of as being spoken by Diotima, though, of course, both she, the heroine of the novel, and her counterpart in real life, Susette Gontard, had died.

214. **'I have enjoyed...' [Das Angenehme dieser Welt; 2, 267]**: Written before 1811, first published in Gustav Schwab's *Collected Works of Hölderlin* 1846. The first transcription of the poem has 'July' in l. 4; Schwab has 'June'.

215. **When out of heaven… [Wenn aus dem Himmel…; 2, 269]**: Written in the early 1820s, first published 1858. Pleasure in images of the natural world is very characteristic of these late poems.

216. **Spring ('When new joy quickens…') [Der Frühling (Wenn auf Gefilden …); 2, 272]**: Still in classical metre, therefore probably not *very* late. First published 1846.

217. **A Happy Life [Das fröhliche Leben; 2, 274]**: Said by Schwab to be 'much earlier than 1841'. First published 1846.

219. **The Walk [Der Spaziergang; 2, 276]**: First published 1846.

220. **The Churchyard [Der Kirchhof; 2, 277]**: Schwab again: 'much earlier than 1841'. First published 1846.

221. **Not all days… [Nicht alle Tage…; 2, 280]**: Around 1830, first published 1923. The poem harks back, in its form too. Hölderlin's landlord, the carpenter Ernst Zimmer, copied out the poem in a letter and commented: 'There can be no doubt that Höld does sometimes feel his condition. A few years ago he wrote the following lines about himself.'

222. **Spring ('How blessed to see…') [Der Frühling (Wie seelig ists …; 2, 283)]**: Not later than 1832, first published 1938.

223. **Autumn ('The stories that are leaving earth…') [Der Herbst (Die Sagen, die der Erde sich entfernen …); 2, 284]**: Written, according to Schwab, 16 September 1837. First published 1846.

224. **Spring ('The new day comes…') [Der Frühling (Es kommt der neue Tag…); 2, 286]**: First published 1909. Hölderlin in the tower would often sign his poems thus and add a fictitious date.

225. **View ('To us with images …') [Aussicht (Der off'ne Tag ist Menschen hell …); 2, 287]**: First published 1870.

226. **'In a lovely blue…' [In lieblicher Bläue…; 2, 372]**: In Tübingen, 1822-4, Hölderlin was much visited by a young man called Wilhelm Waiblinger. Waiblinger wrote a novel, *Phaëthon*, published 1823, in which, to depict his hero, a mad poet, he used Hölderlin's life and writings. He gives 'In a lovely blue…' which he got from the Zimmer family, as an example of his hero's work.

231. **Chorus from Sophocles' *Oedipus at Colonus* (5, 32)**: Lines 668-94; translated 1796, first published 1911. Here Hölderlin keeps far less close to the word-order and lineation of the Greek text than in the following passage from Euripides.

232. **From Euripides' *Bacchae* (5, 41)**: Lines 1-24; translated, autumn 1799, with strict adherence to word-order, lineation and metre; first published 1913. The manuscript is a single sheet of paper having on one side ll. 1-22 of the translation and on the other ll. 23-24 – immediately below which Hölderlin drafted the poem 'As when on a holiday...' (p. 113), his first and only attempt to write a metrically strict Pindaric hymn and drawing on the myth of Semele and Dionysus.

233. **Chorus from Sophocles' *Antigone* (5, 42)**: Lines 332-52; probably 1799, first published 1911. Compare this version with that in the Sophocles translations published in 1804 (p. 332).

234. **From Sophocles' *Oedipus at Colonus* (5, 275)**: Lines 14-19, 38-59; 1803, first published 1913. Hölderlin translated these lines, and the three extracts from *Ajax* that follow, in the same close fashion as his *Antigone* and his *Oedipus Rex*. It is likely that he intended to translate all seven of Sophocles' extant plays.

236. **Three extracts from Sophocles' *Ajax* (5, 277)**: Translated 1803; first published 1913.

1. Ajax went mad with rage when the arms of dead Achilles were awarded as prize to Odysseus and not to him. In his madness, and in the dark, he fell upon a flock of sheep and cattle, thinking they were the Greeks who had slighted him. In this first extract, watched by his wife Tecmessa, he has come to his senses and grieves over his disgrace.

2. Ajax was from Salamis. Here a chorus of the men who came with him to Troy lament the harm he has done.

3. The Chorus, deceived by a new reasonableness in Ajax's manner, jump to the conclusion that all will be well. In fact, he has decided to kill himself.

240. **Pindar Fragments (5, 281)**: Written, most likely, in 1803. 'The Sanctuaries' and 'The Life-Giver' were first published in 1910, the others in 1916. Each of the nine texts consists of a

fragment of Pindar's verse, closely translated into Hölderlin's own late language, and a passage of prose set below it as though to explain and comment. But that comforting relationship – text + exegesis – is belied by the practice. Out of the fragment of a poem, elusive in its peculiar beauty, Hölderlin derived a poetic prose which itself reads like translation from a strange elsewhere and itself seems to call for exegesis. The whole sense of each piece is generated in the interplay of ancient text and modern reading. The manuscript is a beautiful fair copy. These nine texts and the nine 'Night Songs' (pp. 73-82), which were composed or at least revised for publication in the same year, have much in common.

240. 'That wild ocean creature' (in 'Wisdom's infidelities') is the octopus, good at camouflage. But much of the sense of these fragments is generated by and contained in 'collision', 'contraries', 'living relations'. That working mix is embodied in the Centaurs, horse and human, savage beasts and teachers of the arts, creatures who cross over, to and fro. The texts resist any exegesis which would allow us to get out of them, have done with them, commodify them for particular ends. The one abstractable teaching is that of 'thorough interplay'.

OEDIPUS THE KING

260. 'the songstress': The Sphinx, whom Oedipus destroyed by answering her riddle.

263. CHORUS: The Chorus, made anxious by the message brought from Delphi, call on Athene, Artemis, Apollo and, finally, Zeus and Dionysus also, to defend the city against Ares, here understood as a bringer of the plague.

264. 'the evening/ God': This must be Hades, into whose kingdom the dead are flocking.

274. 'Zeus's son': Apollo; 'the wise birdscrier': Tiresias.
'Polybus's son': Oedipus (as they still believe).
The Chorus imagine the guilty man pursued by divine justice. They express their worries but still put their trust in Oedipus.

275. 'the winged maid': The Sphinx.

279. 'the sign-diviner': Tiresias.

286. 'But if that stranger…': The worst Oedipus has grasped so far is that he may be the murderer of Laius (and so the object of his own curse), but not that Laius is his father.

288. CHORUS: The Chorus reflect on the nature of divine laws, on the dangers of impiety, especially in the great, and pray that the truth will be revealed and the honour of the gods and their oracles thereby restored.

289. 'the earth's / Untouchable navel': Delphi.

296. CHORUS: The Chorus, with a quite groundless optimism, look forward to more revelations and associate one or other of the immortals with Oedipus' birth.
'Cyllene's/ King': Hermes.

298. 'three whole moons': The text Hölderlin used is corrupt here. He translates it correctly, but the real sense is that the herdsman served three whole seasons of six months each, from spring to autumn.

300. CHORUS: Now facing the facts the Chorus bewail the precariousness of human happiness, and the fate of Oedipus in particular, in which they feel personally involved.
'the prophesying virgin': The Sphinx.

302. 'childless': So Jocasta had thought herself, having agreed to the murder of her one child Oedipus.
'two husbands made of one': Of her husband Laius she made a second husband, Oedipus.

309. 'they are men': Eteocles and Polynices.
'my troubled girls': Antigone and Ismene.

312. 'μηχανη': Mechanics, calculable procedures.
'moyen': French for means, medium.

313. 'nefas': Latin, here meaning especially that which must not be uttered.

317. 'Της φυσεως γραμματευς ην τον καλαμον αποβρεχων ευνουν': An abbreviated and slightly altered quotation from the *Sudas*, there referring to Aristotle. Here, applied to the tragedian, its meaning is: He was the scribe of Nature, dipping in his well-intentioned pen.

321. 'the Earth's Father': Zeus. An example of Hölderlin's 'inter-pretative' mode of translation in *Antigone*. See his own notes, pp. 368 and 369.
'the General': Creon.
'the Argive army': The army led by Polynices from Argos against Thebes.

324. CHORUS: The Chorus review the fighting which has just ended, and give thanks to the gods for the successful defence of Thebes.

324. 'the White Shield': A singular title for all the forces of Argos. The city's name was associated with the word *argos*, which means bright or gleaming, here as it might be of their shields.
'the seven mouths': The seven gates of Thebes.

325. 'the battle wraith': Ares.
'the abominable...that pair': Eteocles and Polynices.
'Creon, king': Creon becomes king now after the deaths of Oedi-pus' two sons.

330. 'Lord of the Earth': Zeus.

332. CHORUS: The Chorus reflect on the powers, achievements, limitations and errors of humankind. Hölderlin did a version of these famous strophes in 1799 (see p. 233). Comparison with the version here shows how radical his translating had become.

340. CHORUS: The Chorus lament the ruin of the house of Labdacus and, more generally, the lot of humans liable to fits of madness and at the mercy of the gods.

346. CHORUS: The Chorus reflect on the power of love, perhaps construing Haemon's opposition to his father as an effect of his love for Antigone. She herself then grieves that she will die unmarried.

347. CHORUS: The Chorus offer Antigone the cold comfort of dying famously. She associates herself with Niobe. She will be entombed in rock, Niobe was turned to stone.

350. 'a light...angrily, pityingly': The Greek text has *Persephone*, a goddess of the underworld and herself forcibly married to Acheron. Hölderlin's interpretative translation (*zornigmitleidig...ein Licht*) derives chiefly from his associating the first part of her name with

pertho, meaning 'to destroy', and the latter part with *phaos*, meaning 'light'.

352. CHORUS: The Chorus evoke three figures from the myths: Danaë, imprisoned by her father in a tower; Lycurgus, driven mad (so that he killed his children) and imprisoned in a cave by Dionysus whose worship he had resisted; the two sons of Phineus, blinded by their stepmother ('the wild wife') and joining their pain to that of their repudiated and imprisoned mother, Cleopatra, daughter of the North Wind. The general relevance of these stories to Antigone's is clear and almost banal: there is no escaping Fate; specifically, the connections are at once crueller and less certain.
'the Father of Time': Zeus.

353. 'the butcher god': Ares, in whose home territory these things happened.

356. 'God's/ Own crones': The Furies.

359. **Chorus:** The Chorus sing an optimistic hymn to Dionysus, praying that he will come and purify Thebes, the city of his mother Semele.
'**Earth's father**': Zeus.
'**the dragon**': Killed by Cadmus at the founding of Thebes.
Cocytus: The Greek text has *Corycia*, which is a cave on Parnassus. Hölderlin's Cocytus, a river of the underworld, is an error; but in his poem 'Bread and Wine' he alludes to Dionysus' descent into Hades to bring out Semele, so perhaps that connection surfaced and misled him when he was translating.
'**the mother the lightning struck**': Semele, killed when Zeus appeared to her in the lightning.

367-69. In this section of his Notes, Hölderlin gives a series of commentaries on quotations from the play. The procedure is strikingly similar to that in his *Pindar Fragments*, composed at the same time. A Greek text, in his own radical translation, is followed by an exegesis itself inviting exegesis. See p. 401.

368. Here and on p. 369 Hölderlin justifies his own interpretative translation. Given the shift in the times, from Greek to our own (which he calls Hesperian), it is, he says, necessary to alter the texts into a language we will better understand.

369. '**aorgic**': In Hölderlin's usage the word means a condition or

forces antithetical and inimical to conscious and individualised human life. Loose synonyms might be 'anarchic', 'formless', 'unconscious'. **'managed for Zeus the coming of the streams of gold'**: This would be closer to the Greek and refers to the form Zeus assumed in order to impregnate Danaë.

370. *'antitheos'*: The Greek word as an adjective means 'equal to or hostile to the gods'; as a noun it may mean 'hostile deity'; Hölderlin's meaning seems rather to be 'God's opponent'.

371. **'factive'**: Hölderlin's word is *faktisch* and he seems to mean by it 'causing something to be or to happen'.

371. **'For us etc'**: As often in letters and poems of this period Hölderlin seeks to distinguish our modern conditions from those of the Greeks.

371. 'δυσμορον': The word actually means ill-fated.

372. **'The plot in *Antigone* etc'**: Here Hölderlin must be thinking of his own times, and of the total reversal caused by the French Revolution and in 1803 still under way.

372. 'προφανηθι θεος': Literally, 'Appear, God'. From the last strophe of the chorus that opens Act V, pp. 359-60.

373. **'The rational form here developing etc'**: Again, Hölderlin seems to be viewing the conflict between Creon and Antigone in the light of his own times.

GLOSSARY

Abae, city in Phocis having an oracle of Apollo even older than that at Delphi.

Acheron, one of the rivers of Hades.

Achilles, a Greek hero, son of Peleus and Thetis, he died young at Troy.

Aeacides, family of Aeacus, among whom are Peleus, Achilles and Ajax.

Agora, the marketplace and civic centre of ancient Athens.

Ajax, a Greek hero, fought bravely at Troy. In a bout of madness he disgraced himself and committed suicide afterwards.

Alcaeus, lyric poet of Lesbos, born *c.* 620 BC, contemporary and countryman of Sappho.

Alpheus, river in Elis, flowing past Olympia.

Amphion, a former king of Thebes and the husband of Niobe.

Amphitrite, wife of Poseidon, god of the sea.

Anacreon, lyric poet, born *c.* 570 BC in Teos, Ionia.

Antigone, a daughter of Oedipus and Jocasta.

Aphrodite, goddess of love, daughter of Zeus.

Apollo, god of light, poetry, prophecy.

Arabia, its coastal parts were known as *Arabia felix* (happy, fortunate).

Arcturus, brightest star in the constellation Boötes, its appearance marking the beginning of autumn.

Ares, god of war.

Argos, chief city of Argolis in the Peloponnese, from which the Seven came against Thebes.

Artemis, goddess of the hunt and of childbirth, sister of Apollo.

Aspasia, born 470 BC in Miletus, Ionia, cultured and beautiful woman, the lover of Pericles, her house in Athens became a renowned intellectual centre.

Athene, goddess of wisdom, protector of cities, worshipped in Thebes.

Atreus, father of Agamemnon and Menelaus. The whole House of Atreus, beginning with Tantalus, were cursed down the generations.

Attica, the region surrounding Athens.

Bacchus = Dionysus.

Bactra, capital of Bactria, powerful trading centre in the Persian Empire, roughly equivalent to modern Afghanistan.

Boreas, the north wind.

Bosporus, straits joining the Black Sea and the Sea of Marmora.

Briseis, the female captive allotted to Achilles and taken from him by Agammenon, with dire consequences for the Greeks at Troy.

Cadmus, founder of Thebes.

Calauria, the ancient name of Poros, an island in the Saronic Gulf, home of Diotima in Hölderlin's novel *Hyperion*.

Capitol, smallest but most celebrated of the Seven Hills of Rome, the city's ancient religious and political centre.

Castalia, a spring under Parnassus, at Delphi, sacred to the Muses.

Cayster, a river of Asia Minor rising on Mount Tmolus and entering the Aegean near Ephesus.

Centaur, a mythic beast, half human, half horse.

Cephissus, a river flowing to the west of Athens, near Col-onus.

Cerberus, monstrous three-headed dog who guards the gates of the Underworld to prevent the dead from leaving.

Chaeronea, in Boetia, where Philip of Macedon defeated the Thebans and Athenians in 338 BC.

Chariclo, wife of Chiron.

Charites, another name for the Graces.

Chios, an island near Lesbos, close to the coast of Asia Minor, famous for mastic and wine.

Chiron, centaur, tutor of many Greek heroes, among them Achilles, Jason and Peleus.

Cithaeron, mountain range between Attica and Boeotia, sacred to Dionysus and where Oedipus was exposed.

Cnossian, after Cnossos, town in Crete famous for its labyrinth and festivals of dance in honour of Ariadne, wife of Dionysus.

Cocytus, one of the rivers of the underworld.

Colchis, on the east coast of the Black Sea, where the Argonauts went after the Golden Fleece.

Colonus, outside Athens, where Oedipus came when he was banished from Thebes. Its horses and natural beauties are celebrated by Sophocles who was born there.

Corinth, city on the Isthmus of Corinth, where Oedipus grew up.

Creon, brother of Jocasta, ruler of Thebes after the deaths of

Polynices and Eteocles.

Cyclops, a race of single-eyed giants, one of whom, Polyphemus, Odysseus deceived and blinded (*Odyssey*, Book 9). They kept sheep and goats.

Cyllene, mountain in Arcadia, birthplace of Hermes and a home of Pan.

Danaë, daughter of Acrisius, imprisoned in a tower by him and there visited by Zeus in the form of a shower of gold.

Daulia, city in Phocis.

Delian, an epithet of Apollo who with his sister Artemis was born on Delos, one of the Cyclades.

Delphic = of Delphi, on the slopes of Parnassus, famous for the oracle there and the worship of Apollo and known as the navel of the earth.

Diana = Artemis.

Dionysus, god of wine and intoxication, closely associated with Thebes through his mother Semele, also with Mount Cithaeron and the Mysteries at Eleusis.

Dioscuri, the twins Castor and Pollux, sons of Leda, the first fathered by a mortal, Tyndareus, the second by Zeus. When Castor was killed, Zeus transformed them into the constellation of Gemini.

Diotima, the seer or priestess who, Socrates says, taught him the philosophy of love.

Dirce, a nymph, a devotee of Dionysus, who gave her name to a stream near Thebes.

Dodona, in Epirus, north-western Greece, where Zeus spoke through the wind in the oak tree.

Doris, small mountainous region of Northern Greece, traditional homeland of the Dorian Greeks.

Dryas, father of King Lycurgus.

Ecbatana, the ancient capital of Media, the summer residence of the Persian kings.

Edonians, a people of Thrace.

Eleusis, near Athens, famous for the Mysteries in which seasonal rebirth was celebrated.

Eleutherae, Mnemosyne's town, on Mount Cithaeron.

Elis, a region in the western Peloponnese. Near the town of that name, at Olympia, the Games were held.

Elysium, a place for the afterlife of the blessed, imagined as fields, a plain or islands, somewhere westerly.

Enodia, the word means 'by the road' and is a euphemistic name for Hecate, a goddess of the underworld.

Ephesus, ancient city at the mouth of the Cayster in Asia Minor, associated particularly with the worship of Artemis. In early Christian times it became one of the Seven Churches.

Erebus, a primordial god of darkness, or the Underworld itself.

Erechtheus, fabulous, perhaps divine, founder and king of Athens.

Eteocles, the elder son of Oedipus and Jocasta.

Etruria, a region of Central Italy whose people spread out from what is now Tuscany to make a great civilisation long before that of Rome.

Eumenides, the Furies, three female deities (their name means 'the kindly ones') who punish without mercy all transgressions of primordial laws.

Eurydice, in *Antigone* she is the wife of Creon.

Evius, a name for Dionysus, after the cult-cry 'evoi!'.

Furies = Eumenides.

Ganymede, a herdsboy on Mount Ida, he was carried off by Zeus' eagle to be the gods' cupbearer on Olympus.

Hades, the underworld and the god of it.

Haemon, son of Creon and Eurydice, betrothed to Antigone.

Haemus, a mountain in Thrace where writings of Orpheus were said to have been found and a temple and college built in his honour.

Helicon, mountain west of Thebes, sacred to the Muses.

Helios, the sun god.

Hephaestus, god of fire and of work that uses it.

Heracles (or Hercules), a notable Greek hero, performer of the Twelve Labours, he visited the centaur Chiron, with fateful consequences.

Hercules, Pillars of, Straits of Gibraltar.

Hermes, god of ways and means, messenger of the gods.

Hesperides, guardians of a paradise garden on the edge of the world.

Hestia, Greek goddess of the hearth and domestic life.

Hymen, a god presiding over marriage.

Icarus, his father Daedalus made him a pair of wings, but he flew too close to the sun, the wax in them melted, and he fell into the sea near the island of Icaria, not far from Samos.

Ida, a mountain near Troy.

Ilissus, a river of Athens, on the south side of the city.

Ilium, another name for Troy.

Indus, a great river flowing through China, India and Pakistan. Dionysus is said to have reached it on his progress through Asia, teaching the peoples the cultivation of the vine, and to have returned from there into Greece, establishing his cult.

Ionia, the coast of Asia Minor, locus of the beginnings of Hellas. Homer was thought to have been born there and several very eminent poets and philosophers certainly were.

Ismene, Antigone's sister.

Ismenus, a stream flowing through Thebes, there was temple by it in which the ashes of sacrifices were used for divination.

Ister, the Danube, in some accounts especially its lower reaches.

Isthmus = the Corinthian Isthmus.

Jason, robbed of his birthright by his uncle Pelias, was falsely promised he should have it back again if he would first fetch the Golden Fleece from Colchis.

Jocasta, daughter of Menoeceus, wife of Laius, mother then wife of Oedipus.

Jupiter = Zeus.

Kos, one of the Dodecanese, Peleus was shipwrecked and died there.

Labdacus, the father of Laius.

Laius, a king of Thebes, first husband of Jocasta, father of Oedipus.

Lethe, one of the rivers of the Underworld, drinking from it brought forgetfulness.

Loxias, a name for Apollo.

Lycian = of Lycia in southern Asia Minor, Apollo and Artemis were worshipped there.

Lycurgus, a king of the Edonians, driven mad by Dionysus for opposing the introduction of his cult.

Lydia, an ancient and powerful kingdom of Western Asia Minor, in the sixth century BC taken by the Persians and in the second by the Romans.

Maeander, river of Asia Minor notable for its windings, enters the sea below Miletus.

Maenads, frenzied women, followers of Dionysus.

Marathon, where the Athenians defeated the Persians in 490 BC. The soldier Pheidippides ran the 26 miles into the city with the good news.

Mars = Ares.

Medes, an ancient people whose territory (in Iran and Mesopotamia) was annexed into the Persian empire in 550 BC.

Megareus, son of Creon and Eurydice, he sacrificed himself for the good of Thebes.

Menoeceus, father of Creon and Jocasta.

Merope, wife of Polybus, Oedipus' foster-mother in Corinth.

Messogis, a mountain in Asia Minor, between Sardes and Ephesus, in a region known as Asis.

Mnemosyne, Goddess of Memory, mother of the Nine Muses.

Morea, The: the name for the Peloponnese in Medieval and Early Modern times.

Muses, the nine daughters of Mnemosyne, each of whom was the proctectress of one of the arts or sciences.

Naxian = of Naxos, one of the Cyclades, an important site of the worship of Dionysus.

Nemesis, Goddess of Retribution.

Nile, according to Ovid (*Metamorphoses*) the Nile fled when Phaethon crashed and set the world on fire.

Niobe, the wife of Amphion, an early king of Thebes, when she boasted that she had more children than Leto they were all killed by Leto's children, Apollo and Artemis, and she herself in her grief was turned to stone.

Nysa/Nysian, a nymph, and a mountain of the same name (possibly near Helicon), both associated with the upbringing of Dionysus.

Oceanus, a primordial god, the ocean stream, the vast ever-flowing body of water that encircles the earth.

Oedipus, son of Laius and Jocasta, his name means 'swell-foot'.

Oeta, a mountain in Central Greece on which Heracles immolated himself. Below it, to the east, is Thermopylae where in 480 BC the Spartans held out against but were finally slaughtered by the Persians.

Olympia, in Elis, site of the Olympic Games.

Olympieum, the Temple of Olympian Zeus in Athens.

Olympus, in Thessaly, the highest mountain in Greece, seat of the gods.

Orcus, a Latin name for the Underworld.

Ossa, a mountain in Thessaly. The giant brothers, the Aloadae, tried to storm Olympus by piling Mount Ossa on Mount Pelion.

Pactolus, a gold- and electrum-bearing river, rising on Mount Tmolus.

Pallas = Pallas Athene.

Palmyra, a city in the Syrian desert, destroyed by the Romans in 273 AD. Its ruins were rediscovered by Robert Wood and James Dawkins in 1751.

Pan, Arcadian god of the herds and fertility.

Parcae, the Fates.

Parnassus, mountain behind Delphi, sacred to the Muses, also to Apollo and Dionysus.

Patmos, island just off the coast of Asia Minor, south of Samos. St John wrote the Book of Revelation there.

Patroclus, whilst Achilles sulked Patroclus fought and died wearing his armour.

Peleus, husband of the sea-goddess Thetis, father of Achilles.

Pelias, having usurped his brother's kingdom (Iolcus, near modern Volos) he withheld it then from Jason, his nephew.

Pentelicus, a mountain to the north-east of Athens famous for its marble quarries.

Persia, vast empire in the East, competing and warring with the Greeks, they sacked Athens in 480 BC.

Phaethon, son of Helios, he persuaded his father to let him drive the chariot of the Sun, but couldn't control it, went off course, set the earth on fire, and Zeus put an end to the adventure with a thunderbolt.

Phasis, a river flowing from the Caucasus into the Black Sea.

Phidias, Athenian sculptor, painter and architect (*c.* 480-430 BC).

Philoctetes, famous archer, inheritor of the bow and arrows of Heracles. On his way to Troy he was bitten by a snake and the wound stank so much his comrades marooned him on the island of Lemnos.

Phineus, a king of Salmydessus, his sons were blinded by their stepmother and – some say – entombed by her and left to starve.

Phylura, mother of Chiron.

Phocis, the region around Delphi.

Phoebus = Phoebus Apollo.

Phrygian = of Phrygia, district of Asia Minor, epithet of Niobe, who was born there.

Pluto = Hades.

Polybus, king of Corinth, Oedipus' foster-father.

Polydorus, son of Cadmus and father of Labdacus.

Polynices, brother of Eteocles.

Pontus, a pre-Olympian sea-god, or often just the sea itself.

Poseidon, son (like Zeus) of Cronus and Rhea, god of the sea.

Prometheus, a Titan, he stole fire from the gods and gave it to mankind.

Prytaneum, the magistrates' hall in Athens.

Pythagoras, Ionian Greek philosopher and mathematician (*c.* 570-495 BC).

Pytho, earlier name of Delphi, where Apollo killed the Python.

Salamis, Ajax's birthplace. Off Salamis the Athenians defeated the Persians in 480 BC.

Salmydessus, city of Thrace on the Black Sea.

Sardes, capital of Lydia in Asia Minor on the gold- and electrum-bearing river Pactolus.

Scamander, one of the rivers of Troy.

Semele, daughter of Cadmus, loved by Zeus, she was consumed in fire when, at her request, he revealed himself as a god. Dionysus was born out of the flames.

Sipylus, mountain near Smyrna in Asia Minor.

Smyrna, ancient Greek settlement on the Aegean coast of Asia Minor, the Turkish Izmir.

Sounion, the southernmost headland of the Attica peninsula, the Temple of Poseidon on it is a landmark for sailors.

Sparta, ancient city-state in the Peloponnese, the dominant military land-power, rival of Athens.

Sphinx, hybrid creature terrorising Thebes until Oedipus answered her riddle which caused her to kill herself.

Stoa, in Greek cities, usually around the agora, a covered walkway or portico for public use. The Stoics took their name from the building.

Styx, the river that is the frontier between Earth and the Underworld.

Tantalus, famous for his torment, he was a king of Lydia and the father of Niobe.

Tartarus, an abyss in Hades used as a dungeon (the Titans are in there, for example) and said to be as far below Hades as heaven is above it.

Taurus, a great chain of mountains extending down the Aegean coast and then, roughly opposite Rhodes, bearing away eastwards.

Taygetus, the mountain above Sparta.

Tecmessa, wife of Ajax.

Tempe, a beautiful valley in Thessaly between Mounts Olympus and Ossa.

Tenos, one of the Northern Cyclades.

Thebes, capital of Boeotia, setting of Sophocles' *Oedipus the King* and *Antigone* and of Euripides' *Bacchae*, home of Tiresias, birthplace of Dionysus whose mother was Semele, daughter of Cadmus, King of Thebes.

Themis, the Titan goddess of divine law and order, the traditional rules of conduct first established by the gods.

Thermopylae: see Oeta.

Thetis, a sea-goddess, mother of Achilles.

Thracian = of Thrace, in the extreme north-east of Greece.

Thyades, like the Maenads, female followers of Dionysus.

Tiresias, blind seer of Thebes, from Cadmus' time into Creon's.

Titans, twelve primeval deities, the children – six sons and six daughters – of Uranus and Gaia.

Tmolus, a mountain between ancient Philadelphia (modern Alaşehir) and Sardes (modern Sart).

Tyre, ancient Phoenician city in Lebanon, always a major port and centre of trade.

Vulcan = Hephaestus.

Xanthus, a city of ancient Lycia on the site of modern Kinik in the province of Antalya.

Zeus, chief of the Greek gods.